THE FEMINIST CHALLENGE

THE MOVEMENT FOR WOMEN'S LIBERATION
IN BRITAIN AND THE USA

THE
FEMINIST CHALLENGE

The Movement for Women's
Liberation in Britain and
the USA

DAVID BOUCHIER

Schocken Books • New York

First American edition published by
Schocken Books 1984
10 9 8 7 6 5 4 3 2 1   84 85 86 87
Copyright © 1983 by David Bouchier
All rights reserved
Published by agreement with
The Macmillan Press, Ltd., London

Library of Congress Cataloging in Publication Data

Bouchier, David.
   The feminist challenge.

   Bibliography: p.
   Includes index.
   1. Feminism—Great Britain—History.   2. Feminism—
United States—History.   3. Feminism—Philosophy.
I. Title.
HQ1597.B69   1984   305.4′2′0941   83–14296

Printed in Hong Kong
ISBN 0–8052–3881–6

For D. L. B.

Contents

Acknowledgements

This book reflects the work of many women. The knowledge on which it is based comes from the writers, historians, journalists, theoreticians, academics and political activists who created and recorded the women's movement. Many are named in the text, but many more must be anonymous; my debt to all of them is acknowledged unreservedly.

Equally indispensable were those individual women who gave their time for interviews and discussions, and to read and comment on various drafts of the emerging book. Participants in the Women and Men seminar at the State University of New York and many academic colleagues, feminists and friends – among them, Liz Bargh, Kay Gough, Joyce Gelb and Susan Squier – provided insights, nuggets of information and constructive criticism.

Research in the USA was facilitated by a period of leave from the University of Essex, and the libraries of the Women's Research and Resources Centre, the Fawcett Society and the State University of New York provided much of the material – some of it rare and difficult to obtain – on which the narrative is based.

It is no small irony that male authors so often acknowledge a friend and critic who made the whole thing possible, and that that person is almost invariably a woman. I can offer no variation on this traditional and slightly shameful theme. Diane Barthel read the manuscript line by line, challenged the arguments point by point, raised my consciousness on the frequent occasions when this was needed and provided the essential daily reassurances which every writer wants but not all are lucky enough to get.

DAVID BOUCHIER

List of Abbreviations

ACAS	Advisory, Conciliation and Arbitration Service
ACLU	American Civil Liberties Union
ALRA	Abortion Law Reform Association
APEX	Association of Professional, Executive, Clerical and Computer Staff
ASTMS	Association of Scientific, Technical and Managerial Staff
AUEW	Amalgamated Union of Engineering Workers
CAG	Cleaners' Action Group
CHE	Campaign for Homosexual Equality
CND	Campaign for Nuclear Disarmament
COHSE	Confederation of Health Service Employees
EEC	European Economic Community
EEOC	Equal Employment Opportunities Commission (USA)
EOC	Equal Opportunities Commission (Britain)
ERA	Equal Rights Amendment
FEW	Federally Employed Women
GLF	Gay Liberation Front
GMWU	General and Municipal Workers' Union
HRW	Human Rights for Women
IMG	International Marxist Group
IS	International Socialists (Socialist Workers' Party)
LARC	Labour Abortion Rights Campaign
NAC	National Abortion Campaign
NALGO	National Association of Local Government Officers
NARAL	National Abortion Rights Action League
NAWSA	National American Women's Suffrage Association
NCCL	National Council for Civil Liberties
NOW	National Organisation for Women

NUPE	National Union of Public Employees
NUSEC	National Union of Societies for Equal Citizenship
NUT	National Union of Teachers
NWPC	National Women's Political Caucus
OWL	Older Women's Liberation
PWC	Professional Women's Caucus
SCUM	Society for Cutting Up Men
SDS	Students for a Democratic Society
SNCC	Student Nonviolent Coordinating Committee
SPUC	Society for the Protection of the Unborn Child
SWP	Socialist Workers' Party
TGWU	Transport and General Workers' Union
TUC	Trades Union Congress
WAI	Women Against Imperialism
WAR	Women Against Rape
WARF	Women Against Racism and Fascism
WAVAW	Women Against Violence Against Women
WEAL	Women's Equity Action League
WFH	Wages for Housework
WIRES	Women's Information, Referral and Enquiry Service
WITCH	Women's International Terrorist Conspiracy from Hell
WNCC	Women's National Coordinating Committee
WONT	Women Opposed to Nuclear Threat
WSPU	Women's Social and Political Union
WWC	Working Women's Charter
YSA	Young Socialist Alliance

Introduction

All I say is by way of discourse and nothing by way of advice. I should not speak so boldly if it were my due to be believed.

MONTAIGNE

A decade ago the new movement for women's liberation was riding a high tide of energy and optimism. Traditional attitudes towards women were everywhere under attack, legal and educational battles were being won and even the mass media had begun to give serious and sustained attention to women's issues. Suddenly the question of equality and freedom for women had become a matter of public debate and universal awareness. In such an atmosphere anything seemed possible.

Like so many tides of social change which, at their height, seem irresistible, the women's movement has strangely receded from consciousness. The press no longer pays it much attention. The dynamic, politically active women who were its driving-force have largely vanished from the public scene. The organised feminist groups are politically becalmed and divided by deep theoretical disagreements. To the outsider their debates are largely incomprehensible, and the movement itself is almost invisible. For a political movement which hopes to change people's lives and minds, such obscurity is a serious matter. Still more serious, the gains which have been made – over pay, career opportunities, financial independence and personal freedoms like contraception and abortion – are threatened by a wave of regressive conservatism on both sides of the Atlantic. Public awareness may have faded, but the need for a visible and active women's movement has not. Most women still suffer severe limitations on their life-chances simply because they are women, sexual stereotypes have visibly and offensively returned to popular entertainment and to advertising, and the level of violence against women has continued to rise.

The women's liberation movement is *not* dead. The consciousness which it has aroused among women and men is too potent a force to be smothered. But it may be that the fight for women's full human rights faces a period of stagnation, and that new kinds of theories and political action will be needed in the coming crisis. This book is offered in the spirit of a contribution to a dialogue, most of which will necessarily take place among women, but which profoundly involves the attitudes and lives of men. It has both a clarifying and a critical purpose. First, it aims to set out the origins and history of modern feminism in such a way that its distinctive intellectual and organisational forms can be identified and compared. Second, it analyses the processes by which the movement has sought to intervene in society and politics on behalf of women, and suggests why some of its interventions have been more successful than others.

The fragmented, elusive nature of the women's movement makes it necessary to define at the outset what is to be described. Women's liberation is a label which has been over-used by the media, often in a negative way. Nevertheless it is still used self-descriptively by sections of the movement, especially in Britain. Many individuals, and groups, however, prefer the broader and more neutral term 'feminism', which is used in this book to embrace the whole movement. Feminism is still a fundamentally disputed concept, in so far as no general agreement exists about its boundaries. My initial strategy will be to adopt a highly inclusive definition which will cover the whole range of feminist beliefs and activities, from the most moderate to the most radical. *Feminism includes any form of opposition to any form of social, personal or economic discrimination which women suffer because of their sex.* Within this definition, therefore, the feminist movement includes all forms of collective action against such discrimination, from political organisation to cultural separatism.

There have been two great waves of feminist activity in recent history. The first began in the USA in the 1830s, spread rapidly to Europe and ended when women achieved the vote in the 1920s. The second wave also appeared first in the USA in the early 1960s, and has had its major cultural impact there. Soon afterwards a new feminist movement appeared in Britain which took some of its inspiration from the American experience, but developed along very different lines. At the same time, in many other countries, women launched campaigns for their own equality which took their forms from their different cultural settings.

While the core of this book is the history of modern feminism in Britain, a comparative perspective will be provided by the parallel development of the movement in the USA. The influence of the American movement on the British, both positive and negative, has been immense, and their histories are intimately linked through a shared English-language literature and through a great deal of direct political and intellectual contact. American society is sufficiently like the British to be immediately understandable, but sufficiently different to produce a distinctive feminist response. Comparisons, in short, are both possible and fruitful.

The history begins with the period of stagnation which followed women's first great triumph, the achievement of the vote. Indeed, it was not merely a period of stagnation but a time when, especially after the Second World War, women found themselves increasingly restricted by their traditional roles as housewives and mothers. Their frustration, boredom and emptiness provided the catalyst for a re-born feminist movement.

The new movement emerged in America, at a time of great political turbulence. Civil rights agitation was at its height, and many thousands of young people were challenging traditional American values by adopting new life-styles or by involving themselves in left-wing and anti-war politics. Women, caught up in this exciting political atmosphere, began to organise quietly around the equality issue in 1966. The following year, more radical feminist groups were born out of the student new left, and the movement was on its way.

By 1968 women in Britain, Germany and France had become active in causes like equal pay, job discrimination, abortion rights and child care, and by the following year the movement for women's liberation was international news. Terms like 'sexism', 'feminism' and 'male chauvinism' entered everyday language, and significant gains were made in the area of civil rights. Some men feared and detested the new feminism, but for many involved in libertarian and egalitarian causes, it seemed like the natural culmination of the 1960s' movement towards human emancipation. Chapter 2 deals with this exciting period of emergence, when the ideals of contemporary feminism first began to take shape.

In order to understand the history which follows, it is necessary to appreciate the main intellectual debates within modern feminism, and Chapter 3 is devoted entirely to a summary of these. The general reader may at first find them difficult since they are less concerned with matters of fact than with the correct *theoretical* explanation of the situation of women. Many intellectuals were attracted to the movement, and addressed themselves to basic questions like the origins of male dominance or patriarchy, whether women could be regarded as an economic class, whether equality for women depended on the achievement of equality for all (i.e. socialism), whether political organisations of women must be exclusive (women only), the roles which family and childbirth should play in women's lives, and many more. From these early debates arose the three major lines of feminist thought – liberal, socialist and radical – which were quickly reflected in divisions within the organisation of the movement. The arguments in defence of each theoretical position and the political goals and actions implied by each are summarised in Chapter 3.

However, this book was never planned as an intervention in feminist theory, and the main portion is devoted to describing and explaining the unfinished history of the movement. Chapter 4 deals with the early years, between 1970 and 1975, when feminism was dynamic, optimistic and highly creative, one of the most original and exciting movements for change to have emerged from the ferment of the 1960s. The narrative is continued through Chapters 5 and 7, shifting between Britain and the USA to highlight the alliances and the conflicts, the continuities and the barriers within and between feminist groups in the two nations. Every effort has been made to tell the story without bias towards any particular group or tendency.

By the mid-1970s anti-feminist forces had rallied against the increasingly fragmented movement. Chapter 6 is devoted entirely to an analysis of the threat to feminism from public opinion, from organised groups and from conservative intellectuals. The extent of the hostility has become so great that in 1980 Betty Friedan, first president of the National Organisation for Women, felt it necessary to issue a public warning that the existing gains of the movement were in danger from reactionary forces.

To narrate a history is never a neutral act. One reason why there are not already dozens of books which do as much is that re-telling the history of a movement so passionately divided is itself divisive, no matter how carefully it is handled. Yet it would be a feeble book which did not face up to these divisions and attempt to judge their effect on the movement. The final chapter therefore reviews the situation of feminism as a movement and as an idea. The major questions facing feminists today are the unity of the movement in a period of crisis, the most effective form of organisation for the future and the kind of society which the women's movement aims to create. Is the ultimate goal to reform existing society, or to change it in revolutionary ways, to integrate women into man's world, or to erase the differences between women and men (androgyny), or to separate women from men? How can goals like these be achieved by the existing forms of feminist organisation?

These choices and many more have already been made by individual groups and tendencies within the movement, and their range suggests the diversity of views which exists. The issues are raised because they are essential constituents of an effective theory of feminism. A movement which speaks with many voices on such fundamental questions cannot be clearly identified in the public mind *as* one movement. Nor can it act together towards goals which are so variously defined.

The concluding chapter therefore examines widely debated issues concerning the internal organisation of the movement and its search for political effectiveness: the small group structure and the no-leadership ideal, the dangers of dogmatism and isolation and the problems of reaching out to women in the community.

That a man should comment on such matters will outrage some feminists, who believe that women alone have the right to interpret the women's movement. This is a questionable logic.

All people have the right to *decide* their own fate and *act* in their own interests. But to say that men should not even *write* about things which concern women, because men are oppressors, is to ask for an end to practically all intellectual discussion of inequality. Whites could not write about blacks, middle-class academics about the working class or Third World peoples or indeed anyone about a group to which s/he did not belong, and over whom s/he might have some measure of power. I have every sympathy with the argument that the oppressed are often denied their own voice and that their lives are often interpreted for them by people with privileged access to the power to publish (journalists, intellectuals, academics). But I do not believe that women's situation in Western countries today, bad though it is in many ways, includes the total suppression of the feminine or feminist voice. The movement has produced a very substantial literature on both sides of the Atlantic, and anyone seeking the insider's view of feminism has a choice of many sources, both intellectual and popular. This is a study of the *public face* of feminism as a social movement, not of the internal dynamics of groups or the experiences and consciousness of women. These things are no man's business, and many works are suggested in the Further Reading at the end of the book which will give the enquirer a different, more intimate and more committed interpretation of the meaning of feminism.

The role of outsider, commenting on the actions and ideas of others, contains both danger and opportunity. No man can be neutral in the feminist cause because it is in part a power struggle in which he as a man is involved. The feminist challenge is not least a challenge to men, a demand that they change in fundamental ways, and feminists have learned to be wary of men who claim to be their allies but finally react as men (i.e. as enemies) to concrete claims for equality, freedom and respect. A 'male feminist' is like a middle-class Marxist, always in peril of betraying his chosen cause through a sheer failure of nerve, because he has so much to lose. There *is* a conflict of interest and a deep difference in emotional experience which can at times take the form of real barriers to understanding. Unless one believes in the absolute purity and transcendent power of intellectual activity, these facts are significant to the extent to which they throw doubt on any man's capacity to be an objective and sympathetic observer.

Yet nobody, woman or man, could claim objectivity over such an emotionally charged issue as women's equality. One constructive way in which men can perhaps take up the feminist challenge is to engage in a critical dialogue with the movement, recognising the seriousness and the complexity of the issues which are being raised and responding as men to the new knowledge which women have created.

Recent history is always treacherous ground. Events which must be described are still unfinished, and their meaning is frequently in dispute; ideas and ideologies develop and change even as they are written down; it is all but impossible to discern which movements and events will turn out to be important in the long run, and which will prove trivial. The definitive history of modern feminism will be written long after the event by the people who were involved.

This book will have served its purpose if it helps women and men (perhaps especially men) to see beyond the distorted images of women's liberation which they find in the mass media and to appreciate that this is a movement which touches the lives of everyone. If it can be accepted as a positive response to the feminist challenge, so much the better.

1. False Promises: the Liberation and Domestication of Women

In 1928, after almost a hundred years of struggle against the prejudices, religious bigotry and fears of men, British women achieved full voting rights; their long battle against second-class citizenship seemed to be at an end. In the House of Commons, Prime Minister Stanley Baldwin spoke this epitaph on the suffragette movement:

> The subjection of women, if there be such a thing, will not now depend on any creation of law, nor can it be remedied by any action of the law. It will never again be possible to blame the Sovereign State for any position of inequality. Women will have, with us, the fullest rights. The grounds and justification for the old agitation is gone, and gone forever.[1]

The victory so grudgingly conceded to militant women turned out to be an empty one. In 1978 a new feminist movement would be fighting to secure rights which had seemed assured half a century before and to defend those already won. On the fiftieth anniversary of what men had jeeringly called the 'flapper vote', a commemorative gathering was held in London. At that meeting the younger feminists issued an open letter to the veteran suffragettes, which began: 'Dear Sisters, We are writing to you because you will understand how angry we are. One hundred years after the first feminist movement started, fifty years after we were given the vote, women are still not free.'[2] Among the things which half a century of voting had failed to achieve were: equal pay, equal educational and job opportunities, equal representation in Parliament, protection from rape and violence, freedom of sexual choice and freedom from sexual stereotypes and the domestic burdens which those stereotypes had heaped on women. Like black people in America, they had learned through bitter experience that legal or political equality did not necessarily bring equality of condition. The bonds which some women had believed shattered in 1928 had less to do with the franchise than with the deeper structures of family life, male-dominated culture and the entrenched economic interests of men.

The feminists of the 1970s understood these deep structures of male power, or patriarchy; many of them believed that the antagonism between the sexes was deeper even than the divisions between races or classes. Woman/man, mother/father, goddess/god are among the most primitive and emotionally charged distinctions we learn as children. In attempting to bring these things into consciousness and change them, modern feminism issued a challenge to our culture more radical than communism, fundamentalist religion or any other revolutionary creed.

In this chapter we shall look for the roots of the modern movement in history, at what sparked off the first great wave of feminist protest and at how the apparent success of suffrage carried with it a broader defeat. Because this book is mainly concerned with the renewal of feminism that followed, only a very abbreviated picture of the earlier period is possible, and readers are referred for more detail to the histories listed in the Further Reading. Here we are concerned primarily with untangling the forces which conspired to defeat the high expectations of the suffragettes at their moment of victory, and which led from the liberated 'new woman' of the 1920s to the ultra-domesticated 'happy housewife' of the 1950s. At this, the *nadir* of women's liberation, a combination of political, social and economic changes helped produce the climate for a new and more militant movement.

The First Wave of Feminism

Feminism as a radical protest against the female condition began in America, and has always been strongest there. Although women's role had been questioned by radical intellectuals since the eighteenth century, it was not until the early nineteenth that the conditions for a more widespread protest began to emerge.

In America's early decades women had a special role in the building of the new nation. The pioneers who pushed back the frontiers and opened the west and midwest for settlement prized those few independent women who accompanied them and who carried more than their share of the burdens and hardships. These pioneer women became almost legendary for their toughness and endurance, and it is no accident that it was the western frontier states like Wyoming and Utah which first granted women the vote, a full fifty years before they were enfranchised by the federal government. Even in the cities of the east women were more respected as independent human beings than their European sisters. The French aristocrat and social critic Alexis de Tocqueville remarked during his travels in the 1830s:

> In the United States, men seldom compliment women, but they daily show how much they esteem them. They constantly display an entire confidence in the understanding of a wife and a profound respect for her freedom; they have decided that her mind is just as fitted as that of a man to discover the plain truth, and her heart as firm to embrace it; and they have never sought to place her virtue, any more than his, under the shelter of prejudice, ignorance and fear.[3]

As so often in American history, religion helped reinforce specifically American social patterns. Protestant nonconformism was hardly a hospitable doctrine for feminism as such, but it did allow far more active participation and even leadership in the churches to women than did the rigid hierarchies of the Church of England or the Catholic Church. The Quaker and Baptist sects especially produced many able female leaders, and encouraged the always-subversive doctrine that the individual could relate directly to his or her god. The great religious awakening of the early nineteenth century saw an intensification of women's activity in the churches, and a huge proliferation of associations concerned with charity, evangelical work, moral reform and temperance. The existence of this great female network was to be of decisive importance in spreading the idea of feminism quickly and widely through the population.

But it was the anti-slavery movement which provided ordinary, middle-class American women with both a public forum and a vital insight into their own situation. Christian women were highly active in the abolitionist cause, seeing the condition of the slaves as a religious abomination and a national disgrace. And what was the condition of the slaves? They could own no property, and indeed were themselves treated as property; they had no legal rights to their own children; no right to vote; no right to payment for the work they performed for their masters; no redress against abuse or violence; no access to education, skilled work or independent social status of any kind. It could scarcely have escaped the married women working for abolition that, despite their relative comfort and security, precisely the same restrictions applied to them.

The female abolitionists exposed some of men's deepest prejudices. Strenuous efforts were made to prevent women speaking in public, since this implied their entry into the jealously guarded male realms of politics and power. A key consciousness-raising moment was the exclusion of women from effective participation in the World Anti-Slavery Convention in London in 1840. By the middle of that decade there was a distinct movement for women's rights, based, like the anti-slavery movement, on appeals to the promises of the US Constitution and the Declaration of Independence, which seemed to guarantee freedom and equality to all. More sceptical feminists of the time reflected that the Declaration was no less than honest in its promise that 'All *men* are created equal.' They sensed – and they were right – that slavery might be more easily and promptly abolished than the subjection of women.

Against these forces for liberation, tendencies emerged which created new tensions for American women: modernisation was irresistible, with the growth of industry and big cities, and the general civilisation of the whole, wild continent. The affluent middle classes looked to Europe for a proper life-style, and one of the things they imported and imposed was the

Victorian idea of the lady of the house, dedicated entirely to family, home, religious and domestic pursuits. Generations of women growing up in the 1830s and 1840s never experienced the opportunities and independence which their mothers and grandmothers had known in more expansive times. It is indicative that, in the south, where white women had always been restricted within a peculiarly stifling and artificial role, the feminist impulse was weak.

The American movement was formally launched at a convention at Seneca Falls in 1848 organised by Lucretia Mott and Elizabeth Cady Stanton. The convention issued an Alternative Declaration calling for reforms such as property rights for married women and greater access to education, trades and professions, including the church. An undercurrent of more radical demands for the transformation or abolition of the family and for free love were an embarrassment to the movement in a puritanical and restrictive age, and only effectively resurfaced a century later. In general, the conventional wisdom that women had special duties and responsibilities to home and family was accepted, though this doctrine of separate spheres for men and women later became a source of division between moderate and more radical feminists.

Voting rights, although mentioned in the Seneca Falls document, were also seen as radical in this period but, as the century wore on and other rights were conceded, the suffrage gradually became the main and only issue for the movement. Freed male slaves could vote by 1866, and the women who had campaigned so long and hard against slavery justly expected the same right. Resentment over the race issue divided the movement between 1869 and 1890, when the National American Women's Suffrage Association (NAWSA) was formed to carry forward the struggle for the vote on the federal level. But it was to take thirty more hard years of struggle, hundreds of individual state campaigns, defeats, divisions and uncertainty before the vote was won. The 19th Amendment (or 'Anthony Amendment', after the veteran campaigner Susan B. Anthony) was first introduced to Congress in 1878, was rejected, and continued to be rejected in every session up to 1920, when women finally became full political citizens and the first gruelling phase of the American feminist movement was over.

British women had never experienced the relative independence and respect which had been granted to their pioneering American sisters. Nor did they live under a formal political creed of liberty and equality for all. Nor were they engaged to the same degree in such consciousness-raising public struggles as the abolitionist movement. The evangelical zeal behind anti-slavery was less influential in the British movement than the more moderate 'social conscience' spirit of the established churches.

While middle-class British wives, like their American counterparts, experienced the full-blown Victorian family as a suffocating burden, the change was not as sharp or as sharply-felt in the older, more traditionalist culture. And, unlike their American sisters, they had few other structures or creeds to turn to in their revolt against the restrictions of Victorian home life. In short, the contradictions in women's lives were less keenly experienced, and this was reflected in a later start for British feminism, a smaller scale of organisation and a gentler, less militant tone in the early days.

Not that the British feminists lacked ideas or causes. Some of their inspiration came from the American movement, as later happened in the 1960s. Books, journals and pamphlets from the USA were eagerly read by educated women, and prominent American organisers like Elizabeth Cady Stanton came over to speak and give encouragement. But the philosophical foundation of the British movement was not any single constitutional document but rather the whole rationalistic, liberal, egalitarian spirit of the Enlightenment. If one had to choose one example of that spirit, it would be Mary Wollstonecraft's *Vindication of the Rights of Women*, published in 1792, which would stand as a statement of ideals for women for over a century. Feminism on both sides of the Atlantic was a product of liberal rather than socialist philosophy. After Wollstonecraft, the document which produced the profoundest effect was an essay by the liberal individualist John Stuart Mill, *On the Subjection of Women*, published in 1869. Chartists, socialists, Saint Simonians, Owenites and indeed Marx and Engels themselves all observed the injustice of women's situation, but they were never moved to do much about it; nor were feminists on the whole very comfortable with these revolutionary doctrines. Socialism and

Marxism only became significant for feminism in the twentieth century. In the meantime inequalities of class and inequalities of gender were treated as entirely separate issues.

The specific issues which engaged the attention of women at the outset of the British movement in 1856 were the rights of married women to own property, family welfare and better opportunities for education and employment. Through the remainder of the nineteenth century slow and painful progress was made towards these goals through the tireless organising work of women like Emily Davies, Barbara Leigh Smith and Caroline Norton.

By the 1870s the British movement had begun to take on a different tone and split into two distinct parts, a process mirrored in the USA. On the one hand, there were numerous women's clubs, associations and campaigns directed towards moral reform, based on the premise that women were morally superior to and more refined than men, and had a specifically feminine mission to civilise men's untidy and disorderly world. Women who chafed against the restrictions of the Victorian family were able to move into public life by using the argument that the world was nothing but a larger home into which their purifying and nurturing duties should properly be extended.

In the desperate poverty of those times, the social feminists found endless opportunities for philanthropic works. In Britain the prostitution crusade associated with the name of Josephine Butler, and Annie Besant's pioneering campaign for birth control, were two of the great struggles. But prison reform, public health, working conditions, child labour and all the worst symptoms of early industrialism were tackled by women's organisations, or by organisations in which women were prominent. In the USA in the later years of the century, the Temperance Movement and the Settlement Movement among the city poor engaged the energies of women in the same way. It was of course true that such crusades, based on the notion of the special purity of womanhood, often reinforced the divisions between the sexes rather than dissolving them. But this was no problem for the Victorian reformers, who would have been rather horrified by the idea that men and women were the same. Indeed, the sentiment of the time was that womanhood should become the standard against which men could measure their failings. The Declaration of Sentiments issued at Seneca Falls in 1848 demanded that 'The same amount of virtue, delicacy, and refinement of behaviour that is required of woman in the social state should also be required of man.'

In 1903, the long and apparently hopeless struggle of the Suffrage Societies gave rise to a new and more militant organisation, Mrs Pankhurst's Women's Social and Political Union (WSPU), and the vote became more and more the all-consuming feminist issue. The treatment meted out to the suffragettes, especially in the last years of their campaign, is one of the more shameful episodes in British history. The violence practised on these women, whose 'crimes' were never more than trivial, vividly illustrates the fear and loathing inspired in men by the modest claim for the vote. It was more than a claim for equity; as men well knew, it was a fundamental attack on privilege.

But it was an attack which, after the catastrophe of the First World War and the inescapable contribution of women to the war effort, the government had lost the will to resist. In 1918 the Representation of the People Bill granted the suffrage to women aged over 30 and, ten years later, the franchise was finally equalised by the inclusion of younger and unmarried women aged over 21.

In Britain as in America victory brought mixed emotions. Most ordinary women and the men who had supported them felt that the battle had indeed been won, and that the normal processes of politics would now ensure full and substantial equality. The exhausted suffragettes themselves, having confronted the system for many years, were less certain that this would be the end of the fight or that the vote would bring utopia. The dreadful war and the bitterness of the suffrage struggle had brought a sober realism. Sylvia Pankhurst wrote in her autobiography: 'Gone was the mirage of a society regenerated by enfranchised womanhood as by a magic wand.'[4] The campaign to turn the vote into more tangible benefits for women was work for a new generation of feminists.

After the Vote

What happened next is a poignant reminder of the limitations of democratic politics. Just as the vote had failed to bring equality to working-class men or to American blacks, so it failed for women. After several years of being nervously sensitive to women's issues, politicians realised that women were simply not voting on such issues as a group; nor did they have an effective political party of their own; nor were women entering politics in significant numbers. All three conditions are necessary before a group can begin to turn the democratic system to its own advantage. In Britain as in America the torch which the suffragettes had laid down was simply not picked up.

If politics is where the power is, and if we look at the levels of female participation in national politics, the figures are startling. In 1929, the first general election after full suffrage, 69 women candidates contested seats and 14 women MPs were elected (2.2 per cent of the total). In the 1979 election, with the victorious party led by a woman, 210 female candidates stood and just 19 MPs entered the House (3 per cent). Simple arithmetic tells us that, at this rate of progress, the House of Commons would be equally balanced in just a little under 3,000 years. The highest number of women MPs ever was 29 after the 1964 election, so the present figure actually represents a sharp decline. In the USA the picture is, if anything, worse. Nine women were elected to the House of Representatives in 1928 as against 19 in 1980, in which year there were only two female senators in the elected upper house.

These figures can be interpreted in many ways. Anti-feminists claim they prove that women are incompetent at or uninterested in politics, and should stick to their kitchens. Yet the obstacles facing women who try for selection as political candidates are often overwhelming and, once in the electoral arena, they face the daunting reality of prejudice from both men *and* women. Women do not vote as a bloc any more than do men, and they certainly have not used their votes to elect other women.

We can also speculate that, for many of the old-time feminists, the vote was more symbolic than strategic. They believed that the true destiny of a woman was not to become an ersatz male, fighting for petty advantage in politics and commerce and war, but to contribute her distinctively feminine qualities fully to society. High-minded as it was, this attitude did nòt encourage women to pursue economic or political power. What was distinctively feminine all too easily became defined as women's issues and women's interests, things which had never much threatened the central sources of male power and which men, once they had learned the new rules of the game, could generously concede to the domain of women. If anything, women had become less visible as political actors than they were during the suffragette agitation.

Historians disagree about the extent to which women's lives really changed in the 1920s. The popular press image of womanhood in that febrile decade was that of the 'flapper', sexually provocative and emotionally hard. Wearing short hair, short skirts and the flat-breasted tubular look, smoking cigarettes, driving cars and flying planes, the flapper embodied a new and more exciting life possibility for women. In Britain the terrible decimation of men in the First World War added an extra dimension to independence. There now appeared a big surplus of females who remained unmarried, or married to men so damaged that they could not play the traditional masculine role. These women learned by necessity to be more androgyn-ous, less traditionally feminine. But the much-publicised 'new woman' of the 1920s probably represented only a small, young and privileged minority; most ordinary women led lives of quiet domesticity or enforced celibacy.

Nor do we see in this era much evidence of substantial progress for women in education, work or the professions. In Britain in 1919 the Sex Disqualification Removal Act gave access to professions and professional associations, and in both countries the proportion of women employed professionally went up two or three percentage points in the decade; but they remained clustered in the traditional female occupations, especially teaching. It was hardly a period of liberation or equality in the sense in which those terms are used today, and for working-class women virtually nothing changed.

Meanwhile, feminists had by no means ceased to be active in women's causes, and were generally scathing about the kind of 'new woman' represented by the flapper. In the USA, after suffrage, the National American Women's Suffrage Association transformed itself into the League of Women Voters, and set out to educate women into their political roles and responsibilities. Women's issues in Congress were co-ordinated by a Women's Joint Congressional Committee, and legislators found themselves facing a steady stream of bills on welfare for women and children, birth control, abortion (on medical rather than libertarian grounds), divorce and allied family issues. The whole movement, in fact, had become welfare-oriented, with the exception of the small Women's Party led by Alice Paul which continued to press for equal rights, and introduced the Equal Rights Amendment (ERA) into Congress for the first time in 1923.

This was a somewhat bitter division in the movement, for it was more than just a matter of priorities. The welfare feminists fully accepted the notion of separate spheres for women, and were concerned with issues like protective legislation and child care which tended to reinforce the role of women as home-makers. The equal rights feminists, on the other hand, were convinced as they always had been that women would be oppressed until these traditional roles were broken down absolutely and by law, and regarded things like protective legislation as barriers to equality. Both groups saw the other as an unwitting enemy of women, and both were weakened by the conflict. As the 1920s turned into the 1930s and peace and survival became the overriding concerns, both welfare and equal rights activism languished.

In Britain we see a similar pattern of development after the first phase of suffrage ended in 1919. While some prominent suffragettes like the Pankhursts abandoned the movement for new endeavours, many others continued to be active. Their prime target was full suffrage (which came in 1928), and this goal tended to keep the organisations alive. Aside from the suffrage, the movement was divided about equally between those groups concerned with the extension of equal rights, such as the Fawcett Society, and those more interested in welfare, but, until the end of the decade, no sharp conflict developed between them as it had in the USA.

This was in part because the new Labour Party acted as an umbrella organisation and parliamentary representative for feminism, pulling together the different groups in the cause of effective action. The National Union of Societies for Equal Citizenship (NUSEC), the Women's Co-operative Guild, the Women's Freedom League and many others campaigned with as much energy as their American sisters on a whole range of causes from the guardianship of children to pension plans. Politicians – perhaps still anxious about the power of the women's vote – were willing to go along with these reforms, and substantial welfare gains were made through the decade.

Protective legislation again provided the occasion for a break in the movement in 1927 when NUSEC split over the issue of welfare *versus* equal rights. In the British case the welfare current was clearly dominant so that, after full suffrage, the weakened movement moved forward into the threatening decade of the 1930s with its egalitarian goals muted in favour of piecemeal social reform.

Depression and War

Nevertheless something had been gained and, on these slender beginnings, much more might have been built. But, as so often happens, history ambushed and negated the advances made. In 1929 the whole industrialised world was cast into a depression which allowed women no chance to grasp their opportunities, and the fragile continuity of their progress was broken long before new valuations of their roles could become securely established in the culture.

The depression affected employed middle-class and working-class women differently. In many working-class families in Britain, and perhaps even more among poor and black families in America, the unemployment of the breadwinning male resulted in the wife becoming the sole support of her family, since low-paid domestic and sweatshop work was more easily available to women. Bereft of his traditional authority, the unemployed husband might find himself sharing domestic chores which his father would not have deigned to touch. In these depression years some working women thus achieved a new authority in their families; but male resentment and the breaking of the tradition of male responsibility more than cancelled out these gains.

Most middle-class women experienced no such exchange of roles. On the contrary there was a concerted effort to get them out of the employment market altogether. The previous slow growth in the employment of women in professional and managerial capacities was reversed, and under the British Anomalies Regulations of 1931 married women were cut off from unemployment benefit, forcing them back into total dependence. The media, quick to go with the tide and almost entirely controlled by men, cynically revived the idea that the truly feminine woman did not work, and that the working wife was selfish and perverse. A rash of new women's magazines boosted this old/new ideology of femininity. Fashions lost the practical severity of the 1920s and became frilly and awkward once more. The fully employed, competitive 'new woman' had become a luxury which societies in the throes of depression could not afford.

In America the same dismal story was repeated, though New Deal programmes like Aid to Dependent Children and maternal care brought some benefits to women. Educated and professional women were eased out of their jobs, but the worst sufferers were the poorest, mostly black women, thousands of whom were left homeless and utterly destitute by the economic collapse.

To explain how such severe changes in employment are managed, some sociologists and economists suggest that work in industrial societies is organised as a 'dual labour market'. According to this theory women as a group, along with some ethnic minorities, function as a reserve army of workers which can be called into action in times of war or economic boom and returned to idleness when times are bad for employers. This apparent callousness is justified by the assumption that these are secondary workers who (in the case of women) should properly be looked after by their husbands or (in the case of both women and ethnic minorities) are unskilled, unreliable newcomers to the workforce who have to be sacrificed for the sake of the real producers, who usually turn out to be white males. During the depression trade unions, dominated by white males, did little to defend women workers against this abuse.

But the sacrifice of parts of the female workforce during the 1930s was a temporary expedient. When the Second World War broke out women were summoned back into the man's world of work by the pressing needs of wartime production. In the services and in the civilian labour force women once again demonstrated what they had clearly shown in the First World War, that they could do any man's job. They drove trucks and buses, operated cranes and heavy machinery, learned to be welders, radar operators, electrical engineers and anti-aircraft gunners. Many women already in the labour force as unskilled workers received training for new and more satisfying jobs. The rhetoric of 'a woman's place is in the home' was temporarily shelved as yesterday's housewives became today's heroic war workers.

The most significant change, however, was in the numbers of married women working for the first time. Between 1939 and 1945 the proportion of married women who earned a wage rose from one in seven to one in four in the USA and in Britain. Immediately after the war in both countries there was a panic over jobs for returning soldiers, and a wave of propaganda urged women to go back to their homes. Many did, and many were forced out of work. As one woman put it, 'We were no longer comrades [with the returning men] but competitors for what little there was.'[5] But by the early 1950s booming reconstruction economies were pulling women back in, and by 1954 a quarter of married women in Britain and America were again employed. The working wife had become an accepted fact, and the consequences in terms of living standards, expectations and the nature of traditional marriage were to be profound.

Post-War Affluence: Women as Consumers and Producers

In 1945 the citizens of a devastated Europe emerged into a new world, or at least the promise of one. In the grey days of post-war scarcity, Britons were encouraged to dream utopian dreams of the peacetime affluence which was to be their reward. The model was America, already unimaginably rich in

British imaginations and scarcely touched by wartime austerity. Big coloured magazines mailed from the USA showed pictures of the ideal families with detached houses and cars and washing-machines and boats and televisions. All this – so went the fantasy – would be Britain's future, with the added bonus of a nurturing welfare state to blunt the sharp edges of capitalism.

In America itself the war had brought a decisive end to the depression and, during the late 1940s, a veneer of affluence spread more widely through the middle and working classes. What was reflected in those magazines, and taken to be the norm, was in fact the first wave of mass American consumerism, a dozen years ahead of its British counterpart. Suburbs of single-family houses mushroomed around all the big cities, and here real families, with two jobs and massive hire-purchase debts, struggled to be like those ideal families in the magazines, on television and on the cinema screen.

This pre-eminence of America as a model of the new affluent culture thrust before women (and men) a materialistic ideal impossible to achieve, not least because it was largely imaginary. Historically, social movements have often been grounded in relative deprivation, a feeling that one's just and legitimate expectations are not being fulfilled. The American utopia produced both a desire to imitate and a guaranteed backlash of jealous disappointment when those dreams were frustrated. Tiny British cars with tail fins and chrome teeth, the cocktail craze, the gadget crazes, the slavish imitation of American casual fashions, pop music and Hollywood films all reflected the obsession with things American. And the tough and glamorous American woman who lived confidently in the midst of all this plenty, she too was an image to conjure with.

The Festival of Britain in 1951 and the coronation of Queen Elizabeth II in 1953 were two high points of post-war optimism. With the new welfare state to watch over the health and security of families and new machines to take the worst drudgery out of housework, the country seemed to be heading for a golden age of sexual equality. Sociologists believed they detected a new phenomenon, the working-class family grown affluent on a double income. It was widely assumed that such families, by acquiring consumer goods and middle-class expectations, would help consolidate the classless society of the

Labour Party manifesto by eroding the sharp differences which gave rise to class conflict. And the working wives themselves, with some financial independence and the chance to get out of the house and meet people, were expected to be more emancipated than the housebound and dependent women of an earlier age.[6] Events were to prove these predictions wrong on all counts.

The irony was that, in the scramble for security and better living standards, affluence and freedom somehow became confused. The notion took root – not without energetic help from governments and mass media – that material goods were literally and psychologically liberating, the physical proof of our free-world status. Overwhelmingly in America, and through paler imitation in Britain, the home and its appurtenances became the showplace of family achievement. This had always been the arena in which women could legitimately express their creativity and establish their identity in the world. Now, millions of women working as producers generated extra income which could be ploughed back into the home in their alternate role as consumers.

When the consumer boom began, its appeal was directed squarely at women. Retailing became a sophisticated art designed to make buying a pleasure and a vocation; modernised department stores with open shelves, soft carpets and background music, shopping malls with unlimited parking (in the USA), every device was deployed to tempt the housewife and working woman into the new temples of consumption. Advertising was the driving force, and the marketing techniques developed after the war helped promote an explosion of glossy women's magazines directed towards home and family; these magazines consisted – and still do – mainly of advertising matter.

While men were equally caught up in the consumerist fantasy, it was a special burden to women. By far the greatest volume of consumer goods were connected with home and home-making, and the advertisers were 100 per cent agreed that this was women's business. The complexity of choices now facing the housewife (which extended from housewares into clothes, cosmetics and accessories) reinforced the separation of women by making femininity an even more richly specialised art. This elevation of the domestic role served to cut women off from other options; affluence helped give that role a spurious content. What in meaner circumstances was manifestly drudgery now became invested with a certain glamour.

The advertising industry itself thus became a deadly enemy to women. Not only were they portrayed almost universally as silly creatures, totally engaged in the unserious business of cleaners and cake mixes but, in so far as they were allowed any existence at all outside the home, it was as sex objects. Advertising's most durable discovery was that women's bodies can be used to sell anything and that the sexual appeal of a woman and the material appeal of an object can all too easily be confused in people's minds. Pornography proves that this discovery works both ways.

The counterpart of this orgy of consumption was a massive expansion of productive and service industries. At the very moment when people most acutely felt the need for a second family income, changes in technology and the employment structure made millions of suitable jobs available to women. After the low point immediately after the war, a steady increase in female employment began which has continued with minor upsets until the present time. If we look at the proportion of all adult women working in Britain and America decade by decade, the figures are remarkably similar: 1950, 30 per cent; 1960, 35 per cent; 1970, 42 per cent; 1980, 51 per cent (approximations). The statistics for *married* women working showed an even steeper rise, from around 20 per cent in 1950 to over 50 per cent today. Many of them were mothers, including the previously inactive group of mothers with young children, though there was no parallel improvement in flexible working hours or child-care facilities to make the life of the employed mother easier.

These figures do not, of course, show any dramatic equalisation of women's work *status* in the post-war world, simply that more of them held paid jobs outside the home. By and large the growing female workforce remained in female-dominated occupations and, by and large, they were very badly paid. The vast majority were occupied in lower clerical and shop work, cleaning, unskilled factory work, nursing, primary school teaching and similar traditionally female roles, and many of the new jobs were on a part-time basis, without security or benefits. Although opportunities were undoubtedly improving, the proportions of women holding posts as managers, doctors, head teachers, research scientists and so forth remained dismally low. The Royal Commission on Equal Pay issued an ambiguous report in 1946 which implied that only professional women really deserved the same pay as men, and even they were a long way from getting it. In the 1950s and early 1960s a woman doing an identical job to a man could generally expect to receive 60 per cent of the man's earnings (or at best 70 per cent) and her wage or salary might be entirely swallowed up by the cost of the domestic arrangements which allowed her to earn it.

For a while the affluent society was self-sustaining, consumption generating full employment generating profits generating investments in a classic capitalist boom cycle. For the first and possibly the last time ordinary working people began to think in terms of ever-rising material standards of living within a paternalistic and secure framework. Encouraged by the growth of the welfare state in Britain and the high tide of liberal reform in America, the last remnants of the puritan ethic succumbed to the more attractive belief that the world owed us not just a living, but a good one.

But yet another painful squeeze was on the way. Just as the massive, better-educated post-war generations began to flood the labour market, the world economy began its long downward slide. The first tremors of serious inflation and unemployment began to be felt in Britain around 1965, and some years later in the more resilient American economy. Once again the economic switchback was about to pull women down.

The Liberalisation of Sexuality

In this brave new world one essential item of consumption was sex. Since the 1920s the rigid sexual rules which had helped to preserve family life in Victorian and Edwardian society had increasingly been disregarded. The social upheavals of the First World War and the shortage of men which followed, revealing fashion styles and new social freedoms for women, the declining influence of religion and, above all, the availability of effective female-controlled contraception in the form of the diaphragm had all contributed to the changing morality. Women's sexuality had always been controlled by fear – fear of social disgrace, fear of hell fire and fear of pregnancy. As these sanctions lost their power, and the ignorance which went with them was dispelled by more and more explicit information about sexual matters (under the guise of psychology or marriage guidance), some women at least gained the confidence to make their own sexual choices.

The process was hastened and spread through the class structure by the family dislocations and cultural traumas of the Second World War, and the soldiers came home to a culture saturated with sexual feelings, which advertisers and film-makers were quick to exploit. In Britain the rationed drabness of war had not done much for feminine fashions. As rationing ended and materials became available, an impulse to femininity appeared in visible form. In 1947 Christian Dior introduced the long-skirted 'new look'; in 1952 he launched the lethal stiletto-heeled shoe and, through imitation and mass production, a whole new ultra-feminine and restrictive style of dress emerged. The feminine mystique of an earlier time was being re-born, but this time with an undercurrent of explicit sexuality.

For the teenage generation better health brought earlier sexual maturity, and physical mobility provided the opportunity for sexual adventures. Before she had reached the age of 20 a young woman might have had all the life experiences which previously defined mature womanhood. For many the new freedom brought dismal experiences of exploitation and abandonment by men, pregnancy and abortion.

The widespread relaxation of attitudes towards sex was fundamentally based on improvements in the technology and availability of contraception. Traditional attitudes had been built up over the centuries when every act of intercourse could mean yet another miserable, perhaps fatal, pregnancy. Fifty years of technical progress and political campaigning for birth control had made these attitudes increasingly redundant. By the mid-1950s married women in Britain had access to Family Planning Association clinics in many cities and, in ten more years, the female contraceptive pill was widely available, though its dangers were not yet realised. The pill, however, was not responsible for the end of the baby boom – births had already peaked and started to decline by 1957. In 1967, the same year as the Abortion Act, the Family Planning Act empowered local authorities to give birth-control advice and supplies, and in 1970 the Family Planning Association decided to offer contraceptive advice to all women over 16, whether married or not. For a privileged minority male vasectomy (and to a lesser extent female sterilisation) had also become available as secure alternatives. This was something infinitely more revolutionary than any philosophical notion of liberation or equality because it offered women an elemental power which only celibacy or age could previously have given them: the power to control their own bodies.

Two significant exceptions to this liberalisation were homosexuality and lesbianism. The Wolfenden Report of 1957 paved the way for the decriminalisation of private homosexual acts in 1967, and this was a step in the direction of full acceptance. But lesbianism – the love of women for other women – remained deeply hidden from public consciousness and hardly discussed.

Not everyone concerned with human liberation welcomed the liberation of sexuality. The neo-Marxist philosopher Herbert Macuse argued that it was merely a device used by capitalist societies to distract people from more serious political and economic oppressions. Many old-guard feminists were as profoundly unhappy with the new permissiveness as they had earlier been with the antics of the flappers, for along with this apparent liberation of female sexuality came a reinforcement of the image of women as creatures of a separate and powerless sphere – feminine, delicate and dedicated mainly to the romantic and/or sensual pursuit of men. The Victorian stereotype of feminine purity had at least the merit that it rendered women special (if inferior) in men's eyes. In the pursuit of equality and freedom even this dubious moral advantage was lost, and the way was open for a new and less flattering stereotype. It was no accident that the most ardent supporters of the *Playboy* style of sexual liberation were men.

The Dream of Domesticity: Woman as Housewife and Mother

The sexualisation of culture did not imply a diminished interest in marriage and the family. On the contrary, as the numbers of each sex reaching marriageable age equalised and finally stabilised with a slight surplus of men, more young people married earlier than ever before. Sexual experience did not seem to dent the romantic view of marriage; if anything, the marital experience was expected to be even more romantic and blissful than before.

In considering the ideology of marriage and womanhood during this period, the popularity of Doris Day's movies pinpoints the collective (male) fantasy. The glamorous, sexy, competent, tough woman gives her man or men a thoroughly hard time, threatening their masculinity and challenging their prejudices. In the last reel she discovers true love and undergoes a Pygmalionesque transformation into a happy, obedient, housewife. This less than innocent nonsense was, to be sure, written and produced by men, and it may have sparked off a certain anxiety in women less versatile than Ms Day. But for the millions on both sides of the Atlantic who sat through *April in Paris* (1952), *Calamity Jane* (1953), the *Pajama Game* (1957), *Teacher's Pet* (1958) and a shoal of near-identical productions, the message was loud and clear: a woman might be as strong, as free and as clever as a man but her *real* destiny and happiness lay in being a wife and mother. Popular television series like *I Love Lucy* and *Father Knows Best* reinforced the same dream-image of domesticity, and the magazine market was flooded with new titles dedicated to romance and home-making.

Despite the increasing number of married women in employment, this ideal of woman-as-housewife was endorsed by governments and happily embraced by many women. Eager to make comfortable lives after the deprivations and uncertainties of war, many middle- and working-class women opted for home and motherhood, marrying quickly or settling down for the first time with returning husbands they had scarcely seen. The men, filled with dreams of peacetime family life, were only too happy with this trend.

The Labour governments of 1945–51 accepted the conventional wisdom that stable families were the basis of a stable society and necessary to raise the worryingly low birth rate. As it happened, little propaganda was needed and the birth rate in both Britain and the USA shot up to an all-time high in 1947 and continued rising until 1957. Sociologists set about idealising the warmth and supportiveness of the family – especially what they conceived to be the traditional working-class family – and social welfare policies were tailored to make the institution still more attractive. The Children Act of 1948 in Britain, for example, provided a safety-net for hard-pressed mothers unable to cope with their children, and National Health and Child Benefit programmes gave desperately needed financial relief to poorer families. A family-rescue service appeared, in the form of professional marriage guidance clinics with government and church support.

But domestic work itself, the daily routine which dominated the lives of married women, was a less manageable problem. The government could hardly provide domestic help on a national scale, nor could it contemplate the cost of what later became a key campaign in one sector of the feminist movement, wages for housework. Women's labour in the home continued to be unpaid and unrecognised, and little had changed since Friedrich Engels remarked in 1854 that 'The modern family is founded on the open or disguised domestic slavery of women.'[7]

Above all, the redomestication of women was made possible by a new ideology of child care and child–mother relationships. Dr Benjamin Spock's best-selling baby manual, *Baby and Child Care*, hit the American bookstores in 1946 and arrived in Britain a year later, just in time for the baby boom. The closest British equivalent, John Bowlby's *Child Care and the Growth of Love* (1953), was more theoretical than practical but the emotive keyword was the same, 'maternal deprivation'. Babies needed their mothers, and deprivation of constant maternal care in the early years might ruin a child's whole development. A monstrous weight of guilt was thus heaped on working mothers, while those who stayed at home were assured that their child-rearing task was more challenging and worth while than the vain pursuits of any career woman.

Indeed, for Spock, the ideal remedy for maternal deprivation lay in government allowances to mothers who would otherwise be forced to work, for 'Useful, well-adjusted citizens are the most valuable possession a country has, and good mother care during early childhood is the surest way to produce them. It doesn't make sense to let [sic] mothers go to work.'[8] Spock revised the book in 1973 to correct this bias.

Sceptical as many British mothers were of the new child-centred orthodoxy, its influence was profound. Popular newspapers, always quick to seize an opportunity for righteous indignation, published pathetic articles about 'latchkey children' left to fend for themselves on the streets by heartless working mothers. Every form of deviance, from juvenile delinquency to pre-marital sex, was blamed on the absence of mothers from the home. There was no evidence to support any of this reprobation, but it was a powerful emotive argument for the domestic confinement of women.

Despite the avalanche of good advice, things were less than perfect on the home front. The family, in its newly elevated role as a haven of romance and arbiter of future human character, was showing signs of stress. Domestic work and child-rearing had always meant isolated drudgery for women. Now, at the time of headlong growth and technological progress, when men's sphere of action was constantly expanding, women's sphere shrank once again to the four walls of the home. Their segregation was heightened by the decline of wider family ties and the fragmented life of suburbs, new towns and estates. It was just such a sense of confinement which had in part motivated the feminists of the mid-nineteenth century, cloistered in the stifling Victorian family while men were out building the empire and creating a new industrial world.

Middle-class housewives in the 1950s and 1960s also shouldered burdens which their Victorian sisters had not suffered. The more tedious drudgery of domestic life had previously fallen on the servant class. Rebellious Victorian ladies like Florence Nightingale complained of domesticity because it was claustrophobic and dull, not because it was hard work. But now the housewife, whether or not she had a university degree or a professional qualification, was expected to cope with the unrelieved round of shopping, cooking and cleaning dishes, floors, sinks, lavatories and clothes. Not only was she oppressed by the insult to her intelligence, but also by the constant drain on her physical energies and time.

The baroque elaboration of the full-blown American suburban life was beyond the reach of all but a few British families, and the ideology of the ultra-feminine housewife and mother was slower to take root in the more spartan climate of British society. But it served none the less as a cultural model of the ideal family and the ideal home. For many of the pre-war generation it was the long-delayed fulfilment of a dream; for some younger women and men, it was a claustrophobic nightmare. When the new feminist movement emerged, one of its most difficult tasks would be to reconcile the differences between those women who regarded the family as a haven and a refuge, and those who saw it as a repressive trap.

The experience of marriage and family life continued to change at a breathtaking pace for each succeeding generation. Traditions of decades and centuries were uprooted and discarded, sometimes with deliberation and sometimes by force of circumstances. By the end of the 1950s, and even more by the mid-1960s, women were marrying later and having fewer babies. As the puritan ethic faded, the search for happiness became increasingly a legitimate personal goal, and a bad marriage was a cruel obstacle to happiness. The divorce rate had risen steadily but slowly through the 1950s and early 1960s, but shot up between 1968 and 1978, doubling in the USA, where 'no fault' divorces became possible after 1970, and tripling in Britain following the Divorce Reform Act of 1969. In both countries now it is estimated that 40 per cent or more of first marriages will end in divorce. The high expectations of romance, companionship and sexual fulfilment which the post-war generations had inherited led to an epidemic of divorces after they reached marriageable age in the middle and late 1960s.

This changing valuation of the marriage tie had three important implications. First, it loosened the traditional bonds between parents and children, giving some women new life-chances and condemning many others to the dismal experience of abandonment and single parenthood. Second, it forced people to think in new ways about sexual relationships and to consider alternatives to the traditional family. Young women began to lose their taste for mother's domesticity, and for the security which turned out to be no security at all. The early 1960s saw a rash of trendy new women's magazines like *Woman's Mirror* and *Nova* which catered to the single and divorced working woman, and painted a somewhat richer picture of life's possibilities. Third, the fragility of marriage threw into sharp relief the archaic workings of the divorce laws themselves, in particular the ways women were discriminated against in matters of property, taxation and social security. In America for many years marriage had been a highly conditional and revocable contract, and American divorce rates a British national joke. After the 1969 reform British women found themselves in the same situation, with much more freedom at the cost of much less security. These changing attitudes to marriage may be seen as one of the essential preconditions of the new women's liberation movement.

Women's Life-Chances in a Changing World

In our society, individuals and groups are presumed to have access to economic opportunities, status and power largely according to their access to education. Feminist campaigners on both sides of the Atlantic had assumed since early in the nineteenth century that the education of women must be a crucial condition for their emancipation. By the time of the Second World War political pressure had ensured that free primary and secondary education was almost universally available on an equal basis to (white) girls. In America, college education also had been opened up to the extent that, by 1920, nearly half of all college students were (white) women – a figure which fell to 35 per cent in the domesticated decade of the 1950s.

In Britain the barriers against women entering higher education were more formidable. The monastic traditions of the ancient universities meant that all the most talented females could aspire to was the secluded ghetto of the women's college and, in any case, the whole system was much smaller and more elitist. In the 1920s less than a fifth of all university students in Britain were women, and by 1965 the figure had risen only to a quarter.

The first major breakthrough came with the 1944 Education Act, which established a grant system enabling young women to continue their education on the basis of merit in direct competition with men. The great expansion of the university system in the early 1960s, and the steady integration of all-male colleges, also made it more practical for qualified girls to aspire to a university place. By 1981 women made up more than a third of all British university students.

But important reservations have to be made about this apparent success story. The vast majority of female undergraduates were choosing to follow courses in the arts, humanities and teacher-training rather than in sciences, professional or vocational subjects. Partly as a consequence, women with degrees could expect to earn perhaps only half the salary of qualified males.

In the area of graduate and professional schooling, the gateway to the most prestigious and secure career opportunities, these trends in subject choice continued. Even more important, very few women were encouraged to continue beyond the undergraduate level at all. In 1965 women accounted for less than a quarter of all British postgraduate students (half of them in advanced teacher-training courses), one in ten PhD students and university teachers, and one in fifty full professors.

In terms of the number of trained and educated women available to be mobilised by a feminist movement, it is worth recalling the scale and scope of the American higher education system in contrast to the British. At this time some 30 per cent of all young American women were going on to some form of higher education, while in Britain only 5 per cent of women were able to enter the elite training grounds of the universities and polytechnics.

The basis of these striking differences in the educational choices and opportunities for women was not only the masculine tradition of the universities but the built-in bias of elementary and secondary education. In both Britain and America a predominantly female teaching force continued to regard the education of girls as something distinct and special.

The Crowther Report of 1959 and the Newsom Report of 1963 sustained the conventional wisdom that, while really gifted girls might benefit from academic education, most would be happier learning more ladylike and domestic skills which would prepare them for their future lives as housewives and mothers. This attitude, hardly challenged until the 1960s, ensured that most girls learned almost nothing which might be of use to them in the competitive world outside, and that those who made it into college would be steered towards the gentle but relatively useless fields of the arts and humanities.

But the slow evolution of education, work and marriage was to be overtaken by a change as sweeping and unstoppable as depression or war. On the tide of prosperity and optimism following the war, a long historic decline in birthrates had been abruptly reversed. Between 1946 and 1957 the average number of children per family doubled, and by the late 1960s the first wave of this unprecedented baby boom was reaching maturity. This was the largest, tallest, healthiest, best-educated and freest generation in history, and probably the most demanding. Schools and colleges expanded to digest them. As teenagers, they grew up in the era of unquestioned affluence, and became almost a race apart with their spending money, their own styles in clothes, music, dancing, films, magazines and sex. In Britain they acquired mobility with motor-cycles and scooters, in America they had their own cars. Parental authority over these alien creatures waned and vanished as the teenagers vocally and explicitly rejected the grey world of depression and war which had shaped their parents' lives. They could not relate to the struggle for security; the world for them was already too comfortable, safe and secure, a trap beyond which lay infinite possibilities. 'We don't want to be like you' was their cry; they became the vanguards of a youth revolution. The generations born after 1945 embraced such protest movements as existentialism, the literary iconoclasm of the 'angry young men', the anarchistic counterculture of the new left and, of course, feminism.

But it was into their parent's world of struggle and responsibility that, like it or not, these liberated teenagers were heading, for the total structure of society had not changed. Far from increasing to absorb them, the employment market steadied and began to shrink at all levels, and many were forced to accept jobs below the level of their skills. Highly qualified middle-class women of the baby boom began to emerge from college in the 1960s to find not the satisfying and lucrative careers which they had been led to expect but a fierce competition with men of their generation (and in America with qualified blacks and other minorities) for a decreasing number of jobs. As it turned out, education was not quite the panacea for inequality that people had supposed it to be. Opportunity also depends on free access to desirable jobs and careers. The managers, professionals and officials who act as gatekeepers in the labour market are, almost universally, men. When opportunities became scarce, their traditional assumptions about the proper roles of the sexes guaranteed that men would be favoured over women. Thus, as the long recession began, the security and rising living standards which this generation had seen as its birthright were snatched away the very moment they were grasped. Without disappointed dreams, there are no revolutions.

Literary and Intellectual Debates

In the two decades following the war the contrary pressures of work, sexuality and family on women's lives became the subject of passionate intellectual debate. A group of women novelists, among them Rosamund Lehmann, Iris Murdoch, Doris Lessing, Edna O'Brien, Margaret Drabble and Penelope Mortimer, made this their central theme. They wrote of the problematic nature of love, marriage and dependence, of the disappointment of sex, of the anger of educated women at the condescension of men, of the impossibility of fulfilling the conflicting roles which society demanded of them.[9]

The growing intellectual interest in the 'woman question' can be partially attributed to Simone de Beauvoir's *The Second Sex*, which had first appeared in English in 1952 and in a cheap paperback in 1961. The influence of de Beauvoir's work on a whole generation of literate men and women can hardly be overestimated and, although some feminists have subsequently attacked it as a book which blamed women for their own oppression, it remains a powerful consciousness-raising work. *The Second Sex* is an extended cultural, anthropological and biological analysis of how the feminine gender came to be defined as less than fully human, and therefore inferior. The American feminist Roxanne Dunbar wrote, 'For many of us, *The Second Sex* changed our lives . . . [it] is still the most intelligent, human and thorough document written on female oppression and masculine supremacy.'[10]

The spread of ideas from America brought works like Mirra Komarovsky's *Women in the Modern World: their Education and their Dilemmas* (1953) to British intellectuals and, in 1956, social scientists Viola Klein and Alva Myrdal produced a widely read book called *Women's Two Roles* which investigated the inherent conflict between work and motherhood. In Britain a similar pioneering work was Hannah Gavron's *The Captive Wife*, which appeared in 1966. In 1964 the highly respected journal of the American Academy of Arts and Sciences, *Daedalus*, produced a whole issue on the theme 'Women in America'. All at once it had become intellectually respectable to talk seriously about women.

The debates extended into questions of sexuality, and perhaps had their strongest public impact there. A steadily more permissive climate allowed the publication of fiction and non-fiction works which explored themes previously forbidden to the average reader. The novels of D. H. Lawrence provided high-culture justification for passionate and satisfying sex as every woman's right, and the Lady Chatterley trial of 1960 turned private uncertainties into a public debate which aired the whole question of the sexuality of women. The novels of Colette and the *Diaries* and *Erotica* of Anaïs Nin gave glimpses into a secret female world, while the popular novels and films of suburbia, Grace Metalious's *Peyton Place* (1956) being the prototype, introduced the public to a new era of frankness in (hetero-) sexual relationships.

More scientific curiosities were fed by the psychologists, sociologists and sexologists who made it their business to comment on the changing sexual scene. Alfred Kinsey's reports on *Sexual Behaviour in the Human Male* (1948) and *Sexual Behaviour in the Human Female* (1953) were the first of a genre which led to Master's and Johnson's dramatic clinical findings, published in 1966 as *Human Sexual Response*. There was an almost evangelical zeal to spread abroad the good news of women's sexual capacities. Low-grade imitations of these pioneering works continue to occupy the best-seller lists in the 1980s.

Thus, as the domesticated 1950s merged into the more turbulent 1960s, many educated women were experiencing deep ambivalence about careers, sexuality and family life. Old patterns were dissolving, and nothing identifiable was taking their place. One thing was clear, that women were going to have to compete in the man's world far more than hitherto – for jobs, for security, for power and for sexual satisfaction.

Women and Public Policy

Great social changes seldom have dramatic beginnings. When any group rebels against its condition, the historian can trace a long chronicle of change, of frustration, of learning and of hidden discontents leading to the final explosion. And, against all common-sense expectations, it is usually the most privileged among the dissenting group who express their anger first; so it was with feminism. Women of the intellectual and professional elites in Britain and America were fully aware of the handicaps which they and less fortunate women suffered. By the early 1960s they were applying energetic pressure on government and its agencies to do something about them. So the prelude to the appearance of a new women's *movement* was a period of discussion and legislation about women's issues which served to raise consciousness and expectations at the same time.

After the Second World War many women's organisations had continued to work for equality, but they existed quietly with a few dedicated followers and meagre resources. In Britain one might point to the Fawcett Society, the Status of Women Group, the Women's Freedom League and to women's caucuses in the trade unions and the Labour Party. In America, organisations like the National Women's Party and the National Federation of Business and Professional Women's Clubs fulfilled similar functions. The voice of traditional feminism was being heard in government and, though slow to respond, legislators did show some willingness to improve the situation of women.

In the USA the prime motive for government action on women was economic. Expanding employment in the 1950s' boom had created an acute shortage of labour. While the ideology of domesticity encouraged married women to stay at home with their children, more pragmatic voices urged that educated workers were going to waste. In 1957 the Ford Foundation financed a major report on working women, *Womanpower*, which stressed the need for child care, and in 1961, under pressure from professional women's organisations and individual politicians, President Kennedy set up a Commission on the Status of Women.

This was by no means a radical development, and some have suggested that it was merely a device to distract attention from the far more significant Equal Rights Amendment, which would remove all legal discrimination against women in one sweep. Nevertheless the Commission's temperate report in 1963 did document the major areas of discrimination in equal opportunity, equal pay, marriage and property laws. State Commissions and a Citizen's Advisory Council on the status of women were also established. These became important political training-grounds and helped keep women's issues in the public arena.

Even before the President's Commission issued its report, Congress had approved the Equal Pay Act of 1963, which established the principle of equal rewards in the private sector, and which was extended in 1966 to cover some public-sector workers. Tens of thousands of pay complaints have now been investigated, and the struggle to have those laws fully implemented continues.

The Civil Rights Act of 1964 was directed mainly at racial discrimination, but it included a section, Title VII, which prohibited discrimination by private employers or unions based on race, colour, religion, national origin or *sex*. The word 'sex' had actually been introduced into Title VII by a southern congressman, who saw it as a certain way of blocking the entire Act. But the legislation was passed, and the implications were profound. The Act was to be administered by a five-member Equal Employment Opportunities Commission (EEOC) and by satellite Commissions in each state. In 1967 the ban on discrimination was extended to cover employment by the government or its contractors, through President Johnson's Executive Order 11375.

In Britain in this period we see similar concessions by government preceding the revival of feminism. Although the Labour Party has never had a particularly sparkling record on women's issues, its welfare state legislation after 1945 brought many direct benefits to poorer families, notably medical care, free school meals and child allowances. By 1961 the equal pay principle had been established in teaching and in the civil service and, by 1970, a Labour government voted full equal pay legislation. In a sense, the Fabian/Socialist current in British politics made a moderate civil rights feminist movement unnecessary. Organisations like the National Council of Labour Women, the Child Poverty Action Group, the National Council of Civil Liberties and the TUC Women's Congress between them eventually took up most of the legal and egalitarian issues which in America required separate and more specifically feminist pressure groups.

Beyond the area of equal pay two other important reforms preceded feminism in Britain. Most significant was the Abortion Act of 1967, which came after the thalidomide scare of 1962 and a concerted campaign by liberal and humanist groups. The new law, while still restrictive, was an enormous improvement on what had gone before. It later became a focus of dispute between feminists and anti-feminists, and many campaigns have since been waged over whether the remaining restrictions on abortion should be removed or the old restrictions reimposed.

In 1969 the Divorce Reform Act removed many of the more degrading and unequal restrictions on women and men seeking to free themselves from bad marriages. This also had important secondary effects, freeing many women to start new lives, but also raising the issue of the rights of displaced home-makers who might not have the experience or the skills necessary to find a new source of income in late middle age.

These remarks on reform should not be taken to imply that the main feminist victories were already won. In substance, and in operation, the laws on equal pay, divorce and abortion still left a great deal to be desired. However, it is clear that public discussion was growing on issues related to women's inequality, and that governments were beginning to listen.

Conditions for a New Feminist Movement

This brief outline of events and changes shows how the conditions for a new feminist movement came together in the 1960s. For forty years women had been subjected to a series of violent and unpredictable transitions, in each phase of which their 'femininity' was defined by men in different terms. In the end the traditional mould of femininity was entirely broken, opening the way for a new definition of womanhood.

From the stifling bonds of the Victorian family to the unshackling of women in the First World War and the political triumphs of the suffragettes in the 1920s, women's lives had come almost full circle. Depression and renewed war had halted their economic and political progress and, after 1945, women had become the victims of a new ideology of domesticity and motherhood which served both to stabilise the damaged social structure and to provide a passive class of consumers for renascent industry. In America this process of domestication went further and faster, incarcerating in their homes a whole generation of women who were generally better educated and more prosperous than their British counterparts.

But this domestic idyll was undermined by new pressures on women as producers, and especially by the increasing participation of married women in the labour force. The baby boom, and the ideology of domesticity which went with it, ended abruptly as they had begun, killed off by the necessities of women's work and by the intrinsic emptiness of the domestic life to a more educated generation. Once more, the roles of women and men were thrown into doubt, each sex searching for a new identity and a new relationship. The emerging ideology was reminiscent of the 1920s, equal opportunity and partnership in work and in marriage. But these high hopes, fed by a liberal trend in politics, could not quickly be matched by reality. The brief period of economic euphoria ended, and the expectations of educated women collided with the economic interests and powers of men. The multiple demands which women now faced seemed to be bringing few rewards, and served only to highlight their powerlessness. American women, further advanced along the road to equality, felt more keenly the barriers which men raised against them. It was not surprising that the first explosion of understanding and anger happened in the USA.

2. New Beginnings: the Rebirth of Feminism, 1963–9

Women's lives were therefore changing dramatically even before the first new feminist texts were published or the first groups formed. Social movements are rarely sudden things, but emerge when a long process of change has caused some part of the population to expect and demand better life-chances. Many changes combined to produce this liberating consciousness in women: an atmosphere of liberal reform which tantalisingly half-opened many doors; the coincidence of a large generational group with high expectations; the flood of married women into the lower levels of the labour market; a rise in the general level of women's education without a corresponding increase in real career opportunities; and a disintegration of the roles and securities of family life.

Many women, of course, learned to live with these changes. They continued to get married and raise families; until very recently, over half did not take a paid job after marriage. Still others responded by acting as individuals to control their lives, by going back to college or getting out of bad marriages. But a significant number of women felt sufficiently cramped by the limitations of their womanhood to ignite an explosive protest. When their protest came, it came from two strikingly different directions – one the liberal tradition of equal opportunity; the other the radical tradition of racial and class warfare.

Betty Friedan and the Revival of Liberal Feminism

Betty Friedan is tired of being saddled with the responsibility for the whole women's liberation movement, but her best-selling polemic, *The Feminine Mystique* (1963), turned the question of woman's place into a popular public issue for the first time since the 1920s. Radio, television, newspapers and magazines seized greedily on Friedan's book and made her overnight into a national celebrity, for she had dared to say something quite outrageous. *The Feminine Mystique* proclaimed that the very substance and centre of the American suburban dream – the contented housewife and mother – was a pernicious and destructive myth. Other people had said it before, but always in the muffled tones of academic debate, never with such passion and style.

As a wife and mother, a woman of education and formidable talent who herself wrote for women's magazines, Friedan had increasingly felt uneasy about the domesticated image of womanhood. So she set out to study both the image and the reality of the housewife's role. From the fiction, the articles and the advertisements of the glossy magazines she constructed a composite picture of the perfect woman *circa* 1960. One cannot do better than quote what she found in *McCalls*, read by five million American women:

> The image of woman that emerges from this big, pretty magazine is young and frivolous, almost childlike; fluffy and feminine; passive; gaily content in a world of bedroom and kitchen, sex, babies and home. The magazine surely does not leave out sex; the only goal a woman is permitted is the pursuit of a man. It is crammed full of food, clothing, cosmetics, furniture and the physical bodies of young women, but where is the world of thought and ideas, the life of the mind and spirit?[1]

As Friedan dissected this claustrophobic world and interviewed psychologists, social scientists and dozens of ordinary women, she uncovered a profound discontent. Millions of wives and mothers nursed a secret, guilty, misery which she labelled 'the problem that has no name'. Lived in reality, the life of the 'happy housewife' was stultifying and meaningless, offering no sense of independence, identity or achievement. And, just because it was *believed* to be the ideal life, the end of the rainbow, women who were unhappy in their role felt that there must be something wrong with them. Their symptoms were evidence for the disease: depression, heavy use of tranquillisers and alcohol, compulsive housework, hypochondria, obsessive fantasies of sex.

How could such a mystique come to be so widely accepted when its results were so demonstrably harmful? Friedan argued that women in all the rich Western societies were victims of the same set of intellectual and commercial pressures. She pointed in particular to the international vogue for Freudian psychoanalysis, defining women as passive, receptive and sexually neurotic; the parallel influence of the then-popular functionalist theories in sociology, which reinforced the belief that the existing division of sex roles was *ipso facto* the correct and beneficial one, because it worked; the reflection of this theory in education, where orthodox sex roles were taught from kindergarten onwards; and the sophistication of the advertising industry, which had learned how to play on the insecurities of women by offering products which would both confirm and perfect their feminine identities.

While books don't start revolutions, they may help people to recognise shared experiences and to question conditions of life which they had accepted as natural and inevitable. By 1970 *The Feminine Mystique* had sold over a million copies in America and Britain; through this one medium, a great many women learned for the first time that they were not alone in questioning the role which society had assigned to them. In her autobiography, Friedan wrote of the explosion of pent-up unhappiness which her book released:

> It was a relief more important to women than I had ever dreamed, to have [their] questions put into words . . . They wrote me personal, impassioned letters expressing their relief . . . I decided that women were sitting on such painful feelings that they didn't dare open the lid unless they knew that they were going to be able to do something about them.[2]

The National Organisation for Women (NOW)

As Friedan had defined them, the problems facing women were both cultural and political. A revolution in social values was needed to dispel the cobwebs of the feminine mystique, and the legal and economic barriers to women's full participation must be swept away so that their newly available potential could be realised. This was a formidable programme, and existing feminist organisations like the League of Women Voters and the Federation of Business and Professional Women's Clubs had no desire to press such radical demands. A fresh and more militant voice was needed, and the formation of the National Organisation for Women in 1966 provided that voice.

The catalyst was the Equal Employment Opportunity Commission (EEOC), which had been set up to administer the US Civil Rights Act of 1964. The Commission's dismal performance on women's civil rights issues (as distinct from those concerning blacks) became a matter of concern to female commissioners and to politically active women outside. At a national conference of State Commissions in 1966, Betty Friedan and a couple of dozen other women decided that a more energetic organisation was needed to ginger up the Commission's flagging efforts. In October of that year the National Organisation for Women (NOW) was formally constituted with some 300 charter members and Betty Friedan as its first president.

NOW revived and carried forward the nineteenth-century tradition of civil rights feminism; NOW's goal was to reform the social system in line with American liberal values, not to revolutionise it. The founding document stated that NOW was formed 'To take action to bring women into full participation in the mainstream of American society *now*, exercising all the privileges and responsibilities thereof in truly equal partnership with men.' The final phrase is significant. Unlike almost every later feminist group, NOW defined itself as an organisation *for* women, not just *of* women. It welcomed serious male support, and about 10 per cent of its members have always been men.

At the outset the NOW strategy was twofold: to use the existing laws and constitutional instruments to fight individual cases of discrimination; and to educate the American public into a different concept of women's roles. The strategy was modelled on the one which had been used so effectively by the black civil rights movement and, perhaps because the sheer unexpectedness of an articulate pressure group for women helped throw the legislature off balance, the first NOW victories came quickly. In 1967 President Johnson, under pressure from NOW, signed Executive Order 11375 prohibiting sex discrimination by government and its contractors. In the same year the EEOC was persuaded to ban 'male' and 'female' categories in job advertisements, and to modify restrictive laws concerning married air stewardesses. Letters and visits to government officials and legislators, meetings and press interviews, surveys, research projects and press releases, petitions and campaigns, lobbies to influence political party policies in election years – these soon became the everyday business of NOW chapters all over the nation. Never had policy-makers been confronted with such an avalanche of demands on women's issues.

In November 1967 the Second National Conference of NOW drew up a Bill of Rights for women. This demanded:

1. An Equal Rights Amendment to the Constitution.
2. Enforcement of laws banning sex discrimination in employment (notably Title VII of the Civil Rights Act of 1964, administered by the EEOC).
3. Maternity-leave rights in employment and in social security benefits.
4. Tax deduction for home and child-care expenses for working parents.
5. Child-care centres.
6. Equal and unsegregated education.
7. Equal job training opportunities and training allowances for women in poverty.
8. The right of women to control their reproductive lives.

This final demand was a source of some difficulty at the Conference, since it implied the right to abortion, which offended the religious or ethical beliefs of many women, and there were some resignations. But, however hesitantly, NOW was the first feminist organisation to call for the repeal of laws limiting abortion.

In subsequent years the specific goals of NOW were extended to include the revision of state protective laws on women, the revision of divorce and alimony arrangements, the participation of women on an equal basis with men in church life and practices, a campaign to change the mass media's portrayal of women and a campaign against rape and violence. But the original set of goals can still be seen as containing the essence of liberal feminism, namely the aspiration to remove legal and economic barriers to women's progress in a competitive world.

More publicity came from a National Demonstration for Women's Rights which NOW organised in December 1967, and which proved to be the biggest demonstration by women since the suffragette days. This public visibility inspired more American women to organise. The Women's Equity Action League (WEAL) arose in 1968 to combat specific discriminations in education, employment and tax laws, and has enjoyed considerable success. Also in 1968, Human Rights for Women (HRW) was launched as an educational and legal aid service, Federally Employed Women (FEW) appeared to represent government workers. We may note the formation in 1970 of the Professional Women's Caucus (PWC) to fight discrimination in professional employment, and in 1971 of the National Women's Political Caucus (NWPC) to press for more women in public office. The cumulative impact of these energetic civil rights groups was to create a genuine sensitivity to women's issues in government, industry and the mass media. During the early 1970s one could almost feel the painful process of discarding stereotypes, and the legacy is an everyday awareness of sex discrimination in America which has no parallel in Britain. It may be that America's agonising self-examination over the treatment of black people prepared the way for a more ready understanding of the sex issue. Whatever the reasons, Britain never developed a similarly reformist and integrated women's movement, and its middle class has not yet undergone a similar challenge to its traditional patterns of thought about women and men.

The growth of NOW from the core group of 300 in 1966 to over 175,000 today has made it the largest feminist organisation in the world. As the more radical sections of the women's movement are tiny by comparison, it is worth noting two characteristics of NOW which contributed to its rapid growth.

First, NOW was based on orthodox principles of leadership

and hierarchy (president, chairperson, secretary, etc.) and was able to attract to its ranks many highly skilled organisers. This meant that the idealistic general principles of equality, common to the whole women's movement, could be translated by the leadership into agreed programmes of action, and sustained over periods of time.

Second, the campaigns and issues chosen by the highly educated, upper-middle-class leaders of NOW were, with the exception of abortion, entirely within American liberal orthodoxy. Equality for women might be unpopular, but nobody could argue that it was unconstitutional or un-American. So NOW became accepted as an honourable opponent, a legitimate if irritating factor in the political equation. Part of the anxiety felt about the abortion issue was precisely that it might damage this legitimacy.

In both respects the more radical feminists who came later were less traditional, and found it correspondingly harder to gain acceptance.

The Radical Politics of the 1960s

Some people now talk with a certain nostalgia about the 'revolutionary sixties'. It was a curious and deeply disturbing decade for the generations who had survived the depression and the war. All over the Westernised world, they saw their daughters and sons rebelling against the very values and political institutions which they felt the war had been fought to defend, and rejecting the very affluence which had been the promised reward of peace. It is impossible to understand why a radical movement for women's *liberation* arose without knowing something about the political ideas which came out of this conflict between the generations.

With hindsight it is possible to see the various protests of the 1960s as one protean social movement for greater human freedom. Some of its manifestations were noble, some silly, and some vicious, as is usually the case. But despite the frequent posturing and some measure of humbug, freedom was the central value and the driving-force. Feminism was a latecomer to this movement, and we can see its roots more clearly by identifying the other main currents of dissent which came before and contributed to it. These were: the peace movement; the black civil rights movement; the black power movement; the neo-Marxist new left and the youth counter-culture or hippie movement.

Peace, like temperance, has traditionally been a moral issue, and therefore one associated particularly with women. In Britain, women were prominent in the protests of the Campaign for Nuclear Disarmament (CND), which reached its height in the late 1950s and early 1960s and, after about 1966, merged with the anti-Vietnam war protests. A network of women's peace groups had developed and it seems that many British feminists had their first political experience in the peace movement.

This was less true in the USA, where the Vietnam campaign was closely tied to the issue of the draft, and so was a more overtly male movement. A group called Women Strike for Peace had formed in 1960, but many, if not most, of the American women who were subsequently radicalised had their political baptism in another crusade, the struggle for black civil rights. Just as a radical feminism had emerged from the anti-slavery movement in the 1830s and 1840s, so now a new wave would be inspired by renewed black unrest and the consciousness which came with it.

When the Civil Rights Movement surfaced in 1956, it became a *cause célèbre* for young people long deprived of satisfying political action. Thousands of white college students from the north became passionately involved with the southern blacks in their fight for basic human rights, and this unlikely alliance finally brought victory in the shape of the Civil Rights Act of 1964. But the inevitable limitations of that victory created frustration among younger and more militant blacks who threw out their white student allies and adopted the revolutionary ideology of black power.

This was a painful moment for white radicals generally, but it conveyed an especially symbolic message to women. The black radicals had concluded that the liberal, ever-flexible, integrationist politics of civil rights led only to the smothering of real inequality under the rhetoric of equal opportunity. An authentic radical alternative could only be created by an oppressed group which set itself apart from its oppressors and attacked the total structures of racism and capitalism. The neo-Marxisms of the Third World provided a rhetoric of imperialism, colonial dependence and guerrilla struggle which adapted well to the needs of American blacks.

For many radical women this was a lesson they could not ignore. As they saw it, the liberal policies of NOW simply played into the hands of the oppressor by accepting his rules. While men might grant women (like blacks) equality in theory and in law, they would do everything in their power to prevent the coming of equality in fact. In any case, the option to pursue a satisfying career was no option at all for most women, tied down by children or lacking the right educational and personal skills. Civil rights was simply a confidence trick on women, as it had been on blacks. Thus the impulse towards separatism and revolutionary solutions was planted in the American radical feminist movement from the beginning.

By contrast, the influence of black consciousness in Britain was almost entirely indirect and derived from the American experience. Despite the Notting Hill race riots of 1958, the Powellite backlash against immigration and a long series of anti-racist campaigns by the left, the impact of the issue on women was far less immediate. In Britain it was the rhetoric of class, not of race, which became the foundation for militant feminism.

The relationship between socialism and feminism will be traced in more detail in the next chapter, but part of the general political ferment of the 1960s was a resurgence of socialist and Marxist movements under the general label of the 'new left'. Racism, the exploitation of the Third World and the apparent stability of corporate capitalism demanded a renewal of Marxist theory, which began with the appearance in Britain of the *New Left Review* in 1960. The humanistic quality of this neo-Marxism, with its stress on the role of culture and ideas in sustaining the power of ruling groups, made it especially adaptable to the needs of feminist theory.

Many feminists had always been socialists, believing the oppression of women must be grounded in the inequalities of capitalism; Marx and Engels had said as much. Since long before suffrage, socialists and trade unionists had expressed generalised support for women's equality, but had seldom done much about it. The fact that the intellectual new leftists of Britain and America failed yet again to take women's issues seriously provided one more cause for politically active women to organise themselves separately.

Broader and more formless than any of these political movements was the so-called 'youth culture' or 'counter-culture'. From the beats of the 1950s to the hippies, flower children and yippies of the 1960s, this disorganised rebellion of the young pervaded the whole period. Lacking theory and structure, it nevertheless created a diffuse climate of libertarian ideas which, given a false concreteness by writers like Norman O. Brown, Paul Goodman, Theodore Roszak and Charles Reich, had considerable influence on the radical consciousness of the time. Younger feminists found two things in particular which spoke to their concerns: the anti-Freudian, revisionist psychology of Wilhelm Reich and his followers which stressed the importance of a liberated sexuality; and the ultra-democratic, co-operative ethos of the youth culture which challenged the whole exploitative, power-obsessed structure of Western societies. The hippies went some way towards reject-ing traditional male/female sex roles, and implicit in their life-style was an almost cosmic notion of personal liberation and a unification of personal and political concerns which were later to become hallmarks of the women's movement.

Again, these were the movements of the post-war genera-tion, and especially the children of the baby boom. Brought up in peace and increasing affluence, with their ideals unsullied by the compromises of hard times, they arrived at maturity in the middle and late 1960s to find themselves in a crowded and less than ideal world. Whatever its expression, their anger depended on one fundamental belief: that the world was within sight of the end of scarcity; that, materially speaking, anything was now possible; that the old conflicts over resources between rich and poor, black and white, men and women could and should become a thing of the past. Sociologist Daniel Bell called it 'the end of ideology',[3] and nobody can understand the radical impulse in feminism who does not remember the unique hopes and experiences of that generation.

The Beginnings of Women's Liberation in the USA

The phrase 'women's liberation' seems to have originated about 1964 in an American civil rights group called the Student Nonviolent Co-ordinating Committee (SNCC). It began as a mildly satirical expression, coined by SNCC women to dramatise how they felt about their own treatment within a movement dedicated to liberating blacks and Third World peoples. The satire went unheeded. It was at an SNCC Conference in 1964 that the black militant Stokely Carmichael refused to discuss a paper about the position of women in the movement. 'The only position for women in SNCC is prone', he replied, a remark which became notorious. Attempts to raise women's issues in the new left group Students for a Democratic Society (SDS) during 1965 and 1966 received similarly contemptuous responses. Women's issues were not defined as serious or political matters. As a result of such treatment, small groups of women began meeting to discuss their frustration with the behaviour of their fellow male radicals.

In Britain the situation was no better. The mainly Trotskyist new left, obsessed with imperialism, racism and industrial conflict, paid no attention to women though it had many female supporters. The prestigious Dialectics of Liberation Conference in London in 1967 had nothing to say about sexual oppression. In the memoirs of the period one finds, over and over again, the growing realisation that women in the radical sub-culture were being used by the men as secretaries, tea-makers and sexual partners, and their status in the supposedly egalitarian organisation was as low as it would be outside.

The spark to ignite this underground resentment could have come from anywhere, but it finally came from another American conference on alternative politics. The National Conference for a New Politics was scheduled in Chicago in 1967 to bring together the activities of diverse new left groups. It was a big occasion, and an independent women's caucus led by Jo Freeman and Shulamith Firestone came to introduce a motion on the problems of women. Instead of being allowed to speak, they were patronised, ridiculed, and effectively excluded from the business of the meetings. It was their rage at these events that led directly to the formation of the first radical feminist groups. In Chicago, Freeman launched the Chicago Westside Group with a newsletter called *Voice of the Women's Liberation Movement*, which announced that 'the liberation of women from their oppression is a problem as worthy of political struggle as any other that the New Politicians were considering'. In New York, Firestone founded a group called Radical Women (later New York Radical Women).

When, today, men criticise women's liberation for being anti-male they should recall that its founders began by asking over and over again for a *dialogue* with men which would simply treat women's issues with the same seriousness as issues affecting black or white males. When women began leaving organisations like SNCC and SDS to form their own, separatist political groups, the men had only themselves to blame; by the time some of them realised their past mistakes, it was far too late to convince many women of the good faith and seriousness of any male, radical or otherwise.

Small women's liberation groups began forming in cities all over America but, in the first months of their existence, they attracted little attention. Their first business had to be to decide how to organise themselves and how to analyse their own experiences of oppression.

Perhaps their first moment of public visibility came on 15 January 1968. At a peace march in Washington a coalition called the Jeanette Rankin Brigade (named after the first woman elected to Congress in 1919) split off to stage a 'Burial of Traditional Womanhood'. In a piece of pure street theatre, they invited women to join a funeral procession to the national cemetery at Arlington, to lay to rest the traditional woman who has 'passed with a sigh to her great reward . . . after 3,000 years of bolstering the egos of Warmakers and aiding the cause of war'. The few women who joined the procession found that the radical magazine *Ramparts* joined the rest of the press in reporting their demonstration as a joke.

The next event of this type rated major media coverage, if only because the press were present in force beforehand. In September 1968 the annual Miss America Contest was held at Atlantic City, New Jersey; New York Radical Women, led by Robin Morgan, demonstrated outside the hall by filling a trash can with bras, girdles, make-up, women's magazines and other articles symbolic of women's traditional treatment as sexual objects. A reporter with more imagination than integrity reported that the demonstrators had 'burned their bras' (they hadn't), and it is a reflection of the male obsession with breasts that discarded brassieres became, from that moment on, a perverse symbol of women's liberation. In some ways the movement has never lived down this curious style of entry into the people's consciousness. On similar lines, an imaginative group called WITCH (Women's International Terrorist Conspiracy from Hell) had a brief public career in 1968–9 with such enjoyable fancies as the hexing of the New York Stock Exchange (causing a slight downward move in share prices) and the levitating of the Pentagon (without results).

Because of their brevity and sudden impact, these tactics were called 'zap actions' and they were both a gift and a curse in the movement's early days. Many politically sophisticated women disagreed with them as a tactic, but were hard-pressed to suggest alternatives. The radical sub-culture at large had shown itself entirely unwilling to take the new cause seriously, and the small groups had few resources to publicise their ideas in other ways. Any dramatic public act *by women*, however odd it might be, was bound to get national news coverage; the *rationale* was that, while men might sneer, other women would get the point.

But the damage to the movement's long-term image was considerable, and the sense of craziness generated by some of these early radical actions was never quite dispelled. In 1968 a woman called Valerie Solenas tried to castrate Andy Warhol with a pistol, and subsequently issued a manifesto under the title SCUM (Society for Cutting Up Men). All this was gleefully seized upon by the media to prove that women's liberation was a movement of lunatics.

But the energy and support for a radical movement were none the less there, and groups continued to appear through 1969. The ex-president of the New York chapter of NOW, Ti-Grace Atkinson, broke away to form the October 17th Movement (later called The Feminists), with an anti-elitist, strongly separatist ideology. A breakaway group from New York Radical Women constituted itself as the Redstockings, whose main contribution was to establish consciousness-raising as a central feminist activity.

Although some groups in the American movement emerged from the neo-Marxist left, most of them preferred to develop their own theory outside the traditional confines of Marxism. Revolutionary socialist groups like the Socialist Workers' Party (SWP) and the Young Socialist Alliance (YSA) started to establish their own affiliated groups in 1969, and specifically socialist feminist journals like *Off Our Backs* began to appear. The dialogue between socialist (mainly ex-new left) and radical feminists (mainly ex-civil rights) became known as the 'politico/feminist' debate and, as we shall see in the following chapter, came to define one of the main divisions in the women's liberation movement.

From this time onward the proliferation of groups of every kind was bewildering; at least 500 had formed by the end of 1969. Every city and most towns had their feminist group, some of them active in local politics, some devoting themselves to special campaigns or programmes for women, others (especially in the universities) concerned with building theory and publishing feminist journals and pamphlets. If ever there was such a thing as an idea whose time had come, feminism was it.

In New York on 24 November 1969 an attempt was made to pull all this together in a Congress to Unite Women. Ten demands were issued which largely paralleled the Bill of Rights devised by NOW three years before, focusing on equal job and educational opportunities, the right to abortion and media images of women and women's liberation. The main additional demand was for free 24-hour child-care centres throughout the nation. Apart from the NOW network, however, feminist groups maintained their complete autonomy to believe in or campaign for whatever they liked, and the next few years saw an explosion of creative feminist activity in America.

The Beginnings of Women's Liberation in Britain

To see why feminism in Britain turned out so very differently, we must begin by looking for its political roots. The liberal tradition which underscored even the most radical of American feminisms had small influence in class-conscious Britain. Here feminism was a revolutionary movement from the start, and posed its challenge in explicitly socialist or Marxist terms. In the *annus mirabilis* of 1968 it was natural that politically concerned women should join in the general demand for greater equality. This was, after all, International Human Rights Year, the fortieth anniversary of full suffrage, the year of the Race Relations Act, of student sit-ins everywhere, of the great anti-Vietnam war demonstrations and of the May revolution in France, which itself had generated a militant women's caucus.

The women who formed the movement were mainly young – between 20 and 35 years old – mainly university graduates or students and almost without exception already active in politics. They brought with them a broadly Marxist sympathy, but especially a concern with alienation as a product of industrial society, a longing for more communal and expressive human relationships and a deep mistrust of all authoritarianism and dogma.

The British movement was not launched at any precise moment or by any particular event. Rather, women working in different causes began meeting together and talking about their own problems as women. By the beginning of 1968 rumours had been heard of movements in France and Germany, and the existence of feminist groups in America was well known. The American influence was quite direct; the early writings quickly found their way across the Atlantic via the network of radical journals and book distributors, and one of the seminal London groups was formed by American women working in the Vietnam solidarity campaign.

At this time left-wing politics in Britain was in a highly fluid and amorphous state. Old-style communism (and even Stalinism) were by no means moribund, and the spectrum ran from the stolid Labour Party and the trade unions, through Fabianism, numerous varieties of Trotskyism, Maoism, intellectual neo-Marxism to the quasi-anarchistic grass-roots politics of Agit-Prop. Socialists, and especially young socialists, were trying to put new life into the old dogmas; just such a fertile period was needed to allow the voice of women to be heard.

It is instructive that the voice was first heard not from the intellectual radical community but from the working class. In a sense, working-class women served the same liberating function for British feminists as did blacks for the Americans – by articulating their grievances, they made legitimate the grievances of other groups who could identify with their cause.

In the early spring of 1968 a group of fishermen's wives began to organise in the north-east coast port city of Hull. Under the leadership of Liz Bilocca, they set up a committee to improve safety conditions on the trawlers, and the unusual spectacle of female militancy attracted wide (largely negative) media publicity and considerable local abuse. Middle-class women with political interests joined the confrontation and helped form an Equal Rights Association which evolved into a continuing women's liberation group, though without its original working-class base.

If the trade unions were not doing their job in Hull, neither were they at the huge Ford motor works in Dagenham, near London. Sewing machinists at the plant staged a three-week strike for equal pay in June, which rated slightly more favourable publicity than the actions of the fishermen's wives. So also did a militant revolt by London bus conductresses who wanted to be drivers. This outburst of industrial militancy among working women shook up a complacent trade-union movement. A union committee was established under the title of the National Joint Act Committee for Women's Equal Rights (NJACWER) to press for more energetic action, and an Equal Pay Bill was piloted through the House of Commons by Barbara Castle and finally passed by the Labour Government in 1970, to be implemented by 1975.

The publicity given to these confrontations had made the situation of women a matter for discussion throughout the left. The Joint Committee was a moderate group, consisting mainly of older trade unionists and Labour Party people. Thus it was no accident that further-left organisations should decide to take up the issues and translate them into more militantly socialist terms. They also provided the in-place network of contacts and communications which the women's movement needed in order to attain an independent identity.

The Trotskyist International Marxist Group (IMG) must take credit for first recognising the importance and potential of the women's liberation movement in Britain. In the autumn of 1968 its theoretical journal *International* put forward the idea of socialist women's groups to make connections between the concerns of women and the wider problems of exploitation in capitalist society. These groups, closely connected to the parent IMG, began to form early in 1969, the first being in Nottingham, and issued a journal *Socialist Woman*. Other groups based within the revolutionary left quickly followed: the Women's Liberation Group of the Revolutionary Socialist Student Federation (RSSF), and groups attached to the International Socialists (journal *Women's Voice*) and the Communist Party (journal *Link*).

Differing in detail, the women's sections of the Marxist parties were united by their common focus on the situation of working-class women, especially those of the industrial sector who were thought to have the most revolutionary potential. From the beginning they campaigned most strongly on issues like equal pay, unionisation, free nurseries, price and rent controls and better welfare benefits. In part because of their close ties with male-dominated organisations, they tended to focus less sharply on sexism and male power than on the exploitation of women by capitalist bosses and government.

Beyond the confines of existing revolutionary socialist groups, but still within the general ambience of the left, other developments were taking place. In January 1969 the anarcho-socialist paper *Black Dwarf* published a whole edition on women which tried to relate sexual oppression to Marxism. At a Festival of Revolution at the University of Essex later that same year a liberation group was formed and, in London, yet more groups began to emerge piecemeal from the radical background. The American activists already mentioned constituted themselves as the Tufnell Park Group and, early in 1969, they got together with two or three other small groups to form a loose collective called the London Women's Liberation Workshop, open to women of all political persuasions and of none. The Workshop, which at its peak in 1971 included seventy small groups, was to be an influential part of the early British movement, not least through its newsletter *Shrew* (briefly called *Harpies Bizarre*), which was edited in turn by each small group in the collective:

The Women's Liberation Workshop believes that women in our society are oppressed. We are economically oppressed: in jobs we do full work for half pay, in the home we do unpaid work full time. We are commercially oppressed by advertisements, television and press; legally, we often have only the status of children. We are brought up to feel inadequate, educated to narrower horizons than men. This is our specific oppression as women. It is as women that we are, therefore, organising.[4]

The early issues of *Shrew* demonstrate the variety one would expect from a newsletter produced each time by different people, but they do show that specifically feminist concerns were more important to the Workshop than Marxist politics. The first six issues, for example, took up themes already widely discussed in the American movement: female separatism; developing feminist theory; the politics of housework; sex, contraception and childbirth; Freudian psychology; make-up and deodorants. Indeed, there is an undercurrent of real hostility to the male left borne out of the same kinds of negative experiences which had driven American women from the Marxist parties:

The support of the male radical is always conditional. As long as you dedicate yourself to his political causes and accept his buck-passing analysis of your oppression (it's capitalism, not me sweetheart) you will be given some time off and occasionally – when politically expedient – some patronising interest . . . It's an interesting fact that on no other issue than their unanimous dismissal of the Women's Movement as 'revisionist' does the male left agree.[5]

In the small world of alternative politics, the London Women's Liberation Workshop was a success story, providing much-needed focus and co-ordination to the fragile movement. And the word spread outside London. In addition to the early Socialist Woman Group in Nottingham, others appeared in Coventry, Birmingham, Liverpool, Leeds, Oxford, Cambridge and Bristol. By the end of 1969 there was at least one group each in Scotland (Aberdeen), Southern Ireland and Wales.

As a final point of contrast, there was to be little support in Britain for zap actions on the American model. The first two street demonstrations were relatively modest: a picket at the Miss World demonstration in London and some leafleting outside the Ideal Home Exhibition. But, late in the year, some women got together to plan a national conference at Oxford for 1970. This was to be the public and political baptism of the women's liberation movement in Britain.

Conclusion

What is missing from this dry account of the movement's first days is what only a participant could put there – the euphoria. Over and over again women who were involved recall their sense of discovery, of whole new horizons opening, of a true feeling of liberation when they first came into contact with the movement. 'Do women entering the movement now, when feminist ideas have become fairly common currency, experience the same sense of revelation and exhilaration that we did then?', wondered a member of one of the earliest London Workshop groups.[6] Many of the autobiographical accounts sound almost like religious conversion experiences; for thousands of isolated women the movement came literally as salvation. It was especially attractive to young mothers breaking out of claustrophobic marriages, providing the support they needed to assert an independent identity. The key word was 'sisterhood', women being together for the first time and developing that sense of solidarity and purpose which is the hidden binding-force of social movements.

Within that broad solidarity we have seen how feminist groups developed from the earliest days their very distinctive identities. The American civil rights or liberal current in feminism grew out of the profound frustration of capable women with the restrictive roles and stereotypical images available to them in the post-war world. Their resources and skills helped launch a number of specialised pressure groups – of which NOW was and still is the largest – which the government was unable to ignore. By 1969 even the not too liberal President Nixon had found it expedient to establish a 'task force' on the status of women.

The second major current also appeared initially in America as younger women politically committed to radical and libertarian causes began to identify themselves as an oppressed group. Lacking the resources and the legitimacy of the big liberal women's organisations and determined not to compromise their high ideals, these radical feminists or women's liberationists aimed for nothing less than social revolution. With unorthodox tactics and a stinging rhetoric, they made a public impact far greater than that of the liberals, an impact out of all proportion to their numbers. But the extremely radical nature of some of their demands limited their influence to changing consciousness rather than changing public policies.

The force of both these currents was felt in Britain, where the conditions affecting women were essentially the same but where certain features of the society and culture disposed the feminist movement to develop differently. The civil rights issues were largely pre-empted by satellites of the Labour Party and trade unions, but the backwardness of the economy made progress in these areas painfully slow. More traditional, more class-ridden, more elitist, British society appeared to offer a poor prospect of achieving reforms which might produce anything like equality for most women. The existence of a powerful tradition of revolutionary socialism (and the involvement of many women in it) made it natural for the new movement to focus first on Marxist and neo-Marxist solutions, in which the liberation of women would be one aspect of the transformation of the whole socio-economic structure.

In subsequent years these three currents in feminism – the liberal, the radical and the socialist – have been vastly elaborated internally and have greatly influenced one another. All three coexist in America and Britain, and in almost every country where a women's liberation movement has taken root. But they remain discrete and identifiable as political themes and, in order to give context to the history which follows, it is necessary to describe just how each tendency in feminism views the situation of women, and what goals and programmes they offer towards creating a more equal society.

3. Mixed Messages: Theories of Modern Feminism

There is no single feminist theory. Like any complex political philosophy, feminism has generated a rich variety of ideas on the situation of women. This variety is reflected in the structure of the movement, a deliberately dispersed network of small groups, campaigns and intellectual tendencies which have no single focus, apart from their common concern with women's inequality, and therefore no unified public viewpoint and no official spokeswomen.

Any attempt to classify the theories of feminism in cold print therefore involves the risk of caricature. But there are lines of analysis which are widely accepted, theoretical positions which are widely known, debated and used in practice. It is possible to separate these essential patterns of feminist thought and present them in a distilled and simplified form as types. In this chapter, for the sake of clarity, a sharp division has been made between 'liberal', 'socialist' and 'radical' feminist positions. Each theoretical position entails certain organisational and tactical choices. But they are evolving theories, infinite shades of meaning coexist within and between them and they in no sense represent three separate and opposed feminisms.

It is therefore appropriate to begin with the fundamental concepts and ideals which all feminists share in common.

Basic Principles

Feminism as a philosophy shares with all traditions of progressive thought since the Enlightenment the principle of the equal

62

worth of all human beings. The unequal treatment of women simply because of their sex has come to be called 'sexism'.

The term 'sexism' appeared in the earliest days of the movement as a direct analogy of racism. One thing women learned from the civil rights movement was that they, like blacks, were treated as inferior simply on the grounds that they belonged to a certain biological category. Blacks were defined by racist rhetoric as intellectually inferior, irresponsible, and childlike, and sexism was used in just the same way against women. It was the ideology against which feminist utopias came to define themselves.

Sexism carries the same basic meaning for all feminists. They differ on how it originated and how it is institutionalised in culture, but all use it as a shorthand way of describing prejudice against women. A sexist man may be described as a male chauvinist, 'A man who takes up a position, either consciously or instinctively, of domination (and egotism) over and against women, by virtue merely of his status as a man.'[1]

Feminism as a *movement* was defined in the Introduction as 'any form of opposition to any form of social, personal or economic discrimination which women suffer because of their sex'. The term also encompasses a statement of political priorities on which all feminists agree.

One of the greatest barriers faced by the movement in its early days was to get women's issues taken seriously by anybody, radical or conservative. Feminism declares that women's issues *are* political issues, and that to be a feminist is to define those issues as *the* problem, and to focus one's political energies upon them. Liberals, socialists and radicals give feminism different emphasis – with the latter most strongly committed to an entirely female-oriented movement – but all make it the practical centre of their political action.

One final concept arising from feminism is 'sisterhood' as a symbol for the solidarity of all women, both within and outside the movement. Sisterhood expresses a feeling or a value universally shared by feminists, and carries the same deep meaning for them as does the notion of the unity of the oppressed classes for Marxists.

Liberal Feminism

To speak of a theory of liberal feminism may be misleading. By its nature liberalism resists such attempts at packaging, being simply an open-ended set of egalitarian and humanistic values. Unlike the revolutionary, the liberal reformer does not need a total theory of society, since s/he is aiming to improve what exists rather than to transform it into a new, utopian order. None the less liberalism represents a consistent and recognisable political tradition which can be contrasted against the more highly structured theories seen in other forms of feminism.

Liberal principles have their roots in the eighteenth-century philosophical revolution which we now call the Enlightenment. As Western societies began to rid themselves of the ancient burdens of religious dogma and autocratic government, greater value was attached to the freedom of individual men (*sic*). Rationalism, anti-authoritarianism, democracy, freedom of speech, *laissez-faire* economics and all things which might contribute to the free development of the individual became deeply absorbed into Western political culture.

The link between liberal philosophy and women's inequality was first made in 1792 in Mary Wollstonecraft's *Vindication of the Rights of Women*. The theme was taken up in the Declaration of Rights issued by the Seneca Falls convention in 1848, the rhetoric of which was based directly on the American Declaration of Independence, itself a classic statement of liberalism in the mode of John Locke. But the most comprehensive argument for liberal feminism emerged from the collaboration of John Stuart Mill and Harriet Taylor, notably in the long essay *On the Subjection of Women* (1869). They made explicit the contradictions between the democratic values of liberalism and the subordination of women:

> If the principle [of democracy] is true, we ought to act as if we believed it, and not to ordain that to be born a girl instead of a boy, any more than to be born black instead of white, or a commoner instead of a nobleman, shall decide the person's position throughout life.[2]

Liberal principles thus became an important political weapon in the struggle for female suffrage. When feminism revived in the 1960s, the same principles were used to emphasise the disadvantages of women in the supposedly free and democratic societies. In the USA, with a written Constitution firmly grounded in the liberal tradition, the feminist movement gravitated naturally to those doctrines, and the largest part of it remains committed to them today. In Britain, liberalism was much more ambiguously woven into the adversary pattern of class politics and had no such strong attraction for feminists.

The essential distinction between liberal feminists and the rest is that liberals believe progressive reforms can lead to real and substantial equality for women as individuals without the need for revolutionary changes in the economic, political or cultural realms. Indeed, as liberals, they must argue that existing democratic structures constitute the essential *condition* for successful reform, and that radical change could only diminish the availability of freedom and justice to both men and women.

Beyond these broad ideals of democratic reform and individualism, the closest thing to formal theory which we find in liberal feminist thought is a view of social processes derived directly from the social sciences. This view suggests that individuals are trained – by social institutions like the family, the education system and the mass media – into patterns of behaviour or roles which are performed unconsciously and become an integral part of a person's identity. Thus boys learn to be competitive, unemotional and outward-looking, while girls learn to be submissive, to express their feelings and to look for their satisfactions in personal and family affairs. These socially constructed male/female roles then become the basis of a status system which places women in an inferior position. In de Beauvoir's phrase, 'One is not born, but rather becomes a woman.'

For liberal feminists, there are no real villains in this process, nor is it the inevitable product of biological differences or of any particular social or economic system. Sexual roles have been built up over a long period of historical time and have become embedded in our culture. But, since they were constructed by human beings, they can be dismantled by human beings. This must be done by changing the social training which men and women receive from childhood onwards, and by challenging the role stereotypes which continue to discriminate against women. The outcome of this process, say the liberals, would be a convergence of male/female roles from which both women and men would benefit.

The goal of liberal feminism is therefore a redistribution of existing social and economic rewards (status and power) along more egalitarian lines. For the most part, women who follow the liberal tradition do not shrink from the fact that the world is a competitive place, with winners and losers, and it is consistent with this attitude that most of them also reject unfair advantages for women in the form of positive discrimination in education, hiring and promotion. Like the blacks of the early civil rights movement, they ask only for a fair chance.

Liberal feminism embraces a wide range of political commitments, from single-issue campaigns (women in politics, education, media, equal pay) to more comprehensive demands for the equalisation of sex roles. It is worth noting that although liberal feminists are frequently criticised by those of more radical persuasion, even the *minimal* liberal demands, if conceded, would have profound social effects, and that resistance to them outside the movement remains strong.

Socialist Feminism

Socialist feminism embraces as wide a range of ideas as does liberalism. Fabians, Trotskyists, revolutionary communists, Labour Party activists and humanistic Marxists all fall within the range, and their disagreements with one another often seem as deep as their disagreements with liberals. But these differences are more often concerned with tactics than with the broad outlines of their social analysis, which (for feminists even more than for socialists as a whole) tend to be developed from a Marxist perspective. The following account suggests those lines of thought which are common to most forms and varieties of socialist feminism.

Utopian socialism grew out of the same ferment of eighteenth-century thought that produced liberalism. Before

Marx's time, utopian thinkers like Charles Fourier, and Robert Owen's follower William Thompson,[3] had turned their minds to the question of women's status in the perfect society of the future. These speculations were later refined and elaborated by Marx and Engels, by August Bebel, Charlotte Perkins Gilman, Alexandra Kollontai and other socialist writers of the late nineteenth and early twentieth centuries. Despite these theoretical contributions, the relationship between the early women's movement and socialist organisations remained an uneasy one. Organisations like the trade unions, the Independent Labour Party and the Co-operative Movement had always harboured some women's rights sympathisers, and had frequently sided with the suffragettes. But these generalised feelings of solidarity were seldom translated into wholehearted political support.

When the new women's liberation movement emerged, however, it came with a ready-made affinity for socialism; many of its founding activists graduated from the socialist movements of Britain and America and at a time when rapid developments were taking place in Marxist theory. It was natural that many of them should immediately turn their attention to the question of how Marxist conceptions of class, class conflict and social change could be adapted to serve the needs of women.

The work of Friedrich Engels on *The Origins of the Family, Private Property and the State* (1884) provided a starting-point. His work was more direct and accessible than the few passing comments which Marx and Lenin had made on the situation of women in capitalism. Engels argued that women's oppression originated in the first division of labour between men and women, a division which had been sharpened by the advent of capitalism and the bourgeois family:

> The first class antagonism which appears in history coincides with the development of the antagonism between men and women in monogamous marriage, and the first class oppression with that of the female by the male.[4]

Here we have the first key idea of socialist feminism: the suggestion that bourgeois marriage reproduces in microcosm the conflicts and contradictions of the wider bourgeois society.

Wives take on the character of a subordinated class, or even of slaves, while patriarchal heads of households act out the role of employers or owners. Yet this analysis does not point to men as the main enemy of women, though they are recognised as enemies in fact. Their conflict is a shadowed reflection of a much greater conflict. Women are exploited *within the context of capitalism*, and in this sense men are merely the agents of an exploitative system and are oppressed in their turn. The equality with men which liberals demand makes no sense to socialists, since it would mean equality with an already oppressed group within a corrupt system.

This might suggest that women's demands should simply be one ingredient in a broader socialist movement. In fact, socialist feminists have organised themselves separately for at least two reasons. In the last chapter we saw in some detail how the treatment of women within socialist organisations had persuaded many of them that nothing could be gained for women without creating a separate, all-female political platform: 'It is simply that we are . . . the oppressed people, and around this we organise.'[5] Male power was a reality which had to be confronted on a level distinct from the struggle against capitalism. A separate feminist movement was also felt to be necessary because the exploitation of women by capital was so deep and wide-ranging. Women needed a theory and a political structure which would encompass their double oppression as workers and as housewives. Existing socialist groups had amply demonstrated that they were not interested in these questions.

The main pillars of the socialist feminist analysis may be summed up under three headings: wage labour, the family and ideology.

Wage labour

Socialists hold that the root cause of all oppression is economic, though feminists know from the example of the state socialist societies and from their own experiences that powerful cultural mechanisms also work to perpetuate women's inequality. Like any oppressed group, women provide a pool of labour for low-paid and unpleasant work. In addition, they are considered politically docile, seeing their work as secondary to their families, and therefore more easily hired and fired according to economic circumstances. While the unionisation of women has made some progress since 1968, they remain a very exploitable and exploited section of the work-force.

Given this focus on economic oppression, socialist feminists tend to concentrate on the interests of working-class and black women. Their oppression is considered

> the most potentially subversive to capitalism because it spans production and reproduction, class exploitation and sex oppression . . . Their organisation and militancy is vital not only for women's liberation but for the whole socialist and working class movement.[6]

It is important to distinguish here between the liberal position that women are *discriminated against* because of flaws in the system and the socialist claim that they are *exploited* as an inevitable consequence of the system itself.

Socialist feminists vary considerably in the degree to which they are committed to the classic Marxist class analysis. Since women span the whole range of wealth and poverty, and their interests are by no means obviously the same, crude class analysis is not found in modern feminism. The emphasis is rather on how capitalism gains from the exploitation of working-class women at work and in the home. This exploitation is seen to differ from men's in at least three ways: women form a reserve army of productive labour, with low wages, no prospects and a total lack of security; they perform unpaid work in the family; and they are super-exploited by capitalism as consumers and sex objects.

The family

As indicated above, the critique of the traditional family has a long history in socialist thought. Marx and Engels called for its abolition and, although not all socialists have followed this revolutionary line, modern socialist feminists continue to argue that the family is at least in need of profound transformation.

For example, much of their recent analysis has focused on an aspect of the family all but ignored by earlier economic theorists – its function as a *private* domain of work. In the home, women are privatised, isolated. Their work at home, whether or not it is done in addition to an outside job, is the most isolated form of labour. Moreover, the fact that it is *unpaid* labour emphasises its mean status. Housework, as Lenin wrote, 'chains the woman to the kitchen and nursery, and she wastes her labour on barbarously unproductive, petty, nerve-racking, stultifying and crushing drudgery'.[7]

The debate about the exact nature of work in the home is complex and still developing, but the essential point is that what is done by wives in the home is *not part of the market economy.* Cooking, shopping, cleaning and the upbringing of children are not recognised as commodities which can be sold or exchanged. The labour which they represent is not considered by society as real work, worthy of payment. Yet a simple calculation will show what an enormous amount of labour housework represents. It has been suggested that the wage value for a woman with two young children is £10,000 per year. Women's housework thus contributes vastly to the capitalist economy.

Theories differ over whether the main importance of housework is in providing a free support system for the production of commodities, a kind of hidden subsidy, or whether the essential fact is that families create and train new workers for the capitalist system.

All feminists place great emphasis on the sexual and personal stresses produced by the restrictive patterns of family life and the dependency which is enforced on women by its economic structure. Juliet Mitchell suggested that oppression within the family created in women 'a tendency to small-mindedness, petty jealousy, irrational emotionality and random violence, dependency, competitiveness, selfishness and possessiveness, passivity, a lack of vision and conservatism'.[8] These qualities, she emphasised, were not false stereotypes created by male chauvinism but real, the inescapable result of the woman's powerless condition within the family.

Michèle Barrett and Mary McIntosh have proposed in addition that the monogamous nuclear family exhalts individualist values at the expense of social values, and that a false ideal of 'familism' distorts the whole fabric of social life, defines the priorities of the welfare system and cramps the culture in a narrow cul-de-sac which leaves no room for conceptions of a more communal, sharing life-style.[9]

The divisions between families in terms of wealth, status and opportunities reproduce directly the divisions in the wider society. Children born into each isolated unit inherit the life-chances of their parents. Wealth, education and privilege are thus transmitted directly through the family, as are poverty and disadvantage. For this reason alone, socialist feminists must necessarily believe that a more equal society cannot be built on this foundation.

Ideology

'Ideology' is a much-abused word. Strictly interpreted it refers to the ways in which ideas are used by powerful groups to control and mystify the less powerful. Ideology may come in the form of religious dogmas, political doctrines like communism, nationalism or fascism, or imposed cultural patterns like the 'happy housewife' myth discussed earlier. Modern Marxists have increasingly paid attention to the role of ideology in reinforcing economic forms of power. Some have gone so far as to suggest that, in the modern world, the control of ideas is even more important than the control of capital.

Marxist feminists have been particularly keen to develop the theory of ideology, since economic exploitation at work and in the family do not by themselves seem wholly to explain the long subordination of women. The feminine mystique is deeply embedded in the consciousness of women and men, yet is also a social convention which can be exposed as artificial. The task of the Marxist theorist is not simply to strip away such facades, but to show how, by whom and for whose benefit they have been constructed and maintained. This analysis has led towards a gradual convergence of socialist and radical feminist perspectives.

In Britain the first steps towards such a theory were taken by Juliet Mitchell as early as 1966, two years before an organised women's movement appeared.[10] Her analysis aimed to show how women became locked into their inferior social status, and her answer revealed the complex interplay of objective and subjective pressures generated by the family. Domestic work, maternity, sex and the socialisation of children are more than just practical obstacles to equality; they are manipulated to create a *psychological* state in women which makes their inequality seem natural to them. These intangible mental bonds are the hardest to reveal, and the hardest to overcome, not least because they all work to reinforce one another. Although many feminists reject Freudian theory as anti-woman, Mitchell sought to produce a synthesis of Freudian and Marxian categories which would create the essential bridge between the subjective (psychological) and the objective (economic) aspects of women's oppression.[11]

While the ideology of the housewife and mother was the obvious first target for such an analysis, feminist research has since branched out into every area of culture. The whole symbolic apparatus of femininity, from clothes and shoes, to hair styles and make-up, has been indicted not only as a device for restricting and defining females as sexual objects, but also as a direct form of commercial exploitation which reaches even young children.

An essential aspect of this exploitation is the definition and self-definition of women as *consumers*. The symbol of the 'ideal home' provides the dynamic for an enormous amount of unnecessary consumption. In Western societies the home has become a fetish which it is the housewife's business to serve. Many socialists see the cycle of endlessly self-generating consumption as more than just an economic device; by injecting a phantasmagoric purpose into otherwise empty lives, it confuses political consciousness. Thus the economic functions of the family and its ideological justification as a fulfilment of personal needs neatly coincide. The more isolated and self-involved the family becomes, and the more it can be drawn into status competition with other families, the higher will be the rate of consumption and the more tightly bound women will be to serving the family's purposes rather than their own.

Exposing these ideologies is a far harder task than exposing simple economic oppression, which is usually obvious to the people who suffer from it. The theories which feminist intellectuals have developed in this area tend to be complex, embody-

ing concepts from psychology, linquistics and sociology as well
as Marxism, and are expressed in a specialised language.

However, the question of ideology can be approached by the
more direct route of personal experience. The reappearance of
feminism in the 1960s coincided with a revaluation of the
political significance of individual consciousness. The insight
that 'the personal is political' was universally adopted by the
feminist movement. Despite the scepticism of the (male) left,
which regarded the approach as self-indulgent and tactically
sterile, socialist feminists united in the belief that the experience of women could be a revolutionary force.

Here, the work of Sheila Rowbotham must be mentioned,
since it represents one of the earliest attempts in Britain to
integrate the personal experiences of women into the collective
categories of Marxist theory. It was, as she expressed it, a
matter of bringing to the surface the unspoken feelings which
women had about their situation, and incorporating these into
the theoretical analysis:

> Unless the internal process of subjugation is understood,
> unless the language of silence is experienced from inside and
> translated into the language of the oppressed communicat-
> ing themselves, male hegemony will remain. Without such a
> transaction, Marxism will not be really meaningful. There
> will be a gap between the experience and the theory.[12]

A great deal of the literature of the movement, and many of its
group activities, were directed towards this expression of
experience as a way of understanding the ideological mechanisms of oppression. Experiences of women's work and women's
role in factories and offices; experiences of housework and
child-rearing; experiences of the stultifying world of the nuclear
family – all these were not merely tolerated but their expression
was actively sought and encouraged. These experiences could
not be repeated too often, because it was through them that
women could become conscious of the situation of mental and
emotional debasement which they shared, and could conceive
the possibility of change.

Radical Feminism

The distinction between socialist and radical feminism is a delicate and sometimes elusive one. Although radical feminism arose in part as a reaction to the bad experiences of women in socialist movements, it is rarely anti-socialist. In the USA especially there are some radicals who are openly anti-left but most would argue that, far from rejecting socialist theory, the radical analysis has added a new dimension to it. Similarly, important themes of radical theory have been accepted by many socialists. While both liberal and socialist feminism had a long intellectual history, the radical analysis of the 1960s was new. It had an enormous impact on the older traditions, and has changed them.

When radical feminism first appeared, its distinguishing feature was the way in which it located the origins of women's oppression. Liberals blamed the system of learned sex roles, socialists blamed the economic and cultural exploitation of capitalism, radicals blamed men:

> We do not believe that capitalism or any other economic system is the cause of female oppression, nor do we believe that female oppression will disappear as a result of a purely economic revolution.[13]

For radicals, the socialist revolution was not nearly revolutionary enough. One of the first and still one of the best arguments for radical feminism appeared in Shulamith Firestone's book *The Dialectic of Sex*, in which the author claimed both to encompass and enlarge socialism by grounding Marxist theory more deeply in objective biological conditions. The theory of the class system became the theory of the sex/class system, in which the economic oppression of women was only a secondary result of their biological and psychological oppression by men.

Because it draws on so many sources, including the experiences of individual women, the radical feminist analysis is particularly difficult to encompass with brevity and accuracy. The following sketch describes radical feminism rather as a road map describes a landscape: the bare essentials are there, but a great deal more could be said. The radical theory is here divided into four themes: patriarchy; the family; sexuality and women's history.

Patriarchy

In its original meaning, 'patriarchy' is literally rule by the father, or by paternal right. Radical feminists, however, have used it to describe the historic dominance of men over women. This is seen as being prior to and necessary for the continuation of all other forms of social oppression: of blacks, of the poor, or of working people in general:

> Male supremacy is the oldest, most basic form of domination. All other forms of exploitation and oppression . . . are extensions of male supremacy . . . *All* men have oppressed women.[14]

Thus defined, patriarchy identifies men as the enemy. Men benefit from their power over women in every way: from ego-satisfaction, to economic and domestic exploitation, sexual domination and political power. In the last analysis patriarchy is maintained by violence. One male act which came to symbolise this power was rape. Whether or not an individual woman has experienced rape, she has certainly experienced the fear. That fear became a potent consciousness-raising device, an unambiguous proof that something was seriously wrong with the male/female relationship. More generally, all violence towards women was taken to be evidence of the intention of men to retain their power.

In its strongest form, sometimes called the 'pro-woman line', the theory of patriarchy labelled *all* women as victims and *all* men as oppressors. Gender alone defined the conflict. Socialists, by contrast, have argued that patriarchy was a particular case of capitalist class relations (following Engels) and therefore secondary to class. As the theories have developed, there has been a tendency for these two views to converge towards a model of capitalist patriarchy in which sexual and class oppressions are interwoven and inseparable.

The historic origins of patriarchy are a matter of great

dispute. Some theorists have suggested that it can only be the product of a long process of conditioning;[15] others have imagined an ancient matriarchal society which was over-thrown by men, pointing to the historic evidence that women once held greater power; others look to biology for the answer.

Biology is the supremely delicate subject, almost a taboo issue with some feminists who regard even the discussion of 'natural' differences as a dangerous game. The sexual differ-ence itself is an indisputable biological fact; and if men as a biological group almost universally have power over women as a biological group, it seems plausible to suppose that biology might have something to do with it.

Nothing more can be said with certainty, since the scientific debates are entirely unresolved and, as feminists correctly point out, almost totally controlled by men. So arguments over the true extent of male/female biological differences are inconclusive. Do the physical disruptions of menstruation and childbirth really put women at a disadvantage? Are women inevitably weaker and less aggressive than men? Is their mental capacity exactly the same as that of men? Or equal but different in kind? Each question has explosive implications, and the very difficulty of resolving them helps perpetuate sexism, which (like racism) feeds on half-truths and convenient wisdoms.

Liberals and socialists tend to treat the biological question as irrelevant and insoluble, and argue that the fight for equality must be pursued as if no differences at all existed. Within radical feminism, there are two distinct lines of thought. One suggests that women are indeed crippled by their biology, and especially by childbirth. 'Pregnancy is barbaric', states Shulamith Firestone firmly,[16] and women have simply been brainwashed into thinking otherwise. She locates the origins of patriarchy in the first division of labour, based on childbirth and motherhood, which assigned women to a dependent and powerless role and will continue to do so as long as they continue to bear children. This line implies that women can achieve equality in only two ways: by a technological revolution which will separate childbirth from the female body (the artificial womb), or by abandoning heterosexual activity and childbirth altogether.

The second argument, more widely accepted by both

radicals and socialists, is that women's biology itself is not a disadvantage, but only the *social definition* of it. Patriarchal culture defines everything which is biologically feminine as inferior to that which is biologically masculine: impregnation is superior to pregnancy, the penis is superior to the clitoris, and so on. The culturally assigned role of 'mother' labels the woman as a lesser being:

> In the female role, women are defined by their child-bearing capacity, which is interpreted as their function ... The concept 'maternal instinct' – meaning passivity, unconditional giving, sacrificing, suffering – is used to define women's so-called 'nature', thus it creates the context for her exploitation by men.[17]

A positive revaluation of feminine biology is therefore seen by many radical feminists as a centrally important task. A few groups dissatisfied with the argument that gender differences are purely social have developed a theory of feminine superiority, based on such evidence as the female's higher birth survival rate, longer life, greater adaptability to physical extremes and stronger resistance to many diseases. Combined with a belief in the *moral* superiority of women, this leads to a theory of 'female supremacism', a militant minority tendency within radical feminism. Since female supremacism violates the fundamental principle of the equal worth of all human beings as well as the fundamental goal of sexual equality, most feminists reject it completely or see it as no more than a rhetorical device for exposing the corrupt pretensions of patriarchy.

The family

Radical feminists took up the socialist critique of the family and carried it a stage further. While socialists saw the monogamous, heterosexual family as an important institution *supporting* male power, most radical theorists saw it as among the basic sources, and perhaps *the* basic source, of that power. In the family, they argued, women are oppressed by economic dependence, psychological annihilation, sexual exploitation, child-bearing and housework. Radical feminism's most radical

demand was therefore for the elimination of the role and
function of the mother, and thus of the marriage-based nuclear
family:

> Marriage constitutes slavery for women [and] it is clear that
> the Women's Movement must concentrate on attacking this
> institution. Freedom for women cannot be won without the
> abolition of marriage.[18]

Marriage was for radicals what capitalism was for socialists,
the real institutional source of exploitation. It destroyed the
individuality of women and perverted the minds of children,
while sustaining the patriarchal power of men.

There were many alternative visions of what might replace
the traditional family. Most of them stressed communality and
the benefits to be gained by collective child-rearing; all of them
assumed the absence or the minimal presence of men. For some
groups this was seen as an interim measure, allowing women to
take control of their own lives before readmitting men on a new
basis. For others it was the vision of the future, without
possibility of compromise.

In the latter part of the 1970s a new attitude towards
motherhood began to be apparent in the writings of the
movement. This was that maternity can be a joy and a benefit
to women if it is undertaken as a *freely chosen experience*, and not
within the confines of the nuclear family. Both lesbians and
single, heterosexual women argued that their rejection of
traditional family life should not entail the rejection of pregnancy, birth and motherhood as uniquely female experiences.
This new interest in motherhood was by no means shared by all
radical feminists, and clearly raised some difficulties for the
integrity of the original theory. For example, it might return
women (especially single mothers) to a rather restrictive female
role which is still patriarchally defined as inferior and powerless; and it might present those mothers with the extremely
ambiguous task of raising male children. These problems are
matters of continuing debate.

Sexuality

It follows from their critique of patriarchy and the monogamous family that radical feminists seek the transformation of sexuality. With its attendant myths of love and romance, sexuality provides the biological link between women and men which makes their antagonism unique. Man is the 'intimate enemy', not a distant symbol like the capitalist, but a very real body in the bed.

The minimal demand of radical feminists was that women should have control over their own sexuality. As long as sex was used by men to dominate women or by women to manipulate men, it would be alienating and unsatisfying. This meant an end to the double standard, an end to monogamy in marriage and an end to compulsory sex in marriage, goals shared by many liberal and socialist feminists.

But the presence of large numbers of lesbian women in the movement quickly produced a more radical argument, based on a now-famous article by Anne Koedt, 'The Myth of the Vaginal Orgasm'.[19] The Freudian root of this myth was that the clitoral orgasm represented immature sexuality while only the vaginal orgasm (which required a man) signalled a full and mature sexual experience. The physiological basis for this distinction had been eliminated once and for all by Masters and Johnson in 1966,[20] but it was the political implications which concerned radical feminists. Koedt exposed how the myth helped sustain the definition of women as passive rather than active sexual subjects, and how it reinforced the false belief that men were essential to the full sexual satisfaction of women.

Once the myth of the vaginal orgasm was out of the way, it became possible to conceive a complete sexual revolution which would enable women to escape the sexual domination of men. If women did not *need* men, and could make an unrestricted choice of heterosexual, bisexual, lesbian or celibate life-styles, the resulting liberation of sexual behaviour would break the hold of the monogamous family, the source of patriarchal power.

In practice, this belief has led towards the predominance of lesbian sexuality within radical feminism (although by no means all who subscribe to the radical theory are lesbians).

Some groups have institutionalised this in the form of a quota limiting the number of members who may be in an active sexual relationship with a man; some are open and work for more egalitarian sexual relationships; some are limited to lesbians only. Transforming women's sexuality has come to be seen as one of the major goals of this section of the movement, a necessary basis for the overthrow of patriarchy.

Women's history

History has a special importance for radical feminist theory. Although many feminists have documented the historic exploitation of women as a consciousness-raising device, the radical concept of patriarchy requires a knowledge of the past which goes deeper and further. The origins of patriarchy, if they are not to be located in biological differences or in the economic relations of capitalism, must lie far back in time when women were either the equals or the superiors of men. At some historical moment men must have gained supremacy and instituted the rule of patriarchy. When, how and why this change happened is clearly of the greatest significance to groups which aim to reverse it.

Such concerns have given rise to an intensive effort to recover and record women's history, and especially to a new field of study, the theory of *matriarchy*. Matriarchy is defined as government by a mother or mothers, or an order of society where descent is reckoned in the female line. Study groups both within and outside the universities, like Matriarchy Research and Reclaim in London, have been searching for the historical evidence which might support the theory of a primitive matriarchy, and a body of literature has accumulated. The assumption underlying matriarchal theory is not simply that power should be given to women but that doing so would create a less violent and materialistic society, since the past matriarchal society is conceived as having been more spiritual, peaceful and democratic than our own.

Alongside such studies, interest has grown in retrieving and developing forgotten forms of women's knowledge. Such knowledge is found in ancient goddess worship, in nature cults, in witchcraft, magic and psychic phenomena which are believed to be especially accessible to women.[21] All such knowledge, by providing a counterpoint and an alternative to male-defined history and male-defined science, is seen as a political resource for the reconstruction of society along feminist lines.

Theory and Practice

Political theories and utopias are easy to create but hard to translate into concrete social changes. Social movements offer one way of moving from theory to practice, but what they can do is limited by the values and assumptions on which they are based. Organisation, goals, strategy and tactics are all defined by the theories and beliefs which give the movement its coherence. In the case of feminism it will be obvious that the three main branches of the movement can and must act very differently in pursuit of their different aims.

Strategies of liberal feminism

Liberal feminism is almost entirely concerned with campaigning on specific issues; the issues reflect the egalitarian beliefs which have been described, and also a humanistic concern to alleviate women's immediate problems. Locally, campaigns are based on an assessment of what women need most, and on the kinds of demands which are likely to command the widest support. An area containing many poor or immigrant women, for example, will require different programmes and tactics from a middle-class area surrounding a large university.

In terms of the basic issues, there is little difference between America and Britain except where campaigns concern specific legislative proposals. The long struggle for an Equal Rights Amendment to the Constitution, for example, has been central to liberal feminism in the USA, and has had no British counterpart.

The main issues for liberals are equal pay, equal educational and job opportunities, the abolition of all legislation which discriminates against women, the abolition of sex role stereotypes in the media, and the development of knowledge for and about women. In addition, liberals universally support the wider feminist demands for free abortion, contraception and child care, improved maternity and health benefits, stronger enforcement of the laws against sexual violence and an end to discrimination against lesbians. Large organisations like NOW may campaign on all these issues, smaller groups usually concentrate only on one or two at a time.

These issues may also be taken as a description of the *minimal* demands of feminism as a whole. They are supported by socialists and radicals as at least intermediate and palliative measures, on which further demands could be based.

The wide-ranging nature of this programme is reflected in a great diversity of political activities, many of them supported co-operatively by the whole feminist movement. The following strategies are most typical of liberal feminism.

Legal and legislative actions: individual and class-action suits over the whole range of women's issues; work in political parties and campaigns, especially for the election of women; lobbying politicians; attending political committees and meetings to press women's interests.

Coalition building: working for the incorporation of feminist demands by other political groups and parties (in Britain this is a major area of action, directed mainly at the Labour Party, the new Social Democratic/Liberal Party Alliance and the trade unions; the Rights for Women Unit of the National Council for Civil Liberties is especially influential).

Single-issue campaigns. In the USA powerful professional pressure groups have grown up which work entirely on one or two issues, for example the Women's Equity Action League and the National Women's Political Caucus. The National Organisation for Women also has specialised units like the Media Group which concentrate their energies on one continuing campaign. In Britain single-issue campaigns on such demands as abortion, financial and legal independence and wages for housework, though liberal in their conception and tactics, have tended to arise from the socialist wing of the movement.

Direct intervention. This is most often organised on a local basis by a single group, and would include ventures like women's aid and rape crisis centres, contraception and health advice, day care, resource centres and bookstores. Liberals involved in work of this kind try to keep a low profile and to become integrated and accepted in their local community.

Influencing public opinion. The most traditional of all liberal tactics is to convince people that they should be on your side, and mobilise their convictions in pursuit of democratic change. For any social movement this is a most formidable task. Without a base in a major political party, or free access to the mass media, the movement must somehow publish its convictions and programmes. The feminist movement now has its own journals and publishing houses but (with the possible exception of the mass-circulation magazine *Ms* in the USA) these reach mainly the converted minority. The difficult tactic of using the mass media without being used by them remains the only real option open to a movement which seeks public influence on a scale large enough to create social change.

Those I have called 'liberal feminists' (although they tend to reject political labels) must have faith in a democratic system, the legal system and in the essential goodwill of their fellow (wo)men. They ask for and expect concessions which involve real costs for other groups, on grounds of fairness and equity. Socialists and radicals alike view this as a strategy which ignores the true realities of power.

Strategies of socialist feminism

Socialist feminist groups are distinguished from one another less by their general theory of society than by their programmes for change. At one end of the spectrum the work of socialist groups overlaps heavily with that of liberals; at the other it is ultra-revolutionary and explicitly anti-liberal. Four main tactical choices may be distinguished.

Reformist campaigns. All but a few socialists recognise the value of reformist campaigns 'pending revolution'. Aside from their human value, such campaigns help to build the movement and to raise consciousness, but they are always defined as interim programmes and not as the final goals of socialist feminism. To some extent these campaigns overlap with those of the liberals, and often involve co-operation. But the main focus of socialist feminist activity has been around issues which most directly concern working-class women: wages and unionisation; exploitation by employers; social security and public spending cuts; free and easily available abortion and contraception; and the special problems facing minority women. Campaign styles are combative, and often involve lobbying MPs or local councillors, staging street demonstrations, pickets and sit-ins.

Working within the labour movement. As an integral part of the fight for better conditions at home and at work, many socialist feminists choose (collectively or individually) to join the wider labour movement. They may be found in trade unions, in the Labour Party and in local government, pressing policy-makers to consider women's issues. Tactics of this type are open only to feminists who will work with men, which includes most socialists and Marxists as well as the liberals.

The critique of capitalist culture. Women working in colleges and universities have played a major part in developing a theoretical and practical critique of capitalist culture. Ideologies of femininity and images of women in the mass media have been a major concern, but the theoretical contributions of the past decade have touched on every aspect of Marxist analysis. This work appears publicly in the form of a large number of books, as well as such academic journals as *Feminist Review* and *M/F* in Britain. Feminist intellectual work also appears, of course, in non-feminist journals and collections, and is increasingly becoming a recognised branch of most academic disciplines.

Revolutionary organisation. Ultimately, Marxists and socialists believe that equality for every social group is linked to, and can be achieved only by, a massive transformation of the economic system. Thus the precondition for the liberation of women is the political unification of the whole working class (including women) towards the overthrow of the capitalist state. Because of the complex nature of women's situation, reforms in one area will simply be cancelled out by new oppressions in another; all the structures must be changed.

The unification of the male working class has itself proved a stubborn problem for Western Marxists. The assimilation of women is even harder. The private, individualised nature of most women's lives and consciousness has always worked against their involvement in politics, and socialist feminists face a double challenge: first to create the collective conscious-ness of women *as women*, and then *as workers*. The middle-class basis of the movement (especially in America) has made it no easier, for working-class women naturally resist being organ-ised by those in positions of relative power and privilege. In some cases middle-class feminists have gone to work in offices, factories, shops and telephone exchanges to make contact, but this has been rare.

Nevertheless, the revolutionary goal requires the collective action of the whole working class:

The underlying source of women's oppression, which is capitalism, cannot be abolished by women alone, nor by a coalition of women drawn from all classes. It will require a worldwide struggle for socialism by the working masses, male and female alike, together with every other section of the oppressed ... Men will have to learn that, in the hierarchy of oppressions created by capitalism, their chauvinism and dominance is another weapon in the hands of the master class for maintaining its rule.[22]

In both Britain and America this has meant a close connection between socialist feminism and the wider socialist movement, nationally and internationally. Some feminist groups are affiliated with existing socialist parties, though organised separately; some are actually incorporated within such parties, and others are not aligned to any specific organisation but generally support socialist campaigns. Despite many doctrinal differences, revolutionary socialism is ideally conceived as a single, worldwide movement, which now includes the libera-tion of women among its ultimate goals.

Strategies of radical feminism

In practice, radical feminists work alongside liberals and socialists on most issues, injecting their own political perspective into the shared campaigns of the movement. Beyond this, however, there are practices which – if not unique to the radicals – have been developed and most creatively used by them. These are forms of organisation and activity which arise directly from the radical analysis of the sex/class system, and which are designed to challenge or to undermine it. Three distinctive areas of radical feminist practice are distinguished below: the small group counter-culture; consciousness-raising; alternative structures.

The small group counter-culture. The small groups which form the molecular units of the whole feminist movement began as a practical necessity, and were progressively integrated by radicals as a theoretical necessity. At the start, when women were trying to break with male-dominated institutions, including the political groups to which some of them belonged, it was natural for them to follow the example of the emerging black power movement, and exclude the oppressors (however sympathetic) from their discussions. This had effects which were immediately beneficial. Women who were diffident about entering other types of movement found it easier to come into a small group composed just of other women. They were less intimidated, felt able to contribute, and in particular to contribute ideas and feelings which other women could be expected to understand and to share, but which the presence of men would have stifled.

In rejecting patriarchal culture, radical feminists also rejected the hierarchical power/conflict structure of male politics. From the beginning the small groups were designed to allow fully democratic decision-making and, so long as the groups stayed small and independent, national leaders and co-ordinating bureaucracies could not arise. The movement *belonged* to the women in it, not to some abstract organisational structure, and could appeal to women on the basis of their full participation, rather than junior status in someone else's movement.

In this way the groups became what are sometimes called 'prefigurative structures', i.e. they reproduced within themselves the co-operative, leaderless, all-female culture which radical feminists were working to create. They also enshrined the anarchist principle that, in politics, goals and means must be symmetrical and that the lives and actions of the revolutionary should not contradict the values on which the revolutionary movement is built. Because of its anti-authoritarian values, radical feminism has a natural affinity with social or co-operative anarchism, and a distinct anarcho-feminist theory has developed in Britain and the USA. But the underlying belief in the leaderless group and collective decision-making permeates the whole radical movement: 'The refining distinction from radical feminist to anarcho-feminist is largely that of making a step in self-conscious theoretical development.'[23] The small groups thus represent a self-contained counter-culture in which the political theories of radical feminism can be translated into personal action.

Consciousness-raising. The small all-female groups were thus a means both for making entry into the movement easy and for creating a radical counter-culture; but they also had another purpose. In each group there took place a process of expressing and sharing experience which came to be known as 'consciousness-raising'. Later adopted in various forms by all feminists, consciousness-raising was originated by a New York radical group called the Redstockings. The principle was simple. Women were drawn into the movement on the basis of their own experiences of sexism and, in the small group, were to learn the reasons for those experiences.

Consciousness-raising is the point where theory and action meet, but it is used very differently by the separate feminist groups. For liberals it has a persuasive and therapeutic purpose only, and Marxists use it (if at all) as a learning device to guide new recruits towards an understanding of existing theory. But, as first formulated by the radicals (and still used by the Redstockings, among others), it was an altogether more far-reaching conception, and politically entirely original. Consciousness-raising was to be the basis of theory:

We regard our personal experiences and our feelings about that experience as the basis for an analysis of our common situation. We cannot rely on existing ideologies as they are all products of male supremacist culture.[24]

Theory-building, then, went on anew in each group, usually guided by an experienced member. Participants had the sense that they were not only getting their own problems into perspective but that they were contributing to the general process of development of ideas within the movement. This insistence that the personal is political reflected a particular current of late-1960s' thought, but only the radical feminists made it the basis of their political practice.

Alternative structures. The sheer magnitude of the radical political agenda means that success must be defined in terms of limited victories. It is hard to devise a programme which will show any positive signs of eliminating patriarchy, the sex/class system and the family. At the beginning, when the main problem was to gain attention, 'zap actions' were popular in America; but these showed diminishing returns and in any case laid the movement open to ridicule by the media. Radical groups have also taken part in all the movement's reformist campaigns, being especially prominent in abortion, anti-pornography and gay rights. But these do not promise to change the whole system, or offer any escape from it.

Significant victories can be won, however, by creating alternative structures for women's lives which bypass or ignore the patriarchal culture in which they have to exist.

The most comprehensive form of alternative structure is the all-female commune, which in its ideal form is self-contained. This image of community life, which gained wide currency in the 1960s, harks back to the lost world of the agricultural village and the self-sufficient extended family. Hundreds of communes were started in the USA during the late 1960s and early 1970s, devoted to everything from feminism to oriental mysticism. Only a few survived the perilous passage between the twin rocks of practical inexperience and ill-prepared human nature. Economic constraints in Britain (especially the cost of land and housing) limited such experiments; those that remain and the new ventures still being launched are more in the nature of urban co-operatives than full communes. Buildings and domestic work may be shared, but cash and goods must come mainly from the outside, through work in the regular economy.

Nevertheless, the commune is the logical structure for those women who wish to isolate their lives as much as possible from the patriarchal culture around them. Those who follow this path are usually labelled 'radical separatists' and may be compared with advocates of black power, who argue that racism is inevitable, whites are the eternal enemy and cultural separation the only hope of survival for the black race. In practice, the separatist path is an extremely hard one to follow, not least because the initial step requires a considerable capital investment. Most such all-female living groups remain very small and fragile.

A less drastic strategy is the creation of intermediate institutions to serve as alternate structures for particular areas of life. These would include self-help health clinics; feminist journals and newspapers; bookshops and resource centres; food co-operatives; day-care centres; alternative schools; shelters and rape crisis centres; and so on. Such forms of action are highly developed in the USA and, again because of the less benign economic climate, less so in Britain outside a few big urban centres. They provide ways of using the skills and energies of the group in feminist causes, without implying the engagement with the male world which is inseparable from most liberal and socialist political actions.

Summary and Conclusions

The reader should be aware of the limitations of this account. It reveals only those debates and theoretical positions which are available publicly and in print and relies disproportionately on the work of certain named individuals (mostly intellectuals) who have played major roles in the development of theory. But the grass-roots movement does not always reflect the theoretical preoccupations of these intellectuals, nor are the most organised and articulate metropolitan groups necessarily representative of the movement as a whole. The fact, too, that ideas are more personal than political actions, and are often developed out of the personal experiences of women, means that a man's view of feminist theory must be a view of the surface. Beneath that surface are debates and subtleties accessible only to participants.

But even bearing in mind these reservations, certain clear patterns emerge from which conclusions may be drawn.

Liberal feminism represents the latest development of a long tradition in Western societies. It claims for women the benefits of individual freedom, political influence and equality of opportunity which the democratic system was designed to provide, and has hitherto provided mainly to men. The legalistic and democratic tactics of the liberals have been consistent with these goals.

Britain has no distinct liberal feminist organisations, but the demands and tactics of such American liberal groups as NOW have been assimilated into the socialist strategy, especially by feminists involved with the Labour Party or the trade unions.

In its purest and most simplified form, socialist feminism relates the oppression of women to the class structure of the capitalist system, and draws much of its theoretical material from the Marxist and left socialist traditions. The struggle for the liberation of women is therefore seen as being necessarily a part of the larger revolutionary struggle for socialism and communism. Within this broad definition we find Marxist, Trotskyist and libertarian socialist groups, some independent and some affiliated with (male) left-wing political organisations. Despite these doctrinal differences, socialist feminism has a distinct identity *vis-à-vis* radical feminism.

Radical feminism (and many radical feminists claim also to be unaligned socialists) sees women as the most fundamentally oppressed people, and hence potentially the most revolutionary. Men are perceived as being the major enemy, and radical feminists stress the benefits which men receive from their exploitation of women. The whole Western cultural tradition, rather than the economic organisation of capitalism alone, is believed by radical feminists to support that exploitation. In the absence of a ready-made tradition of analysis, radical feminists generated much of their own theoretical material.

The ultra-democratic forms which they also developed, and the relative autonomy and isolation of the small groups, make it difficult for radical feminists to co-ordinate political action of a traditional kind, and incline this section of the movement towards counter-cultural forms of protest.

When the different theories were formulated in the late 1960s the major theoretical point at issue was that, for socialist feminists, capital used sex (and race) to divide the working class. They argued that radical feminists, by saying that *men* oppressed women as well as (or rather than) capital, were playing into the hands of the bourgeoisie. Radical feminists, on the other hand, held that socialist revolutions had not resulted in the liberation of women, and that there needed to be an autonomous women's movement focusing on the oppression of women alone.

In the following decade, however, there was some degree of convergence between these apparently opposed theories. A major rethinking of Marxism was undertaken by feminist intellectuals, and this produced a recognition that patriarchy was a form of oppression related to capitalism but not reducible *only* to capitalism:[25] in other words, that the subordination of women had two distinct sources – male power and capitalist exploitation. Thus socialists came to accept the need for an autonomous women's movement focusing on patriarchy. Since many radical feminists had always accepted the basic validity of the socialist analysis of capitalism, the sharp lines which were earlier drawn between these forms of feminist theory are now somewhat blurred.

Both socialists and radicals have tended to dismiss liberal feminism as excessively individualistic, and ignorant of the realities of power; it can never result in more than trivial reform benefiting mainly middle-class women.

The easy circulation of books and journals has mingled the ideas of British and American feminists so that the national differences are slight. Perhaps the most significant distinction is that the American movement has been more influenced by theories of racial prejudice, while the British have always stressed class oppression. This has had an important outcome in terms of tactics. Since race is a fixed category, you can either alter the conditions which allow one race to dominate another (*liberal idea*) or overcome or separate from the dominant race (*radical idea*). Class, on the other hand, is a purely economic category which *can* be changed by the transformation of the economic system (*socialist idea*). This helps to explain why America remains the home of the purest forms of liberal and radical theory, while socialist feminism has developed more fully and has been more widely accepted in Britain.

It may be anticipated that there will one day be a full convergence of liberal, socialist and radical ideas into a single but diverse feminist movement. This convergence has not yet happened, and the disagreements which remain play a signifi-cant part in the history which follows. While the factions have certainly influenced one another profoundly, new cross-cutting divisions have appeared, especially over the question of sexuality, which have prevented the movement from speaking with a single voice on women's issues.

4. High Hopes: the Growth of Feminism, 1970–5

If the 1960s was the decade of radical youth, the 1970s became the decade of women. In the early years the sensation of hectic growth was such that a great mass movement of women seemed just around the corner. A new politics was created virtually from nothing, many significant victories were won and feminism staked its claim to be taken seriously as the expression of women's interests and aspirations.

Organising in Britain

The first national gathering of the British movement was held at Ruskin College in Oxford in February 1970. The organisers, themselves uncertain just how many groups already existed throughout the country, were stunned when the Oxford conference attracted 600 delegates. The grass-roots diversity suggested by these numbers made the conference difficult to handle. Women's liberation was not a political party with a programme which could be discussed in the traditional way, and it was hard for women coming from very different perspectives to reach a clear understanding of what kind of movement they had so quickly created, and what was to be done with it.

But the enthusiasm and energy were enormous. The women at Oxford realised that they were the vanguard of a new movement, and the conference established a broad agenda for future action. The first agreed principle was to bypass the conventional forms of parliamentary and pressure-group politics in favour of a movement which operated autonomously entirely outside the system. This principle, which emerged by consensus rather than through discussion, was a critical one for

93

the British movement. Because of it, the political avenues used by the American liberals were closed and British women's liberation was separated by choice from mainstream politics.

The conference set up a co-ordinating committee (the Women's National Co-ordinating Committee) whose main functions were to communicate information between groups and to organise further national conferences. The WNCC became a battleground for left sectarian groups trying to take over the movement and was abolished the following year. No truly national structure has ever replaced it, though regional centres have developed which serve the same functions.

Finally, the Oxford conference defined the most immediate problems and, in doing so, set up the framework for the original four demands of the women's liberation movement. These were hammered out in detail by the WNCC and formed the basis for the first national demonstration. They were:

1. Equal pay for equal work.
2. Equal opportunities and education.
3. Free contraception and abortion on demand.
4. Free 24-hour child care.

These demands were not, it should be noted, a centrally imposed policy. Then, as now, the movement rarely made policy decisions, and individual groups were entirely free to accept or reject ideas which came out of national or regional conferences. Nevertheless, the four demands (later expanded to seven) became the essential starting-point for feminist campaigns everywhere. The first two demands were orthodox liberal 'fair-shares' policies, and aroused little comment or opposition; the more radical demands for free contraception, abortion and free child care were the main sources of conflict and controversy.

The first public demonstration in support of the four demands was held in London on a bitterly cold March day in 1971. Several hundred women, men and children marched from Hyde Park to Trafalgar Square and presented a petition to the Prime Minister. The publicity attending the march can be judged by the expansion of the London Women's Liberation Workshop in the following weeks from 16 groups to 66, only a little short of its all-time peak membership. But the big national demonstration was not to be the typical pattern of action in Britain; local groups and local campaigns were preferred, both for their practicality and because they fitted the decentralist philosophy of the movement.

A remarkable feature of the women's movement in these early years was the way it grew and expanded without formal structures, and with hardly any effective communications outside London. Women simply heard about the idea and organised themselves in small groups, with the most tenuous links to the movement as a whole, no rules, no procedures and no membership lists. A typical small group in 1971 had about a dozen members in their 20s and 30s, employed in middle-class occupations and most frequently single, divorced or with unsettled marriages. They would meet regularly to discuss issues of personal concern, political questions and possible areas of action, but might have few opportunities to meet with other feminists or to share ideas outside the circle.

Another form of organisation designed to overcome the isolation of the small group was the *women's centre*, usually in a house or shop, open to women for meetings, the co-ordination of campaigns, workshops, play groups and special projects. The first of these was the London Women's Liberation Workshop, which began in 1969, and by 1973 there were five in London and others in Bristol, Lancaster, Cardiff and Edinburgh. Some centres obtained council grants, others operated with almost no money in abandoned properties. A centre started in Chiswick in 1971 became a shelter for battered women and, when the need was recognised, others were established on the same lines.

Groups affiliated to the existing Marxist parties such as the International Marxist Group and the International Socialists were usually organised separately along more traditional political lines, but these never accounted for more than a fraction of all the women involved. There was also an attempt to establish a distinct libertarian/anarchist wing of women's liberation in this period, and conferences were held in 1973 and 1974, but this tendency did not gather much strength until late in the decade.

Thus feminism emerged and grew in a totally amorphous way, without financial resources (few women could afford to contribute much) and without an established political pattern to follow. Organisation and theory were built together in a great upsurge of energy and creativity; those who were there remember it as a period of continual excitement, when anything seemed possible.

Organising in America

In America women's liberation had emerged fully on to the national scene in 1970 with a national demonstration which nobody could ignore. The fiftieth anniversary of female suffrage in America fell on 26 August 1970, and NOW proposed a National Women's Strike for Equality on that day to demonstrate the power of the movement. The unofficial slogan for the strike became 'Don't cook dinner, starve a rat today.' A coalition of NOW and more radical groups in New York City organised a march, and a great tide of 50,000 women paraded down Fifth Avenue, making this the largest women's demonstration in history. Simultaneous marches took place all over the country involving tens of thousands more women. It was at this moment that the press began to treat the movement seriously, according the demonstrations wide and respectful coverage.

Just as the British groups had a great influx of support after the 1971 London demonstration, so NOW experienced a surge in membership from 3,000 to 15,000 in the months following 26 August, and to 40,000 by 1974. Expansion at this rate created a number of organisational crises which were not brought under control until mid-decade. Funds were short, experienced staff lacking, and above all, communications between the national office of NOW and its ever-expanding periphery of local chapters were very poor. A common paradox of success is that organisation itself begins to burn up the time and energy which might be going into political campaigns, and this was a complaint frequently heard in NOW during the early 1970s.

These years also saw the hardening of the divisions between liberal feminists, radicals and socialists. The Women's Strike for Equality was the last occasion on which they worked successfully together. Attempts to bridge the differences were made at Congresses to Unite Women in 1969 and 1970, but these only revealed how profound the differences were. So the American movement grew almost from the beginning in two quite distinct directions: the public, highly visible organisations of liberal feminism; and the half-hidden networks of radical/socialist feminism.

The growth of liberal feminism was explosive, much of it consisting of specialised campaigns which originated in NOW, as outlined in Chapter 2. The Professional Women's Caucus (PWC) quickly became an effective force in the struggle for better professional training opportunities. In 1970 we see the first women's caucus in federal government, the founding of the League for Women's Rights to reform marriage and divorce laws, the first civil rights groups for Chicano (Mexican-American) and Indian (Native-American) women. The following year Gloria Steinem and Brenda Feigen Fasteau set up the Women's Action Alliance as the first national women's information and referral system, and in 1972 the *Ms* Foundation became the only nationwide funding source specifically for women. Also in 1971 Betty Friedan, Bella Abzug, Shirley Chisholm and others launched the National Women's Political Caucus (NWPC) to campaign for the election of women at every level. Older women began to organise as Older Women's Liberation (OWL), in 1972, black women in 1973. The National Abortion Rights Action League (NARAL) was founded in 1973 and the American Civil Liberties Union (ACLU), already deeply involved with women's rights, launched their Reproductive Freedom project in 1974.

This almost frenetic pluralism meant that just about any woman could find a place in the movement to match her particular interests and political views. The question whether all women can or do have *common* interests was thus never raised in acute form.

The growth of radical/socialist feminism in these years was as dramatic but much harder to chart with accuracy. The subterranean groups formed, split, vanished and reformed so quickly that no researcher has succeeded in mapping their progress. Even those most intimately involved had no idea how big the movement really was, though it is suggestive that the radical feminist theory collection, *Notes from the Second Year*, sold over 40,000 copies when it was issued in 1970. The indications are that participation in the radical side of the movement peaked in 1971, when groups existed in every town and city in America, and then began to decline sharply in the face of organisational and political problems which the radical theory itself had raised but not solved.

The remainder of this chapter follows the history of the women's liberation movement through the early 1970s, beginning with an account of how the feminist message was communicated and then reviewing the major campaigns of 1970–5 and the state of the movement at mid-decade.

Spreading the Word

No movement can achieve substantial social changes unless it gets its message across to three crucial audiences: political elites who have the power to initiate change; media elites who have the power to portray the movement to the outside world; and the constituency of people who are potential converts to the new movement (in this case, all women).

The channels through which new and dissenting messages can be spread are desperately narrow and almost entirely controlled by wealthy white males. Women, along with blacks, young people, poor people and anyone outside this controlling elite, have always had great difficulty in making their voices heard. We hear about these voiceless sections of the population only when they manage to become 'news' – by protesting, by rioting, by creating an amusing new style, a titillating new idea, or whatever it may be.

Women's liberation first became news by the mere fact of its existence as a novelty, and by public demonstrations and campaigns which had novelty value. It is a sad fact that the first or second march on equal pay or abortion (or black integration or anti-nuclear) will be news to the media, the tenth and the hundredth march will not. In the early months of 1970 women's liberation was big news. Jo Freeman has described the avalanche of publicity, which happened almost simultaneously in Britain and America, as the 'Grand Press Blitz'.[1]

Sunday supplements, weekly news magazines, daily papers and television programmes became infatuated with the new movement and mobilised their best female journalists to cover it.

In Britain press interest was sparked off by the Oxford conference. The coverage was almost entirely negative, stressing the bizarre, extreme and emotional aspects of the meeting and ignoring the issues which were discussed. The April 1970 issue of the newsletter *Shrew* devoted most of its space to a commentary on media images of the movement, and to discussing whether and how the press might be used in a more productive way.

For most feminists, therefore, this sudden notoriety was a mixed blessing. On the one hand, their cause was transformed from a marginal oddity into an international phenomenon in the space of a few months. On the other, they did not at all relish being portrayed by outsiders over whom they had no control and who zeroed in on colourful personalities and dramatic issues that tended to distort the complex and fluid identity of the movement. From this time on there was an unwritten rule against individual women or individual groups speaking to the press on behalf of the whole movement. This minimised the gross distortions, but left reporters with few options but guesswork, caricature or silence on feminist issues.

In 1970 the Women in Media group was formed in London to improve the situation of women in journalism, broadcasting and publishing and, at the same time, to improve the reporting of women's issues. Throughout the early 1970s British feminists kept up a regular barrage of critical comment on sexism in the media, with some effect. By 1973 papers like the *Birmingham Post*, *The Times* and *The Guardian* had been persuaded to abandon their condescending and often trivial 'women's pages' of recipes and fashion and, in general, blatantly offensive stories and images of women were seen less frequently. In 1975 the National Union of Journalists issued a book of guidelines called *Images of Women*. But these improvements were not reflected in the reporting of the movement itself, which continued to be sporadic, ill-informed and sometimes malicious.

As *Shrew* commented, this experience 'Emphasizes once

again our need to develop our own channels of communication, and to establish our own credibility as a movement, so that people no longer look to the establishment media for news about us.'[2] The movement needed to find its own voice. At the beginning it used the existing network of radical journals to build a base, but these were mainly male-controlled. Within a short time the movement had created its own press. The range of British journals is indicated by the following list, which is by no means exhaustive and does not cover local newsletters, occasional and short-lived publications.

Shrew was the first widely circulated source of feminist news in Britain. It was started in 1969 as the unaligned journal of the London Women's Liberation Workshop (at that time only four groups), and was to be edited by each group in turn. Until 1974 *Shrew* was published several times a year and achieved a circulation of about 5,000 copies. However, the growth and diversification of the Workshop made the policy of alternate editorship increasingly unwieldy and politically difficult, and the paper succumbed to these differences in 1974, reappearing briefly in 1976 and 1977. The objective of *Shrew* was not just to communicate information but to give as many women as possible the experience of producing a journal, and this is reflected in the unusually wide range of issues and opinions covered, particularly during the first three years.

Socialist Woman was the second regular journal to appear, in 1970, as the women's magazine of the Trotskyist International Marxist Group. Well-printed and illustrated, the appeal of *Socialist Woman* was nevertheless limited by its narrow political base, and it never achieved a national circulation much above 5,000 copies. The journal concentrated on working-class and militant trade-union issues, and, by its nature, held little appeal for women who were not already committed socialists. Nevertheless, it was an important source of detailed reporting and commentary on socialist and trade-union activities otherwise ignored in the national press.

Spare Rib appeared as part of a flurry of feminist publishing activity in 1972, and remains the only widely circulated national journal of the women's liberation movement in Britain. As such, its influence in presenting the image of the movement to the outside world has been enormous, both in what it has chosen to print and what it has chosen not to. Planned in 1971 by a group of women already experienced in publishing and launched with the minimum of funds, the first issue of *Spare Rib* in July 1972 sold out all 20,000 copies. The editorial collective (the magazine is still edited collectively) made its aim to 'put women's liberation on the news-stands'. In the early years the goal of attracting uncommitted women as readers meant that the more militant aspects of feminism were played down, articles and letters by men appeared regularly and some traditional women's magazine features like cooking and fashion were retained. By 1974 *Spare Rib* had dropped all such features and clearly identified itself as a women's liberation journal aligned to socialism. Yet throughout the 1970s the editorial collective continued to be the focus of many pressures, reflected in published letters, from women who felt the magazine should take a firmer stand on various issues. Some of the most difficult debates in the movement – over wages for housework and the place of lesbianism in feminism, for example – were muted in the pages of *Spare Rib* for fear of deepening existing divisions and giving ammunition to the enemies of the movement. Despite controversies and occasional economic crises, however, *Spare Rib* continues to offer the broadest and least sectarian image of British feminism, and the one most accessible to uncommitted women who may pick up the magazine at their local newsagent. Through subscriptions and public sales, it reaches about 32,000 readers each month.

Women's Voice, also started in 1972, has a far narrower readership than *Spare Rib*. It began as a publication of the International Socialist Party and is currently described as the women's magazine of the Socialist Workers' Party. *Women's Voice* is similar in its format and political concerns to *Socialist Woman* and appeals to the same constituency. In 1982 the independent women's groups were absorbed back into the SWP, but the journal continues publication.

Red Rag was a Marxist feminist journal not aligned to any political party, and was published between 1972 and 1980. More reflective and oriented towards theory than most other journals, *Red Rag* had a small circulation but considerable influence on the movement.

Women's Report was another non-aligned socialist journal of news and events, produced by a collective between the end of 1972 and mid-1979 with a top circulation of about 3,000 copies.

Link was established as the women's journal of the Communist Party of Great Britain in 1973. It has a substantial circulation among members and is distributed in the Soviet Union and Eastern Europe.

Sappho was launched in 1972 and became important as a resource for lesbians, though it was not a radical magazine. Circulating about 1,000 copies, it folded for financial reasons late in 1981.

In the following years the public forum of the movement continued to expand as more and more journals and newsletters appeared: *Women Speaking*, with a Christian emphasis (1974); *Women's Struggle Notes*, from the Marxist Big Flame Collective (1974); *Zero*, an anarchist feminist monthly (1977); *Scarlet Women*, a socialist feminist journal (1978); sympathetic non-feminist journals like *Gay News* and *Gay Left*; local publications like the *Manchester Women's Liberation Journal*, the *London Women's Liberation Newsletter* and Scotland's *Ms Print* – all offered channels for sharing experience, developing theory and making contact with women outside. At the same time, a broader networking service was needed to link the movement together and provide a central source of information. A London group called Action for Women's Advice, Research and Education (AWARE), begun in 1974, was shortlived. But in 1975 the Manchester national conference agreed to establish the Women's Information and Referral Service (WIRES), which still continues to be the main information centre for England and which issues a women-only newsletter to about 500 subscribers.

The growing academic interest in feminism led to the setting up of a library, the Women's Research and Resources Centre, in London in 1975 which, with the Fawcett Library, provides one of the most complete collections of feminist literature in Britain. And academic journals began to appear, *M/F* in 1978 and *Feminist Review* in 1979, concerned mainly with developing the theoretical relationship between Marxism and feminism.

The latest publishing venture (to date) is *Outwrite*, Britain's first national newspaper for women, launched on International

Women's Day, 8 March 1982, and initially planned to be published monthly. The first issues of *Outwrite* show a special concern with international questions and with the situation of black women.

Since the original success of Germaine Greer's *The Female Eunuch* in 1970, commercial publishers have been eager to publish some types of feminist books. The works of Kate Millett, Sheila Rowbotham and many others were quickly issued in paperback and achieved impressive sales. Some bookshops now have sections devoted to feminist works and, indeed, there are a few which sell nothing else. In an effort to take control of their own writings, feminists moved into the publishing business themselves. The first step was a collection of writings called *The Body Politic*, commercially published in 1972 but with royalties contributed to the movement. The next such collection, *Conditions of Illusion*, was published by an *ad hoc* feminist group in 1974. Virago, started in 1975, has been the most commercially successful feminist press and, in 1982, joined a major publishing group. Others such as Women's Press, Sheba and Onlywoman Press have since established themselves firmly in the market.

In Britain, therefore, it could not be said that there is a lack of publishing outlets for feminist ideas. Every significant aspect of the movement is recorded in print and any woman who has wanted to find out about it has been able to do so with little difficulty for the past ten years. The last sentence pinpoints the snag, however. Women's liberation is not 'on the newstands'. Many of the most important sales outlets do not even carry *Spare Rib*, and one would be unlikely to find any of the literature of the movement in the chain stores and big agencies which account for the bulk of magazine and book sales to women. A deliberate and conscious effort would be needed to find most of these journals and books and, in suburbs and small towns, they would simply be unobtainable.

This points up the continuing gap between the power and reach of the women's media and that of the mass media. Traditional women's magazines have circulations in the millions, television numbers its audiences in tens of millions. It is a striking illustration of how modern society can hide an opposition movement, even while allowing it complete freedom of public expression. The sheer weight of mass communications smothers the alternative voice.

In America, feminist publishing has been vastly more prolific, yet hardly more successful in breaking through to a mass audience. From the beginning, energetic attempts were made to use both the conventional and alternative media. In what was perhaps the most-publicised action, a group of women staged a sit-in at the editor's office of *Ladies Home Journal*, and persuaded the management to publish a special women's liberation supplement in August 1970. The same year, the underground paper *Rat* was temporarily taken over by feminists. Female journalists were encouraged to learn about the movement, and many of them became sympathisers.

At the same time, in-movement journals were appearing too fast for anyone to count. The first was a newsletter, *Voice of the Women's Liberation Movement*, published in Chicago in 1968 and 1969. *Women: a Journal of Liberation* was the earliest socialist feminist publication, also in 1969, and radical theory began to appear in the very influential *Notes from the First Year* (1968), followed by further editions in 1970 and 1971.

All over the nation new feminist journals were started: *Off Our Backs* (Washington), *Ain't I a Woman* (Iowa), *Everywoman* and *It Ain't Me Babe* (California) and dozens of others, varying in format from duplicated news-sheets to glossy magazines. The first national commercial newsletters, *Women Today* and *Spokeswoman*, both started up in 1970.

It was inevitable that a mass-circulation commercial magazine would eventually be tried, and this came in 1972, the year of the launching of *Spare Rib* in Britain. Early in the year, after a prolonged struggle to obtain financial support, a collective of women (some but not all from NOW) put out a preview edition of the magazine *Ms*. All 300,000 copies sold out in a matter of days, and the edition became a collector's item; some 20,000 letters were received in response. In July 1972 the first regular monthly edition appeared with Gloria Steinem as editor.

Commercially, *Ms* was a great success. From the start it attracted major advertising revenue – most rare among the feminist journals – and by 1982 had a circulation of half a million copies. How successful it has been in spreading the feminist message is a matter of hot debate. Like the *Spare Rib* collective, the editors of *Ms* were criticised from all sides. Too radical for many liberals, far too liberal for many radicals, the magazine steered an uneasy course. To readers accustomed to British feminist journals, current issues of *Ms* look extremely moderate, although clearly feminist. Articles and letters by men are published regularly and political positions are muted. The policy has enabled the magazine to attract a wider readership among women who do not necessarily define themselves as feminists.

Academic women's studies journals like *Quest* (1974) and *Signs* (1975) soon began to appear, and feminist publishing flourished with houses like Daughters Inc., Diane Press and Feminist Press. At the time of writing there are approximately thirty nationally available news and opinion magazines and twenty academic journals which deal with feminism, women's issues and women's studies in America.

Even more than in Britain, feminism in America was thus made available as an idea to anyone interested in exploring it. Liberal feminist assumptions were swiftly incorporated into the culture, so that while the moderate feminism of *Ms* magazine or NOW still has its powerful enemies it is an accepted part of the political scene. Not so the radical/socialist critiques of patriarchy and capitalism, which were submerged as much by the success and visibility of liberal feminism as by the hostile silence of the mass media.

Campaigning

The annual Miss World beauty contest at the Albert Hall, London, in November 1970 was disrupted by a loud demonstration from about a hundred women. Five were arrested and fined, comparing their treatment at the hands of the police with that of the suffragettes. This re-run of the famous Miss American protest of 1968 brought the same kinds of negative publicity, and many feminists were unhappy with what they saw as a diversion from the serious business of the 'four demands'.

Civil disobedience was a campaigning style which never

became popular among feminists in Britain or America, though
through the 1970s we occasionally hear of direct actions against
such targets as beauty contests or pornographic shops. Small
groups of angry women taking to the streets made good news
but bad images for the movement in a culture where almost any
public display of feeling generates instant rejection. In contrast
to these sporadic protests, the major campaigns of the first half
of the decade were concerned with economic demands, abortion and sexual liberation.

Economic campaigns

The early 1970s were years of chronic class confrontation in
Britain. The student and anti-Vietnam war movements had
faded, to be replaced by a concerted campaign from the left
against rising unemployment, public spending cuts and the
Tory Industrial Relations Bill. These big issues carried the
danger of making the women's movement seem marginal, but
they also raised the general level of political consciousness and
encouraged many more women to become involved in political
actions.

The Night Cleaners' Campaign was a classic, and one from
which important lessons were learned. Night cleaners, working
mainly in office buildings, were and are mostly poor and
immigrant women who were and are still heavily exploited by
the independent contractors who employ them. Late in 1970
women from the International Socialists began a leaflet
campaign to unionise cleaners in London; they were shortly
joined by supporters from the London Women's Liberation
Workshop and the International Marxist Group. This diverse
coalition, known as the Cleaners' Action Group (CAG),
worked hard throughout 1971 and 1972 to persuade the
isolated and often frightened cleaners to join the Transport and
General Workers' Union, meeting time after time with cleaners
who worked in the same buildings and with union officials.[3]

The results were mixed. The women's liberation movement
received unusually sympathetic publicity for their efforts in
what most people saw as a very worthy cause. But, as the
movement's first major intervention in the working class, it
raised disturbing questions. The middle-class feminists found

it difficult to relate to the cleaners, and to the cleaners' own leader, May Hobbs. Conversely, the cleaners were confused and suspicious about women's liberation. There were wide disagreements with the CAG collective about the correct attitude to unions, and these uncertainties were compounded by the half-hearted response from male union officials to the whole campaign. The movement is rightly proud of the Night Cleaners' Campaign, but it eventually withdrew from involvement and, a decade later, the cleaners are still struggling for full union recognition. At the end, the report of the action reflects a sense of pessimism about the compromises needed to make progress along democratic-socialist lines.

This was only the first of a series of efforts by the women's liberation movement to support the economic struggles of working-class women. The women's occupation of the Fakenham shoe factory in Norfolk in 1972, and their subsequent formation of a workers' co-operative, became a *cause célèbre*. In twelve months during 1973 and 1974 one feminist source documented 54 significant strikes involving women.[4] Night cleaners' campaigns were started in Manchester, Liverpool and Durham.

Clearly there was a new (but not unprecedented) upsurge in female working-class militancy. The problem for the women's liberation movement was to know what to do with it. The socialist groups most involved in these struggles lacked the resources to act independently, and indeed lacked any close organic connection with the working class. They therefore had to look to the existing trade unions for practical support, and their reservations about this were often borne out by experience.

Despite the fact that, in these years, women were joining unions at twice the rate of men, and despite the evidence of growing female militancy, large blue-collar unions like TGWU, AUEW and GMWU were slow to abandon their traditionally negative attitude towards women. White-collar and service unions like ASTMS, APEX, NUPE, COHSE, TASS, NUJ, NUT and NALGO got the message more quickly, and were soon making greater efforts to attract and involve female members.

The Trades Union Congress (TUC), with an overwhelmingly male-dominated executive, responded with caution to the new atmosphere. Just two delegate places out of 41 were reserved for women, and this number was increased to five only in 1981. But the TUC Women's Conference, which had existed since 1926, gained a new lease of life from the movement and became an energetic pressure group within the TUC. Local trades councils began to form special women's sub-committees and, in general, the early 1970s were a period of growing understanding and mutual appreciation between the women's movement, the unions and the Labour Party. The fact remained, however, that concrete economic gains in industrial disputes were seen to be accomplished by trade unions and not by women's liberation, and this contributed to a growing feeling within the movement that it should pay more attention to specifically feminist issues.

One good example of fruitful collaboration between the feminist movement and trade unions was the Working Women's Charter (WWC) campaign. In 1974 a women's rights conference was held at TUC headquarters, and this stimulated considerable discussion between feminists and unionists. One result was a ten-point charter for working women drawn up by the London Trades Council which included traditional union demands on wages, promotion, training and working conditions. Beyond these, however, the charter aimed to make connections between the world of work and the private world of home and family by including demands on child care, maternity leave, contraception, abortion and family allowances.

Unions and trades councils all over the country, encouraged and prodded by local charter campaign groups, adopted the Charter as part of their programmes, and it was debated at the Trades Union Congress in 1975, attracting substantial union support. By this time the TUC had adopted its own charter for women, similar in many respects to the WWC, and in 1978 added the crucial abortion demand, which had been resisted earlier by some male unionists. To some extent this made the Charter campaign redundant, and the local groups turned to other concerns. The Working Women's Charter offers an example of that delicate political strategy, victory by co-operation. Persuading an already-powerful group to take over your programme, one of the more effective strategies open to any social movement, has been rarely used in the recent campaigns of women's liberation.

The National Council for Civil Liberties (NCCL) also became a catalyst in the growing relationship between trade unions and the women's movement. The Council had begun to focus on women's rights in 1973 and, two years later, formed a distinct Rights for Women Unit, which has since become an indispensable source of information on economic and social issues.

Progress on equal pay was slow, however. In the first three years of the Equal Pay Act the average gross weekly earnings of women in full-time manual employment crept up from 50 per cent of men's earnings to 51.7 per cent.[5] In the USA, where legal rather than union action was the preferred method of enforcing equal pay, the results were more dramatic. By 1971 the courts had already awarded $30 million in back pay to women who had filed sex discrimination suits against employers.

In general, the relationship between the women's movement and the unions in America was more distant. Women workers organised themselves separately, beginning with a conference of some 30,000 in Chicago in 1974 which constituted itself as the Coalition of Labor Union Women. While liberal feminists held aloof from this development, some socialist groups tried to divert the Coalition to their own ends and the resulting power struggles somewhat weakened its impact.

Outside the union sphere, the Campaign for Financial and Legal Independence was another specifically feminist economic action programme in Britain. It was adopted as the fifth demand of the women's liberation movement at the national conference in Edinburgh in 1974 and was seen as an important advance beyond single-issue demands like abortion and child care.

The main thrust of the campaign was to reduce the dependency of women in marriage and the legal reinforcement of this dependency by the state. The general tendency of the law was (and to a great extent still is) to treat women as dependants of husbands or cohabiting men when considering their economic circumstances. Thus in areas like occupational pensions and national insurance, supplementary benefit and the notorious 'cohabitation rule' used to deny it, unemployment and sickness benefits, taxation, student grants, mortgages and loans, women were treated unequally before the law.

The Campaign for Financial and Legal Independence, which was launched in London in 1975 and quickly spread to other cities, was conducted along orthodox pressure-group lines, and had considerable success in raising these issues in the political arena. A whole series of reforms helped modify the dependence of wives on husbands: in 1975 the Social Security Pensions Act and the Social Security Benefits Act, plus the Employment Protection Act protecting the right to re-employment after pregnancy. In 1978 limited reforms were enacted to give women greater autonomy in tax affairs, and in the same year an EEC Directive was issued on the equal treatment of men and women in social security. A Supplementary Benefits Review the same year modified the strict definition of the male as family breadwinner.

All these changes were welcomed, but they did not add up to the end of discrimination and were undermined by lax enforcement and regressive legislation in later years. The campaign continued strongly through the late 1970s, concentrating mainly on the position of poorer women and one-parent families and, in 1977, the London group launched a 'Why Be a Wife?' campaign to dramatise the still inferior status of married women in tax and social security matters.

The diversity of the movement in these years is highlighted by another major economic campaign whose goals and assumptions could hardly be more different – the Campaign for Wages for Housework. This has become almost a distinct movement in itself, clearly apart from the mainstream of socialist feminism but having its theoretical roots there. The campaign is based on the belief that women's unpaid labour in the home is the most important form of exploitation, and therefore should be the prime concern of the movement. Supporters of the campaign claim that no progress will be possible for women (especially working-class women) until they gain the independence and dignity which will come from being paid for the work they perform in the home.

The demand was first raised in 1972 by an Italian feminist,

Mariarosa Della Costa, and Selma James in a paper entitled 'The Power of Women and the Subversion of the Community', and presented to the national conference. The idea was rejected, and a considerable debate in the feminist and socialist press ensued. But the suggestion that 'Wages for Housework' should be adopted as one of the demands of the women's liberation movement was rejected at conference after conference, and indeed was seen as both divisive and dangerous. Its opponents argue that any such suggestion simply reinforces the traditional prejudices that keep women in the home, while supporters insist that it is the only *practical* way for unskilled working-class women to become financially independent. 'Wages for Housework' campaigners also offend many socialists by asserting that trying to enrol women in male-dominated unions is a waste of time, especially when this leaves exploitation in the home untouched. On the first things first principle, they believe that no external reforms can achieve much without the recognition of women's unpaid work.

As we have already seen, the debate within Marxism about the real economic nature of housework has become highly complex, though the demand for wages is simple enough. In fact, 'housework' is slightly misleading, since the campaign really focuses on payment for full-time child and husband care.

The Wages for Housework campaign held its first public demonstration in London in March 1975. It was associated with the Power of Women Collective, which linked the campaign to the struggle for lesbian rights, black women's rights, prostitutes' rights and the Women Against Rape campaign.

From the start the campaign attracted considerable publicity because of the novel nature of its demand, some scathing but a good deal of it quite serious. In 1981, the *Sun*, *Daily Mail* and *Daily Star*, among other newspapers, ran major articles based on a survey by *Women's World* magazine which estimated a housewife's wages at £180 per week. Several books have now been published dealing specifically with the issue, and the campaign has been energetic in its publicity. A newspaper called *International Wages for Housework Bulletin* is issued with British bases in London, Bristol, Cambridge and Lancashire.

All in all, it has proved one of the more durable and visible campaigns of the modern women's liberation movement.

In America there has been an equally vigorous campaign for what is there called a Social Security Wage for Housework, and – unusually in the women's movement – the international links are strong.

The fourth of the movement's original demands, for free 24-hour child care, had both economic and welfare dimensions. But its major implications were economic, both in terms of the costs involved and the benefits which the measure would bring to working women. The phrasing of the demand at first lent itself to cruel caricature by the press, since it suggested that feminists wanted to abandon all responsibility for their children. In fact, the demand was intended to imply that nurseries should be open at all hours for women on shift work. Nor had much thought been given to the nature of child care, or to how the government might be persuaded to foot the enormous bill.

In the face of these problems, the child-care demand was a particularly difficult and discouraging one on which to campaign. There was a feeling that even success would bring problems, since child care provided by the state or by employers might not at all be of the kind which feminists wanted. The demand was later rephrased to read 'Free 24-hour child care *under community control'*. But the problem of finance was never solved, and could not be solved in a period when the welfare state was contracting. In practice, organising child care became a collective and voluntary effort of individual feminist groups, sometimes with local government support but more often without.

The abortion campaign

Abortion is a uniquely feminine and feminist issue, in so far as it is grounded in women's capacity for bearing children. It thus gives rise to a politics of health, or body politics, which is very different in style and substance from the politics of economic inequality.

In Britain, following a long campaign by the Abortion Law Reform Association (ALRA, founded in 1936) and public concern at the rising numbers of illegal abortions, abortion was legalised on specified grounds in 1967. From the beginning the women's liberation movement aimed to extend this legislation to allow free abortion on demand. By writing this into their programme, however, the movement was going beyond what any government of the time dared offer. The 1967 Act was legitimised as a humane reform in response to widespread middle-class pressures; any extension of it would pit the government of the day against powerful opposition lobbies, including the medical profession, so that no conceivable political credit could be got from supporting further reform. In a 1975 opinion poll, for example, 62 per cent of those asked agreed that abortion should be available 'in particular circumstances', but only 18 per cent endorsed abortion 'on demand' and 12 per cent said 'never'.[6]

As it turned out, the real issue for the feminist movement was not to be the 'third demand' but the need to fight the backlash against even the moderate concessions of the 1967 Act. By the time the movement was organised on the political scene, the numbers of abortions under the Act were rising fast to accommodate the previously unfilled need, and foreign women were entering the country in order to obtain legal abortions. The anti-abortion lobby once again began to make its voice heard.

The London Abortion Action Group took the initiative against the backlash in 1972 by forming the National Women's Abortion and Contraception Campaign (NWACC), in 1975 transformed into the National Abortion Campaign (NAC) with the strong support of the National Council for Civil Liberties (NCCL). The key phrase of the campaign was 'A woman's right to choose' and in its early days it was concerned with such changes as the equal availability of abortions (much less in the north of Britain than in the south, for example) and of contraception. The latter ceased to be a major issue in April 1974 when National Health Service contraception was finally made available, though it was not free, and the free services previously provided by some local authorities vanished under the new legislation.

The major action began in 1975, with news of James White's parliamentary private member's bill to restrict the 1967 Act. 'Right to life' groups such as the Society for the Protection of the

Unborn Child (SPUC) mobilised behind White's initiative and, for the next seven years, the movement faced an almost continuous series of attacks on the right to abortion. After the defeat of White's bill in 1976 there came others by William Benyon (1977), Sir Bernard Braine (1978), John Corrie (1980) and Lord Robertson (1982), each defeated in their turn but demonstrating the continuing determination of the anti-abortion forces.

The NAC struggle against these bills, which involved the whole women's movement, is one of the most underrated political stories of the 1970s, and deserves to be read in greater detail.[7] The staid ALRA became more radical and joined the fight, adopting the 'woman's right to choose' slogan, and support finally came from the TUC, which, after 1978, urged unions to support the campaign and organised a big national demonstration against the Corrie bill in October 1979.

The relationship between the NAC, the unions and the women's movement as a whole was not entirely comfortable despite the efforts of the NCCL to bridge their differences. Like the Working Women's Charter, NAC was very much involved with the disciplined groups of the revolutionary left, and was organised on similar lines, including the participation of men. This helped it to be effective, but alienated many women who saw it as bureaucratic, authoritarian and male-dominated. The unions, on the other hand, were suspicious of NAC's 'extremism'. By the end of the decade the left had withdrawn somewhat from NAC to concentrate on other issues, leaving the campaign organisationally weakened and unsure where to move next.

Ten years after the 1967 Act the number of abortions had stabilised at about 100,000 per year. The right-wing spectre of millions of abortions and a declining population ceased to have any credibility, and opposition to abortion was now on purely ideological and religious grounds. More private members' bills can be expected. Meanwhile, the campaign concentrates its reduced energies on cuts in the National Health Service which make abortions increasingly hard to get.

In the USA the campaign followed a similar course, with the complicating factor that the 52 states all had their own abortion laws. A National Association for Repeal of Abortion Laws was founded in 1969, a National Abortion Campaign in 1971 and the National Abortion Rights Action League in 1973. These largely liberal coalitions, with radical and socialist support, had rapid success. Hawaii and Alaska had been the first states to liberalise their laws in 1970, and seventeen more states followed the same year. In 1972 *Ms* magazine published a petition from 52 prominent women proclaiming that they had had abortions and demanding a repeal of the restrictive laws, and in 1973 the Supreme Court declared abortion legal on specified grounds. Public opinion was divided on lines similar to those in Britain, though the proportion of those opposed to abortion in any circumstances, mainly on religious grounds, was twice as high.[8]

In 1977, however, Congress outlawed Medicaid (health service) funding for abortions, making it difficult or impossible for poor women to continue to take advantage of the new laws. The women's movement soon found itself fighting a rearguard action against the right-to-life campaigners of the Christian fundamentalist Moral Majority, and against a reluctant and male-dominated medical profession which still retained the essential power of decision whether or not to abort. This is a campaign which is far from over.

Sexual liberation

The impact of the sexual revolution of the 1960s on women was highly ambiguous. On the one hand, changing popular attitudes to sex along with improvements in contraceptive technology gave women infinitely more sexual freedom. On the other, breaking the link between marriage and legitimate sex brought an equally dramatic loss of security, especially for older women and those with children. When the women's movement came along, writers like Germaine Greer[9] and Erica Jong[10] projected an aggressive, heterosexual feminism which would demolish once and for all the myth of feminine passivity and, with it, the sexual subordination of women to men.

These ideas received an enthusiastic public reception, not least from men, and liberated sexuality (heterosexual-style) was spread through the pages of journals like *Cosmopolitan*, *Playboy* and *Playgirl*, and books like Helen Gurley-Brown's *Sex and the Single Girl* (1963). However, within the women's move-

ment on both sides of the Atlantic this particular kind of liberation was quickly recognised as something which benefited men
much more than women. In questioning the new permissive
orthodoxy, many feminists were led to consider a more deeply
hidden problem, the true nature of female sexuality and of the
sexual relationship between women.

Since 1970 almost all feminist groups – liberal, socialist and
radical – have supported the rights of gay people of both sexes
to express their sexuality openly without fear of prejudice or
discrimination. However, there has been less support for the
more recent claim that lesbianism is an intrinsic or central
aspect of feminism and that the way forward for the movement
lies in social, political and sexual separation from men.

The natural affinity which gay women felt for the women's
liberation movement was fraught with uneasiness on both
sides. In the early days gay women felt that heterosexuals were
uncomfortable with them, and that they were discriminated
against within the movement as much as outside. Non-gay
feminists feared that the obvious participation of many lesbians
might damage the movement's chances of acceptance by
ordinary working women. This conflict gave rise to a debate
about sexual politics, which emerged first in the USA and has
had a profound impact on the development of the British
movement.

By 1970 lesbian feminists in America had already begun to
organise separately. A great deal of discussion had been going
on around Anne Koedt's 'The Myth of the Vaginal Orgasm'
(see p. 79), and in 1970 the New York Radicalesbians group
published the equally provocative *Woman Identified Woman*
pamphlet. Kate Millet's polemic against male sexual chauvinism, *Sexual Politics*, appeared the same year.

The more conservative leaders of the National Organisation
for Women (NOW) had viewed these developments with
undisguised distaste, and it was only a matter of time before the
conflict came into the open. This happened in the most public
way possible, during a big New York march for abortion and
child care in December 1970. A group of women wearing
lavender armbands (which had come to symbolise lesbianism)
handed out leaflets saying 'They can call us all lesbians until such
time as there is no stigma attached to women loving women.

SISTERHOOD IS POWERFUL!!!'[11] Since the march was being heavily covered by the press, the equation of lesbianism with feminism was instantly and loudly proclaimed to the world, confirming the worst fears of NOW leaders. By a gesture which was both morally courageous and politically naive, the lesbians and their supporters had brought the whole issue into the open.

The emergence of militant lesbianism in America had an explosive effect. The repression and invisibility of both lesbians and male homosexuals have a long history, and the mere fact that their plight had now become public must have seemed like a liberation. For women, the obvious vehicle to carry that liberation forward was the feminist movement.

In Britain, however, the reaction of many women already in the movement mirrored that of the American NOW leaders. They agreed that sexual preference should be respected and not penalised, but many felt and said that the whole business of sexuality, orgasm and 'bedroom politics' was a dangerous diversion from serious (i.e. economic) political business.

The difference was first openly discussed at the national conference at Skegness in October 1971. Dominated by well-organised socialist and Marxist groups, the conference tried to exclude the lesbianism issue, provoking a confrontation with gay women on the floor and finally leading to an inconclusive discussion. The conflict at Skegness contributed to the demise of the Women's National Co-ordinating Committee, who were the *de facto* organisers, and also to the partial withdrawal of some Marxist and Maoist supporters from the national movement. It was the beginning of a split which was to persist and deepen until the end of the decade. At the 1972 national conference British radical feminists issued a separatist statement which echoed the 'pro-woman' line of the American Redstockings.

But this was much more than an in-movement battle. The chief aim of the emerging gay campaign was to end discrimination, especially discrimination at work. Early in 1971, after some months of preparation, the Gay Liberation Front (GLF) *Manifesto* was published in Britain, becoming an immediate target for press and political attack. The GLF was far more militant than formal pressure groups like the Campaign for Homosexual Equality (CHE), and attracted correspondingly more hostility. In February 1971 the GLF sent a substantial contingent to join a trade-union march against the Industrial Relations Bill, thus signalling their intention to participate openly in politics as gays.

At first a mainly male enclave, the gay movement quickly attracted lesbian women who also longed to be able to express their sexuality publicly and normally. Although participation in groups like GLF was an important step, many women felt that they needed a movement more their own, without the presence and domination of men.

By 1973, therefore, it became clear that gay women were establishing a stronger base in the women's movement. This can be seen, for example, in the greater prominence of sexual politics in journals like *Shrew*. The London Women's Liberation Workshop, which issued this journal, had become an essentially separatist group by 1974, and many socialists had withdrawn from it. At conferences, and notably at Bristol in 1973, lesbian themes and issues were more assertively raised and more seriously discussed.

The following year 300 women attended the first national lesbian conference and, at its Edinburgh national conference later in the year the women's liberation movement adopted its sixth demand for 'An end to discrimination against lesbians and a right to our own self-defined sexuality.' Lesbian conferences were again held in 1975 and 1976. On the latter occasion, again in Bristol, some participants were violently attacked by men, an event which generated enormous anger.

The development of the lesbianism debate and its impact on the movement will be described and discussed more fully in the following chapter. But it is worth noting here that, in the context of campaigning, the 'end to discrimination' demand presented special difficulties in that it is a moral and personal demand on individuals, not a claim on the political state. There were no laws to be changed, few areas where discrimination was fully institutionalised; lesbians were fighting a particular form of the amorphous prejudice which affected all minorities. This made for a hard and discouraging battle, and one where energy could easily be diverted from the indifferent world outside to the smaller, more responsive and more vulnerable community of the women's movement itself. The development of a political theory of lesbianism as feminist practice came later.

Turning-Point: The Movement in 1975

There are moments in the history of any social movement which are fateful, in the sense that its whole future can be changed by small events, or even by the decisions of individuals. After seven years, women's liberation arrived at such a turning-point.

Observers of the scene have variously described 1975 as the year when the movement succeeded, as the year when it entered the mainstream and lost its revolutionary impetus, as the year when it abandoned the mainstream and became revolutionary, and as the year when it finally collapsed. Such an impressive range of disagreement suggests that all these observations were partly true.

The argument that the movement succeeded in 1975 depends on the implementation in that year of two major pieces of civil rights legislation: the Equal Pay Act, which had been in the pipeline since 1970, and the Sex Discrimination Act. With these, many argued, the essential victories had been won, and the role left to the movement was to watch over their implementation, to tidy up the loose ends and to be vigilant in guarding its gains.

The Equal Pay Act was attacked by feminists from the beginning, however, because of its many loopholes and the difficulty of proving cases under it. The Sex Discrimination Act was intended to be more comprehensive, and was preceded in 1974 by the Labour Party's White Paper *Equality for Women*. The paper had been in gestation since 1968, so in itself was not a response to the demands of the women's liberation movement.

The Act was designed to cut to the root of the problem of sex discrimination by outlawing unequal treatment of women in all forms of education – schools, training schemes, polytechnics, universities and professional schools. In employment, the Act prohibited discrimination by sex in job advertising, recruitment, fringe benefits, promotion and redundancy. Trade unions were required to offer full membership, representation and support to women on the same basis as men. The exclusion of women from public facilities was outlawed, and financial services like hire purchase and mortgages could no longer be refused to otherwise qualified women.

This was not an equal rights charter, since it did not unambiguously exclude every form of sex discrimination. There were many areas not specified in the Act, and some notable loopholes such as the continuation of protective legislation restricting women in certain types of work. Nor did it offer any provision or requirement on employers to undertake affirmative action programmes on behalf of women.[12]

Enforcement of the Acts lay largely in the hands of the industrial tribunals and the Advisory, Conciliation and Arbitration Service (ACAS), which aimed to settle cases out of court. The Equal Opportunities Commission (EOC) was set up at the same time to pursue the more active role of promoting equal opportunity and initiating investigations of possible discrimination. It was clear that the effectiveness of both Acts would depend on the energy of these agencies in pressing cases, on the willingness of individual women to initiate them and on the goodwill of employers and unions. In the years immediately after 1975, none of these conditions was fully met.

Nevertheless, the Equal Pay and Sex Discrimination Acts were giant steps forward in the fight for equality. The absolute hostility of large sections of the women's movement needs therefore to be explained. Before it had even become law, the Sex Discrimination Act was described as 'this fraudulent bill'; 'a smokescreen of cant and hypocrisy'; 'a sell-out'; 'miserable tokenism'. There was a National Day of Action against the Bill, on which women chained themselves to the railings outside Parliament.

Their opposition was not just a matter of legislative detail, though they did point to the loopholes and exceptions in the bill, its middle-class bias and the probable weakness of the EOC as an enforcement mechanism. Far more resented was its lack of immediacy; a lesson had been learned from the experience of blacks in the USA. Feminists realised that passive civil rights, no matter how closely defined, would not produce any quick improvement in the situation of women because most were in no position to take advantage of the new opportunities. It was also a cruel irony that the declining economy was making it harder for even the most privileged women to compete in the employment market, with or without the new laws. Immediate .change could be brought about only by enormously expensive provisions like free child care, or controversial changes in abortion or family law. In this sense the Sex Discrimination Act was a cheap concession by government.

Nor was it inappropriate that many feminists feared that, as one newsletter put it, 'If this bill becomes law any further demands for equality will be turned aside', for this was exactly what did happen. In most people's eyes the movement had now achieved all its reasonable demands, and had become redundant. In a 1976 opinion poll 48 per cent of *women* agreed that they now had equal job opportunities with men and no less than 87 per cent believed that their educational opportunities were equal.[13]

Other signs indicated that the movement might be being co-opted into the fringe of mainstream politics. The United Nations proclaimed 1975 to be International Women's Year, and the coming decade to be the International Decade of Women. A huge, expensive and much-boosted world conference in Mexico City brought together 5,000 delegates for what was almost universally agreed afterwards to be a farcical and even frightening affair, with undertones of pressure and manipulation. Radical and socialist feminists and lesbians, according to their reports, felt especially threatened and excluded. It seemed that a number of governments had decided the time had come to defuse the women's movement, and they set about it by the time-honoured method of allocating resources, both to produce ties of dependency and to create internal divisions.

A World Congress for International Women's Year in Berlin aroused similar feelings and, in Britain itself, International Women's Day (8 March) was greeted with only modest ceremonies, the largest being a march of 400 women in east London.

There was anxiety that the movement was being co-opted, made public and made redundant all at the same time. Feelings of deep ambiguity were hardly alleviated by the election of

Margaret Thatcher as a hard-line Tory leader in that same year. The oppression and invisibility of women were beginning to look like grievances from a past era.

At the same time, and not coincidentally, there were indications that significant parts of the movement were moving yet further from mainstream politics into more deeply radical positions. Such radicalisation often happens when reformist demands are partially met and those parts of the programme which remain seem infinitely far from being achieved. In Britain the year 1975 marked a shift of emphasis away from traditional socialist economic concerns (equal pay, equal opportunity) towards a more radical separatist style of feminism. Newsletters and journals become less eclectic and begin to follow a more consistently radical line on most issues. We have already noted the rise of sexual politics in the movement, institutionalised in 1974 as the sixth demand (and in 1978 as the seventh demand, of which more later). What was essentially a socialist movement was, in 1975, beginning to turn into something else.

For outsiders this changing emphasis also made women's liberation less accessible, less visible: thus it was popularly supposed to be dead or dying. Indeed, between 1971 and late 1975 the number of functioning local groups had declined steeply, and growth continued only in the areas where it had been slow to start – Scotland, Wales and Northern Ireland. The structure of the movement had become entirely amorphous, based on a score of local women's centres, each with its associated small groups. At the 1975 national conference in Manchester a proposal to strengthen the movement by establishing a more formal national organisation was voted down, though not by an overwhelming majority.

This appearance of decline was somewhat deceptive, however. What was happening instead was a radical acceleration of the movement's original impulse to decentralise. More and more women were choosing to work in very specific and limited areas of action, creating a network only very loosely linked by common commitments. In this way they hoped to avoid both the centralising tendencies endemic to the left and the destructive experience of factions struggling for control of the movement. Thus the movement was everywhere and nowhere;

anyone could do anything, but no one person or group could take charge. The remaining national newsletter, the radical women-only *WIRES*, was edited in turn by different collectives in order to discourage the accumulation of power.

Typical of the specialised groups which now formed the substance of the movement were those for action on abortion, many women's health groups, lesbian collectives, groups for women in law, psychiatry, teaching, media, film, theatre, history, art, music and literature, groups for black women, information centres, women's aid and rape crisis centres, women's bookshops and collectives producing newsletters, pamphlets and books. The decline of the small consciousness-raising group was matched by the rise of these multifaceted action groups. But the very diversity of their aims and attitudes made it harder to focus clearly on women's liberation as a single, coherent movement.

It is instructive to compare the experience of the American movement by mid-decade. In civil rights terms its achievement had been impressive. As early as 1972 three-quarters of the reforms in the Bill of Rights originally published by the National Organisation for Women (see p. 46) had been either partly or fully conceded. A significant victory was the Education Act of 1972, which prohibited discrimination in colleges and universities. Numerous small pieces of legislation helped to reinforce the principle of equal pay and equal opportunity, and the EEOC had been strengthened to provide better enforcement. Public opinion was swinging behind the basic demands of the movement. A Harris Poll taken in 1975 showed an increase in the number of people favouring improved status for women from 42 to 59 per cent in four years, those favouring legalised abortion from 46 to 54 per cent and those favouring more child-care centres from 56 to 67 per cent. The *Ms* magazine calendar for the years up to 1975 lists scores of victories for women – court decisions, new enterprises, new opportunities – individually small but cumulatively marking a change which was almost revolutionary.[14] Another mid-decade poll showed that 45 per cent of those women asked believed that women's organisations had achieved a 'great deal' of influence, and 39 per cent allowed that they had a 'fair amount' of influence over issues affecting women.

The one great failure was the Equal Rights Amendment (ERA), which was to sweep away all the remaining legal areas of discrimination. The Amendment had been passed by Congress in 1972, and allowed a seven-year period for the required ratification by 38 states. In 1979 this period was extended until 30 June 1982, an extension challenged by one federal judge in 1981 (see Chapter 7).

The fight for the ERA did give the American feminist movement a single, clear-cut goal, and helped to hold it together. Campaigns for ratification had to be conducted at state level, focusing naturally on those states most likely to change their position. These allowed local groups to plan concrete and manageable actions.

The ERA also provided a strong political *rationale* for liberal feminists to de-emphasise issues like lesbianism and socialism which could damage the Amendment's prospects in the conservative heartlands of America. But this liberal effort to keep the lid on radical feminism was only a partial success. In 1975 the radical Redstockings protested loudly and publicly in a journal called *Feminist Revolution* about the liberal effort to suppress them. At the NOW conference in Philadelphia that year, the liberals found the enemy within the gates. The organisation's growth had brought in a broader-based and younger membership, some of whom were unhappy with the staid political style of the NOW leaders. At the conference a radical group called the Majority Caucus made a successful bid for a controlling majority. Their stated programme was to take NOW 'Out of the mainstream and into the revolution', which meant being more active in politics, showing more concern for poor, working-class and minority women, and democratising the structure of NOW itself.

The inertia and size of NOW (40,000 members in 700 chapters) ensured that no sudden and dramatic change of direction took place, but the organisation emerged from the 1975 confrontation noticeably more militant, though hardly revolutionary. A 1974 survey of NOW members showed typically a profile of highly educated, professionally employed, increasingly young women whose interests and inclinations were unlikely to be compatible with ultra-radical political demands.[15] However, the radicals acted as a vanguard, using the logic of their theoretical arguments to pull the liberals towards a wider analysis, and it seems reasonable to interpret the events of 1975 as a partial convergence between the two currents in American feminism in which each side made some concessions.

This partial radicalisation also had the result of reviving some of the negative images of feminism which had been current six or seven years before and creating a new gulf between NOW and most American women. A national women's strike day, 'Alice doesn't', called for after the 1975 conference, was a humiliating failure.

Betty Friedan, now withdrawn from active participation but still a considerable figure, published an 'Open letter to the women's movement' shortly afterwards, warning against the dangers of directing the movement's energies inwards in power struggles, and the growing preoccupation with sexual politics. What would happen to the women's movement, she asked:

> if. . . NOW should in effect go down the drain as new leaders fight each other for power because they have lost heart to fight the external enemy; lost heart to find new allies among former 'male chauvinist pigs' in unions, black organizations, even corporations; lost heart to reach out to those timid, frightened, even antagonistic women who now want to join and feel part of the women's movement, but don't identify with the rhetoric of 'revolution against oppression' [?][16]

The question went unanswered, and feminism as a movement (though not as an idea or as a political issue) lost some of its energy and creativity after 1975 as it entered a period of consolidation and internal dialogue. Socialist feminism had never developed a strong separate identity, except perhaps in Chicago, and was strongest in mixed groups like the New American Movement, the Democratic Socialists and in the autonomous women's unions. A national conference on socialist feminism attracted 1,600 delegates to Yellow Springs, Ohio, in 1975. But the political culture of the USA worked against the tendency, and socialist feminism has remained a distinct current outside the mainstream of both women's liberation and regular politics, its distinctive contribution to American feminism being in the development of theory.

Thus in 1975 both American and British feminism present an image compounded of ambiguity and expectancy, of waiting to move in some new direction.

5. New Directions: Policy Conflicts and Fresh Campaigns, 1976–8

Two factors helped decide what direction the movement would take in Britain. The Equal Pay and Sex Discrimination Acts had shifted the focus of the economic campaigns away from legislation towards enforcement, and a sharply worsening economy and the erosion of the welfare state undermined the remaining social demands. The dissatisfaction with the new equal rights legislation which had been vigorously expressed from the start would continue to grow through the 1970s. In the first six months of 1976 only 31 out of 110 equal pay cases taken to the tribunals succeeded, and only 5 out of 20 sex discrimination cases. The EOC in particular was consistently attacked for timidity, male bias, elitism and its too-close ties with government and industry. Although given wide powers to investigate discrimination and promote equality, it did not take up the issues aggressively. It funded mainly narrow, policy-oriented research, and was unwilling even to touch hot issues like child care.

The slowness of the legislation to take effect, while inevitable, was also maddening. Apart from political constraints on bodies like the EOC, no legislation could sweep away generations of inequality. The British women's liberation movement, as it was constituted in 1975, had no way of influencing the processes of change. To use the legal machinery requires resources, bureaucratic organisation, expensive skills, access to government and close co-operation with male-run institutions and agencies. Hence the day-to-day work of implementing equal rights rested in the hands of ACAS and the industrial tribunals, the liberal but passive EOC, the Women's Rights Unit of the National Council for Civil Liberties and, especially, the trade

127

unions. Some unions with large female memberships like APEX and NUPE were quick to take up the challenge, and the TUC was supportive. But this left the women's movement outside, only able to report the victories and defeats and press for stronger action through groups like Working Women's Charter.

This sensation of marginality and relative helplessness was made worse by the economic climate, especially by the cuts in public spending and the growing ranks of the jobless. All through the latter part of the 1970s, the women's press reported protests against unemployment and underemployment, bad housing, collapsing social services and the worsening plight of immigrant women. But because it was not organised as a political party or pressure group, the movement had no means of acting on these issues, other than simply to let its voice be heard.

In so far as government expenditure was contracting rather than expanding, the social welfare demands of the movement also came to seem more and more remote from reality. Although the demand for free 24-hour child care remained (and remains) on the agenda, nursery education was actually being cut, and every protest was turned away with the formula 'Sorry, the money just isn't there.' Many groups organised their own programmes, seeking and sometimes obtaining support from local authorities. Free contraception and abortion on demand were economically more practical, but in a time of growing reaction against permissiveness and the 'welfare state mentality' were political suicide for whichever party happened to be in power. The main energies of the abortion campaign were thus directed towards defending women's rights under the existing legislation, and the NAC continued to operate almost as an autonomous wing of the movement. Marginal welfare demands like free sanitary protection, free halls for meetings and conferences stood no chance.

More positive and more explicitly feminist forms of action were needed to direct the energies of the movement. What could these be? The answer lay in the debate over sexual politics which had been simmering for years. With the socialist campaigners stymied, and exhausted by the battle for positive economic reforms, another sector of the movement came into the forefront of action, defining their politics in terms of a different set of priorities. British radical feminism was ready to move to the centre of the political stage; but the move was not to be accomplished without a fight.

Unity and Conflict in Social Movements

Every social movement must suffer some degree of internal strife over issues of policy and tactics, and the modern feminist movement has been no exception. Movement organisations find many ways of reconciling these differences. Typically, they may do so through the strength of their leadership, especially if the leader is a charismatic figure; through some system of electoral representation; through binding conference decisions; or (as is frequently seen on the sectarian left) simply through dividing into smaller and smaller units until the group is cohesive enough for everyone to agree about everything.

But the British women's liberation movement could use none of these devices. It had no national organisation, no leaders, no electoral structures, no rules which imposed obedience to conference decisions. Nor was it narrow enough to be called sectarian, though some sects had developed. It was a broad-based, pluralistic movement without a comparably broad-based organisation. There was a feeling that women should be able to agree at least on basic principles. Yet there was no reliable mechanism for reaching agreement.

The search for new policies and new directions in the late 1970s therefore sparked off conflicts which were all the more damaging for being uncontrollable. From the earliest days it had been recognised that the no-structure/no-leadership principles could only work in an atmosphere of mutual co-operation and tolerance. But, inevitably over the years, the movement attracted such diverse supporters that tolerance was bound to become strained. Particularly at a time when the movement felt becalmed and troubled in a hostile world, it could be expected that those feminists who felt strongest in their convictions and most confident about their aims would begin to dominate the more tentative and uncertain voices in the movement.

Factionalism had always been seen as a danger. Back in 1971 the shortlived National Co-ordinating Committee had suggested that no group should comment publicly on the politics of another, and this policy was widely accepted. Such public reticence helped to prevent the divisions in the movement from being exploited by its enemies. But it also restricted debate within a narrow circle. Perhaps radical and socialist feminists – like other revolutionaries – found their inward debates becoming more and more charged with the energy which could find no outlet in political action. This is mere speculation, but it might help to account for the growing bitterness of the long-running debate between separatist and non-separatist feminists that came to a head in this period. It might equally be argued that the issue was hard-fought because its political significance was so fundamental. For whatever reason, the separatist debate dominated women's liberation during the final years of the 1970s.

Heterosexual Feminism and Political Lesbianism

The correct labelling of divisions in the women's movement is a difficult matter. No division is ever entirely clear-cut, and all seem to overlap with other divisions. At the very beginning the main split was between the political organisers (mainly socialists) and the libertarian/anarchist proponents of 'no organisation'. After a while this resolved itself into the division between supporters of socialist and radical feminist theory, and by 1976 the lines seemed to be drawn between heterosexual feminists (mainly socialists) and the lesbian feminists (mainly radicals). Yet this oversimplifies the matter, since by no means all lesbians were anti-heterosexual or anti-socialist and by no means all socialists were anti-lesbian. Nor, of course, can all people be neatly defined in terms of their sexuality. The reader must imagine a debate as diverse as the movement itself, with perhaps eight or ten interconnected arguments going on at the same time. All that is possible here is to adopt the terminology of the movement for the line of division which became most significant between 1975 and 1978, namely that between the separatist and non-separatist positions. The key to that debate is the theory of sexuality and sexual oppression, and especially the relationship between lesbianism and feminism.

It is important to recall once more how hidden as a group lesbians had always been. In Western cultures their sexual preference was hardly ever recognised as real, let alone legitimate. Women were expected to be heterosexual or chaste. Lesbian women were alternately subjected to symbolic annihilation, a denial of their very existence, and direct persecution when denial no longer proved possible.

We saw in the last chapter how some lesbian women had been attracted to the feminist movement and, against some resistance, had begun to establish a base in it. At first they were very much a minority, forced on the defensive within the movement almost as much as outside. By 1975 their position was much stronger and was boosted by a revival of radical feminism in the USA. Since most lesbians (not all) supported the radical feminist position, this implied a corresponding weakening of the socialist current within the movement. In 1976 the Women's Day Demonstration, attended by some 1,500 women, excluded men and banned political (i.e. socialist) banners for the first time, provoking sharp protests and anguished discussions.

The centre of gravity of the movement was shifting quite quickly from economic and general egalitarian issues to the specific lesbian separatist demand for liberation *from men*. Although lesbians remained a minority, they had certain important advantages in an organisational sense in relation to the movement. It was less likely that their time and energy would be fragmented by commitments to men or children, more likely that their partners might also be involved in women's liberation. In every sense their commitment was likely to be stronger and their influence greater than sheer numbers would suggest.

A related development was the appearance of a militant 'revolutionary feminism', based on an idea first aired at the 1977 national conference and more fully defined at a special meeting in Edinburgh the same year. Revolutionary feminism was a direct development from radical feminism, and was sometimes called 'revolutionary/radical'. It implied a more aggressive political practice than had hitherto been associated with the radicals, a turning away from mere sexual politics or life-style feminism towards a direct confrontation with the power of men, akin to a revolutionary class confrontation. A number of radical feminist groups formed or reconstituted themselves on these lines.

These developments made the 1977 national conference in London a difficult and stressful one. Many women present felt that the whole movement should be taking a more militant line on issues like sexual preference and male violence, while others felt uneasy and even repelled by the new emphasis. No clear decisions were reached in 1977, but the questions were in the air and were revived at the Birmingham national conference in 1978. If the 1977 meeting had been difficult, what happened in 1978 was almost a catastrophe for the movement.

At the plenary session of the Birmingham conference a group of revolutionary feminists from Bristol opened up a discussion on the nature and purpose of the 'six demands' as a basis for the movement's unity and action. They proposed that a seventh demand should be added or even substituted for the other six. The seventh demand would read:

> Male violence against women is an expression of male supremacy and political control of women. We demand freedom from intimidation by the threat or use of violence or sexual coercion, regardless of marital status. An end to the laws, assumptions and institutions that perpetuate male dominance and men's aggression towards women.

In a rushed and antagonistic debate many objections were raised against the new demand, the main one being that it committed the whole movement to a radical feminist analysis (*men are the enemy*) at the expense of a socialist one (*masculine institutions are the enemy*). Finally, the demand was accepted after the deletion of the initial sentence.

The Brighton women's liberation group then introduced another proposal to split the sixth demand ('The right of every woman to a self-defined sexuality and an end to discrimination against lesbians'). As amended, all the other demands would be preceded by the first sentence, i.e. 'The women's liberation movement asserts the right of every woman to a self-defined sexuality and demands . . .', and the lesbian demand would stand on its own as the sixth demand. Once more there was strong resistance to giving such precedence to sexual choice at the expense of issues like equal pay, abortion, financial and legal independence which many felt were more fundamental to the movement. But the revised sixth demand was also accepted by the meeting.

Both developments signalled the growing power of the radical separatists. The Birmingham conference and the long debate which followed finally made the conflict explicit and public. It was not, to repeat, a conflict between lesbians and heterosexuals *per se*, but between two different and incompatible theoretical conceptions of feminism itself. The dialogue that had gone on for so long had become a confrontation between entrenched political positions. As one report put it, 'Even though alliances were shifting, the battle lines were firmly drawn all the time. There was little sympathetic listening; it was mainly a question of attack and defence.'[1]

Now it was the non-separatist or 'male-identified' feminists, especially heterosexuals, who were on the defensive. They could not win an argument in which the purity of their feminism was defined by their sexuality. The intimidating strength of the radical position was the statement that a woman's feminism must be made consistent with her sexuality, and that only thus could she be an authentic feminist. To be a lesbian, and oppressed as a lesbian, was held to be the only acceptable form of commitment. This kind of argument helped to paralyse the dissenting voices in the movement ('How can we attack the oppressed?'), just as a similar device used by blacks against whites had silenced debate in the American new left ten years before. It also had the effect of putting lesbian socialists, and lesbians who simply disagreed with the separatist line, in an impossible position.

In 1979 the national *WIRES Newsletter* published a paper from the Leeds Revolutionary Feminist Group entitled 'Political Lesbianism: the Case Against Heterosexuality'.[2] The central message of the paper was:

We do think that all feminists can and should be political lesbians. Our definition of a political lesbian is a woman

identified woman who does not fuck men. It does not mean
compulsory sexual activity with women . . . Any woman who
takes part in a heterosexual couple helps to shore up male
supremacy by making its foundations stronger.

The Leeds paper argued that women could not win their fight
against patriarchy while engaging in sex with men. It implied
that heterosexual relationships allowed women to share in the
power and privileges of men at the expense of their more
committed sisters. In the past some collectives had suggested
that lesbians were a relatively small and fixed group who could
act as a vanguard for the movement. The political lesbianism
position was that *all* women were potentially lesbians and that
therefore all women could withdraw support and sexual
privileges from men, with revolutionary results.

The connection between political lesbianism and socialism
was unclear. Some tendencies claimed that lesbianism was *de
facto* anti-capitalist because it subverted the bourgeois family.
But the main thrust of the revolutionary feminist line was that
lesbianism would subvert the power of men, of which capitalism was only a secondary expression.

This was not a new argument. It had been around in the
American movement for years, and had been made in print by
some members of the London Women's Liberation Workshop
in 1974 and 1975. Nor was it in any sense a policy statement,
since the Leeds group was in no position to impose policy on
anyone else. But no British group had so openly declared that
feminism is the theory and lesbianism is the practice, and that a state of
war existed between women and men in which no fraternisa-
tion with the enemy could be permitted: heterosexual relationships were a betrayal of the cause of women. An explosive
debate ensued in which many heterosexual and lesbian feminists responded with outrage to the Leeds statement, and whole
sections of the movement hastened to disassociate themselves
from it.

What most of the opponents found most offensive was the
statement that women *ought* to be lesbians. Whatever happened
to the right to a self-defined sexuality? What happened to the
pro-woman line which argued that whatever women wanted
was right for women? While many of the critics recognised the

rhetorical force of the revolutionary feminist argument about men, they felt that it denied the real diversity of the movement and the ambiguities of the real social world in which it had to exist. The new line suggested that all attempts to change men should be abandoned.

The socialist response to political lesbianism was a stronger version of the response they had always made to sexual politics issues: simply that sexual choice, while an important issue, should not be allowed to divert the movement from its more important political and economic goals, and that to elevate lesbianism as the core value of the movement would cut it off from the rest of society. This pinpointed the real nature of the division, not socialists *v.* radicals or heterosexuals *v.* lesbians but the unbridgeable gulf between those feminists who *wanted* to cut off the movement from the rest of (male) society (i.e. separatists) and those who were committed to changing society through engagement with it.

Socialists might or might not be lesbians, but they could not by definition be separatists or political lesbians. Marxist feminist Beatrix Campbell wrote that 'Heterosexuality has to feature in our politics as more than a guilty secret . . . It is after all the primary sexual practice of most women.'[3] Heterosexuality could not be denied, but it could and should be changed to make it less oppressive to women.

In some ways, what was going on in Britain in the late 1970s looked like a re-run of the politico-feminist debates which had marked the American movement a decade earlier. Women's liberation in Britain has grown out of the 1960s left. It began with a clearly socialist analysis which identified women's liberation with the unity of the working class and the struggle against capitalism. The 1970s brought in women of different political persuasions (or of none at all), and by 1978 socialism had ceased to be the defining characteristic of the movement. Because of the political style of some socialist groups, for example within the National Abortion Campaign, many women found it difficult or impossible to work alongside the male-dominated left groups, especially such competitive and aggressive groups as the Socialist Workers' Party. Also, the weakness of socialism in this period reflected the fact that no theoretical synthesis, of the type which Sheila Rowbotham and others had sought, had yet been achieved. Separate European socialist feminist conferences were held in Paris and Amsterdam during 1977, their different themes highlighting the failure of the movement's theorists yet to find the theoretical integration between patriarchy and capitalism on which a socialist feminist programme could be built. Although the radical analysis had deeply influenced many socialists, no way had been found to connect the radical emphasis on women's unique experiences and consciousness into a socialist framework.

On the margins of the movement, many other women felt threatened by the new trend. Black women charged that issues like racism and imperialism were being lost sight of. Many liberal feminists working in refuges, information centres and other women's service organisations felt that their efforts to help women with everyday problems were being devalued by radical separatist arguments which marked them as collaborators. The conflict, desired by no one, involved every woman who defined herself as a feminist.

Power and Policy Conflicts in the USA

The size and heterogeneity of the American feminist movement ensured that its search for unity would be even more difficult and its conflicts more frequent and more open than those in Britain. A brief sketch of the major divisions will be sufficient to show how differently the American groups dealt with their internal political disagreements.

Looking back to the earliest days, between 1967 and 1969, the American movement was divided by the politico-feminist debate between those who defined themselves mainly as socialists and those who were trying to establish a separate political identity for radical feminism. The American radicals, unlike the British, quickly adopted a rhetoric which was explicitly anti-socialist. These sentiments were fed by the aggressive tactics of groups like the Socialist Workers' Party (SWP) and the Young Socialist Alliance (YSA) which, in 1970 and 1971, made vigorous efforts to infiltrate and take over the women's movement.[4]

This, combined with the generally anti-socialist temper of

American culture and the bad experiences which many feminists had suffered in the socialist movement of the 1960s, led to the rejection of socialism as a total philosophy for women's liberation. Some elements of Marxist theory were incorporated by groups like the Redstockings (the idea of the sex/class system, for example), but by 1975 socialist feminism was not a significant factor in the American equation. The main division was between radical and liberal feminism.

The situation, then, was very different from that in Britain. It was not a confrontation between two entrenched political positions, both relatively powerless, but between the powerful, highly organised and politically orthodox side of the movement and the radical tendency which was powerless and fragmented but deeply committed and politically agile. As their response, the radicals adopted guerrilla tactics.

The account of sexual politics in the last chapter described how the lesbian question had arisen strongly in the American movement from 1968 onwards, giving rise to separate organisations and a prolonged effort by liberal feminists to keep lesbian issues separate from civil rights issues. Betty Friedan was one of the most outspoken critics of what she called the 'female chauvinism' or reverse sexism of some radicals and, until 1975, there was virtually no meeting-ground between the two positions.

It is clear that radical feminists felt increasingly threatened by the power and near hegemony of the liberal side of the movement, particularly NOW. Their resentment found a voice in 1975 with the publication of a collection of papers by the Redstockings under the title *Feminist Revolution*. The collection proclaimed that the limits of liberal feminism had been reached, and aimed to reassert the right of radicals to a significant place in feminist history, and to turn the whole movement towards a more revolutionary politics.

Feminist Revolution revived a dispute which had been simmering since 1972 over who should have the power and the right to speak on behalf of the movement. The Redstockings and many other radical groups feared that the movement was being professionalised and sanitised, its strongest demands hidden by the powerful women who controlled the feminist media.[5] With much justice the radicals claimed that they were being 'written out of women's history' by those who were more interested in using the movement as a power base for themselves than as an instrument of revolution. A major focus of the dispute was a book of collected readings called *Radical Feminism*, edited by Anne Koedt and others,[6] which was supposed to preserve the early radical writings published in *Notes from the First, Second and Third Years*. A comparison of the original journal with the book version shows that the radicals were right: many of their most important contributions on the pro-woman line, consciousness-raising and the debate with the left had been edited out of the book version. *Feminist Revolution* also protested at the highly selective version of feminism which was presented to the public in the glossy, mass-circulation magazine *Ms*.

In 1975, also, the radicals made a partly successful attempt to gain some power in the liberal organisations of the movement. One tactic was to discredit prominent liberals. The editor of *Ms*, Gloria Steinem, who with Betty Friedan was one of the most visible and powerful liberal feminists, was a natural target. In May 1975 Redstockings issued a press release which accused Steinem of involvement in the CIA through her past directorship of a CIA-funded front organisation called the Independent Research Service. Steinem replied through the feminist press, and was supported by other prominent liberal feminists. In the same year, as was recounted in the last chapter, a radical group managed to gain a controlling majority in the leadership of NOW. The disputes continued throughout 1975, deepening the divisions in the movement but reviving the debate over radical theory and tactics which had been all but submerged by the success of the liberals.

Betty Friedan, in her effort to restore some unity to the movement and contain the damaging effects of public confrontations, argued that women must learn the realities of political power not just outside but within their own movement, and that they must learn to live with their differences:

What we have to do as a movement is set up simple democratic channels for open, even impassioned discussion of basic issues and strategies, instead of trying to manipulate each other covertly . . . And if the differences are really irreconcilable, let those who want to talk of guerrilla action in the streets and feminist violence have one kind of organization, and those who believe that equality for women and participation in the mainstream is the real revolution have another.[7]

But the kind of majoritarian democracy which Friedan wanted would indeed have had the effect of smothering the radicals, and the liberal feminist organisations had substantial power and resources which radicals wanted to share. In the wake of these conflicts the mood of the American movement in the late 1970s was one of disillusion and demoralisation. Just as in Britain, the call for a feminist revolution seemed hollow in a time of increasing conservatism and economic decline. Liberal feminists had been put on the defensive by the radical charges that they were government collaborators interested only in highly educated career women, and by the revival of a militant political lesbianism. Further abuse was heaped on the liberals by blacks and Hispanics, who claimed that affirmative action programmes were being manipulated to benefit middle-class white women at the expense of racial minorities.

Yet although the American radicals, like the revolutionary feminists in Britain, had tried to move beyond consciousness-raising and sexual politics towards a more active and class-conscious intervention in the system, they remained too few and too fragmented to act effectively. The liberal organisations, somewhat depleted and disheartened, nevertheless remained firmly at the core of the women's movement, the visible *public* face of feminism. The liberals were steadfast in their conception of the women's movement as a network of community projects, campaigns, service centres and pressure groups solidly rooted in American political culture. More highly professionalised, better funded, committed to democratic and legalistic procedures and dedicated mainly to the advancement of middle-class women, the liberal organisations (NOW, WEAL, NWPC, and the rest) maintained much of their original identity through the 1970s.

The unifying factor was the continuing fight for the ERA, and a coalition called ERAmerica was formed in 1976 to press this forward. By 1978 the process of ratification had stalled at

35 states, just three short of the number required to pass the Amendment into law.

The continuing public visibility of liberal feminism was underlined by the National Women's Conference in Houston, Texas, in November 1977. Far beyond the scale of anything conceived possible in Europe, the conference attracted 20,000 participants and was funded by a grant of $5 million from the US Congress. This proved to be a great public platform for liberal feminism. The 25-point National Plan of Action which emerged confirmed the movement's commitment to equal rights and the ERA, but did dismay some of its government sponsors by its emphasis on the needs of black and working-class women, abortion and homosexual rights. The radicals had not been without influence. Nevertheless, the Plan of Action affirmed the essential liberal doctrine that the goal of social equality could be approached only through influencing government, not through revolution.

In fact, the Houston conference marked the full incorporation into mainstream politics of feminist demands which had *seemed* revolutionary nine years earlier. An important frontier of consciousness had been pushed back, and only the revolutionary sexual politics of the radicals remained as a reminder of how far the cause of feminism could still be carried. But within a few short years after Houston, as the next two chapters will show, liberals and radicals together would be fighting a desperate rearguard action to hold on to what had already been gained.

Old Issues, New Campaigns

In Britain the upsurge of separatist and revolutionary feminism was reflected in the campaign issues which dominated the late 1970s. Far greater emphasis was placed on the demand for an end to discrimination against lesbians, especially in jobs like teaching. And a series of campaigns was launched designed to highlight the destructive power of men and the need for separatism: against male violence, rape and pornography.

In Brussels early in 1976 an International Tribunal on Crimes Against Women was convened to hear testimony from women from thirty countries. Much of the testimony was harrowing and shaming to men and deserved a wide hearing, though the banishment of male journalists reduced press coverage almost to nothing. But it pointed to the growing concern in the worldwide women's movement about male violence.

Since 1971, when Erin Pizzey opened the first Women's Aid Centre at Chiswick, London, and made this private problem a public issue, the British movement had been involved in helping battered women. By 1976 some ninety shelters were operating around the country. There was no uniform interpretation of the meaning of male violence, however. The National Women's Aid Federation, which co-ordinated most action in this area, saw itself as treating the victims of abnormally violent and often alcoholic men. The Federation depended largely on volunteers (by no means all of them self-defined feminists) and was concerned with its image because of its need to raise funds and to work closely with housing and social services agencies.

On the other hand, the escalating level of violence against women was a potent argument for the radical anti-male line; but some women's aid workers were disturbed by the rhetoric which branded all men as incurably violent. Erin Pizzey protested in a public letter that 'Until women stop attacking all men, branding them as rapists and batterers, we will never have a women's movement which truly represents all women. Believe it or not, most of us like men.'[8]

In taking this line Pizzey diverged from the view of many radical feminists, and indeed her organisation kept itself apart even from the Women's Aid Federation. Some participants in the 1977 national conference felt it necessary to criticise women's aid groups for not being feminist enough and for being willing to collaborate with men. It was an obvious paradox that, while violence towards women became a very central feminist issue, the organisations dealing most directly with that violence sometimes seemed to be following a non-feminist or even anti-feminist line.

The Domestic Violence and Matrimonial Proceedings Act of 1976 was passed largely as a result of the publicity given to this problem, and gave women better legal protection against violent husbands and cohabitees. But the need for refuges continued to grow, and Women's Aid groups held a week of action in cities all over Britain in September 1978 to keep the problem in the public eye.

Reinforcing the radical interpretation of male violence was the crime of rape, the reported incidence of which had doubled in Britain in ten years. Rape came to symbolise the coercive roots of patriarchy and the power which men have over women. A book by the American feminist author Susan Brownmiller, *Against Our Will*, published in 1975, contributed significantly to this new awareness.

The first rape crisis centre in London opened in 1976 and was followed by others in many major cities. Women who had suffered rape, either recently or at any time in the past, could come to these centres for support and counselling from women, and they thus provided a unique service. In the 1980s there have been initiatives to provide a similar service for victims of incest.

Like refuges, rape crisis centres needed to keep a low political profile. They were often registered as charities or received grants-in-aid, and considerable resources and organisation were required. Counsellors had to be trained, and service provided on a 24-hour basis. Most centres saw themselves as providing a social service for women rather than as constituting a political campaign against men.

One campaigning group was Women Against Rape (WAR), launched in 1976 to dramatise the problem and to work for changes in the legal treatment of rape victims. Women Against Rape was part of a network which connected with Wages for Housework, the English Collective of Prostitutes, and parallel campaigns in the USA.

WAR first made headlines in 1977 with public protests against the treatment of an army guardsman who had been convicted of a violent assault on a 17-year-old woman but who was released to 'protect his army career'. From this time onwards, the campaign against rape became one of the more visible activities of the movement. Anti-rape campaigns were launched throughout Britain, many by groups which did not agree with the WAR analysis that rape was a symptom of women's economic dependence, preferring the classic radical analysis that rape was an expression of male power.

The pressure generated by these campaigns did help to make legislators more aware of the public ordeal facing women who tried to bring rape charges, and the Sexual Offences (Amendment) Act of 1976 went some way towards making the process less harrowing.

The radical tendency was also reflected in growingly militant protests against commercial pornography and its effects. These protests have two purposes: to highlight the fact that the degradation of women in pornography is a form of violence, and promotes violence towards women; and to make the point that public streets should be a safe place for women at any hour of the day or night.

A group of feminists mounted demonstrations to 'reclaim the night' in Soho, London, three times during 1977 and 1978. The final demonstration itself became violent when the women were confronted by a cinema employee and the police decided to break up the protest, injuring several women and arresting sixteen, labelled the 'Soho sixteen'.

'Reclaim the night' demonstrations were held in Leeds, Manchester, Bristol, York and elsewhere, and continue to be held. But pornography as such provokes an ambiguous response in the movement. When pornography is raised as the main issue, the press, missing the point about violence, invariably label the protesters as puritans and/or supporters of Mary Whitehouse, and many feminists are unhappy to be found in such company. All feminists (probably all women) object to violent or degrading pornography, and there is strong evidence that such material does indeed encourage violent behaviour. But not all are willing to go along with the campaign slogan 'Pornography is the theory and rape is the practice' and to argue for the banning of all sexual representations of women.[9] But the campaign continues to be an active one, especially visible in its guerrilla attacks on sex shops and pornographic cinemas.

Pornography has also become a major issue in the USA, where an inventive group called Women Against Pornography (WAP) have attracted much serious publicity since 1976 by staging educational tours and demonstrations in the sleazy 42nd Street/Times Square area of New York. On both sides of the Atlantic, groups called Women Against Violence Against

Women (WAVAW), formed in 1976 in the USA and 1980 in Britain, have identified pornographic violence with male power in every aspect of culture and politics.

The relationship between these anti-pornography campaigns and prostitution is a delicate one. Prostitutes may be accused of pandering to men's violent and pornographic fantasies. On the other hand, they are exploited by men and are themselves subject to uncontrolled violence and rape, from which it appears that the police will not protect them. In the debate over prostitution, the latter point of view tends to prevail, and links have been made between parts of the women's movement (especially WAR) and the prostitutes' own organisations.

Prostitutes first began to organise in the USA in 1973, when Margo St James and others formed COYOTE (Cut Out Your Old Tired Ethics), to be quickly followed by the US Prostitutes' Collective and many others. The English Collective of Prostitutes was started in 1975 by Selma James, who also co-founded the International Wages for Housework Campaign. Prostitutes' organisations now form a considerable international network, campaigning for legalisation and for better protection against violence. Helen Buckingham helped launch Prostitution Laws Are Nonsense (PLAN) and Programme for Reform of Laws on Soliciting (PROS) to work on the legal aspects. A distinction has to be made between groups like PROS which act as a form of trade union or protection society for prostitutes and more politicised campaigns like the English Collective of Prostitutes. The latter group, which organised a heavily publicised sit-in for prostitutes' rights in a London church in November 1982, probably had very few working prostitutes among its membership and was more concerned to press a particular theory of women's needs and rights.

Sexual politics and the campaigns against violence, rape and pornography were the most highly visible issues of women's liberation in the late 1970s, but they represented only a small part of what was happening. Political work in the trade unions and the Labour Party continued and expanded, and will be more fully treated in Chapter 7. Equally significant was the burgeoning of an entire women's culture based on the sense that women at last had the chance to build a cultural world of their own, free from the historic domination of men.

Long excluded from the arts, or relegated to subordinate roles, women found in the movement a new environment to express their talents and to create specifically feminist works. In music, theatre, painting, pottery, sculpture, design, photography, film, printing and writing, groups and collectives sprang up to share ideas, facilities and skills.

Some of these groups were developed out of earlier consciousness-raising meetings, others from contacts made in political campaigns; but many had no organic connection with the women's movement other than their desire to develop a female or feminist cultural form. Some creative workers were concerned to address a purely female audience; others looked forward to the time when feminist art would be accepted and integrated into the mainstream of culture.

The latter aim has been accomplished mainly in the field of literature, and mainly by American authors. Writers as varied as Adrienne Rich, Marilyn French, Kate Millett, Nancy Friday and Rita May Brown have broken through to best-seller status in commercial publishing, even though their work carries strong feminist messages. The more restricted world of British publishing has offered fewer such opportunities to feminist authors or poets.

In the intellectual realm also, universities and polytechnics increasingly became important centres of feminist activity. Research, especially in women's history, literature, psychology and sociology, has added new dimensions to existing disciplines, and the growth of women's studies has been phenomenal. By the end of the 1970s there were at least thirty degree-level women's studies programmes being offered in Britain, and in the USA a staggering total of 350 full programmes and 20,000 individual courses as well as a National Women's Studies Association. Women's studies have helped to correct the bias against women's knowledge, experience and history which has been typical of the humanistic and social science disciplines.

In a conservative university system dominated by men, research and teaching in such fields occupied a vulnerable position. Some anxiety was also expressed in the movement that intellectual feminists were retreating into an academic ghetto which was entirely alien to the majority of women. In Britain, especially, there was a distinct anti-intellectual back-lash from non-university women who felt patronised and excluded by the mystifications of the academic world.

In the very concept of 'women's studies' there is a risk both of isolation within the university and elitism in relation to those outside. If, however, one takes the view that formal education can change people's attitudes, there is an unanswerable case for extending women's studies (or gender studies) right through the educational system, including the schools. Young women and men could be sensitised to gender inequality and sexism and could learn what feminists are saying through these programmes, provided that they were widely available and well taught. In this sense women's studies could become a spearhead or educational arm for the women's movement. The Feminist Social Policy Group already functions to turn the experience accumulated by academic women to practical account.

Equally important are the intellectual and professional networks which form around any field of study. Intellectual and academic women, individually isolated in separate disciplines from one another and from other professional women, could have little dialogue and few recognised common interests. Women's studies, along with associated activities like the publication of scholarly journals and the organisation of conferences, provided the anchoring-point for female and feminist networks which have become international. The evidence of recent years has been that such intellectual networks have a crucial part to play in the process of social change.[10]

Conclusions

The 1970s were a decade of growth, creativity and energy for the women's movement everywhere. It was not confined to Britain and the USA, but sprang up simultaneously in France, Germany, Holland, Italy, Spain, Australia, Japan and in a number of developing nations. The problems women faced were not always the same (e.g. there are obvious differences between Catholic and Muslim cultures, and some societies lack even minimal political or human rights). But there was a worldwide new consciousness among women which, now it had appeared, would be impossible to repress.

Nevertheless, in the rich nations of the West, the movement had fallen into the doldrums by 1978. In Britain there was a sense of tiredness after the euphoria and the conflicts of the first decade. The movement seemed blocked by economic depression, and mired down in a series of very difficult strategic and theoretical choices:

1. How to maintain the unity of a highly diverse movement without abandoning its basic non-authoritarian principles.
2. How to find the balance between economic demands and sexual politics.
3. How to open up the movement and make it more attractive, especially to working-class and black women.
4. How to carry on national struggles with leaderless and decentralised structures.

The movement had passed beyond the stage of discovering and describing women's oppression, and needed to find new avenues of growth. It had also passed beyond the political culture which gave birth to it – the radical idealism of the affluent 1960s – into an era of political conservatism and economic decline; the gap between 1968 and 1978 was profound in terms of expectations and possibilities. The adaptation needed to respond swiftly and effectively to such changes demanded a degree of unity and co-ordination which the movement simply did not possess. Less an organisation than an organism, it responded with organic slowness and with many internal crises.

Eight years earlier, at the movement's exciting birth, American feminists had celebrated fifty years of suffrage with a march of 50,000 women and men in New York City. The fiftieth anniversary of full female suffrage in Britain fell in 1978 and, by contrast, a far more modest government-sponsored celebration was held. An open letter from the women's liberation movement was addressed to the suffragettes at the ceremony, some lines of which were quoted at the beginning of this book. Since it so well captured the mood and concerns of the movement in 1978, it is worth quoting again from the closing lines of the same letter:[11]

> In order to achieve women's liberation, we intend to take those things that no male law will ever give. We will walk down any street without being assaulted and raped. We will live in our own homes without being battered by men we live with. We will live with other women, as lovers, if we choose. We will not bear sole responsibility for the housework or childcare. We will not take the burden, unpaid, in the home, of caring for the victims of cuts in the welfare state whilst our sisters in the public sector are thrown out of paid work. We will not be labelled as mad when we protest – twice as many women as men are labelled as psychiatrically ill, and women are prescribed twice as many psychotropic (mood-changing) drugs as men. We will not be confronted on every hoarding, in every newspaper and on every TV screen by images of ourselves as ideal sex-symbol, ideal mother, ideal servant, the product of male fantasies we are incapable and unwilling to fulfil. These are only some of the issues we are organising around; they are elements of all our lives which we as women of all ages are angry about, and which will never be changed by acts of Parliament. We want to make it clear that no feminist 50 years ago thought that getting the vote was the end of the struggle. We haven't won – we've only just begun!

6. Hostile Responses: the Enemies of Women's Liberation

The call for women's equality has always aroused a bitter opposition. From the 1840s to the 1980s feminists have had to contend with powerful enemies who have seen their cause as a threat to the basic fabric of society. When the contemporary women's liberation movement first emerged, it flourished briefly in a period of rare liberalism and political openness when many previously oppressed social groups (blacks, youth, gays) were making claims for recognition and equal rights. A decade later the political atmosphere had entirely changed and the enemies of women's liberation had become more numerous and outspoken. Feminists were no longer on the cutting-edge of progressive reform, but defending a beleagured outpost. It seemed in truth as though everyone was against them.

Most opposition to feminism was and is based on very little direct knowledge of what feminists believe and demand. Popular stereotypes spread by the mass media are the only basis for judgement which most people have, or feel they need; in this sense, with some notable exceptions, journalists are among the movement's most insidious enemies. Women's liberation has been made an easy scapegoat for many social changes which people find threatening – rising divorce rates, the competition of women in the job market and their growing autonomy as individuals, the crumbling of traditional sex roles and the increasing stresses of family life. The reader who has come this far will know that these changes were not consequences of the feminist movement but were among its fundamental causes. But the belief is widespread that feminism somehow spoiled a past relationship between women and men which was happier and more stable.

The elites of politics, economics and culture have more pragmatic reasons for using their powers against women's liberation. Any movement which raises questions about the established inequalities of society is a threat, however remote, to powerful interests. To contain such a threat, forces of social control more subtle than simple repression will be called into play. Typically, elites may encourage the idea that the whole movement is composed of pathological misfits. They may try to divide the movement against itself by defining one portion of its demands as legitimate and normal and the remainder as illegitimate or extreme. If this definition is successfully imposed, the regular process of social stereotyping will do the rest. These, in large part, have been the strategies used by elites against the women's movement. In both Britain and America the liberal pressures for equal human rights, for equal pay, educational and job opportunities were conceded as legitimate political demands. To a lesser extent limited rights to abortion and freedom of sexual expression were also conceded. Everything else contained in the movement's critiques of patriarchy and capitalism was defined as outside the realm of rational discourse. In the USA this left the liberal organisations as the only ones with access to the centres of power through conventional political action; in Britain virtually the whole movement was excluded, apart from those sections which chose to work through the Labour Party or the trade unions.

Other feminists had only two options. They might hope to gain a mass base and political influence by playing down some of their most basic principles, or they could reject all compromise, hoping that time and events would validate their position. In taking the latter course the more radical tendencies were forced to exist in isolation from the mainstream of political life. Like all such outsider groups, they became the repository for the scorn, the fear and the anger of 'normal' society.

In this chapter we focus on the main sources of opposition to the women's liberation movement: from men in general, from women, from the state and organised anti-feminist groups, from the mass media and from intellectuals and other social critics.

Opposition from Men

Warren Farrell, in *The Liberated Man*, offered twenty reasons why men should welcome the liberation of women. Among them were that relationships between women and men would become more genuine and therefore more stable, that the emotional and economic burdens of women's dependence on men would be lifted, and that men could stop worrying about their masculine image and express a wider range of needs and emotions.[1] In the movement's early days such arguments were often heard, and are still heard from some liberals and socialists. But these are the faint echoes of the intellectual idealism of the 1960s. For the average working male it was always quite clear that feminism represented an attack on his economic, political, sexual and status privileges which offered only very hazy and uncertain benefits in return.

It is not necessary to assume that all men are biologically destined to be chauvinists, rapists, wife-batterers and woman-haters, or that men are incapable of love and respect towards women, to understand why male opposition to all but the mildest forms of women's liberation is so nearly complete. We need to distinguish the obvious reasons from those which are more deeply hidden in male psychology and in the roles which women and men are assigned.

The most obvious reason is that feminism appears to be as much a zero-sum proposition for men as socialism is for the owners of capital. In education, employment, in politics and at home, men stand to lose a great deal and gain nothing by admitting the justice of women's cause. At a time when opportunities at all levels are static or shrinking, the hard fact is that what women gain men must lose. The qualities of unselfishness and nobility or character which men would need to support a movement so contrary to their own interests are in notably short supply. In this sense the radical analysis which says that men have been and will be enemies of women is correct.

In addition to these pragmatic considerations, the movement must contend with untold generations of male socialisation which have produced a cultural stereotype of maleness as strong as or stronger than its female counterpart. The stereotypes are not merely different, but fundamentally opposed, and much of the recent research of feminists in the social sciences has been directed towards understanding how and why male and female roles are thus created.[2] The broad outlines of this research are now well known. They show particularly how the cultivation of qualities of toughness, competitiveness and emotional distance in young men gives them a systematic advantage over women who are trained in more passive and humane responses. Femininity is constructed in such a way that women are perceived by men not only as different but, in all important respects, inferior. Nobody need be surprised that when women try to move into male spheres of power and influence most men react with hostility. Not only are they facing new competition, but their roles, their purposes in life and their very identities are being challenged.

Men are powerfully attached to their own view of the world and their place in it. Most have no desire to become more like women, nor for women to become more like men (Shaw's Professor Higgins notwithstanding). Women must play out the traditional feminine role to validate the traditional masculine role, and vice versa. It runs counter to centuries of history for men to accept the idea of undifferentiated, androgynous sex roles.

Any movement for women's liberation will therefore produce defensive and aggressive responses from men. But not all such responses are based on rational economic considerations or on the jealous guardianship of the male role. Psychology suggests another component of aggression – fear. Beyond their uneasiness and resentment, many men nurse unresolved anxieties about the whole dark mystery of 'the feminine' which can be brought to the surface in male consciousness-raising sessions.[3]

In some cultures the repression of women has always been strict because they are seen as dangerous, agents of chaos and anarchic nature.[4] The Judeo–Christian tradition still carries traces of this belief, and the myths and legends of all cultures are richly endowed with demonic women, from the Hindu goddess Kali to the Eumenides or avenging Furies of Ancient Greece. The battle of the sexes has a long history, and the feminist challenge raises many strange fears from the depths of men's minds.[5]

Chief among these is fear and resentment of the all-powerful mother, that arbitrary goddess of childhood with her mixed messages of approval and guilt, love and rejection. Some men spend a lifetime and a fortune in psychoanalysis trying to come to terms with the image of mother. Men may fear the mysteries of female biology, especially menstruation and childbirth. Fertility has always and everywhere been worshipped as the greatest magic, and feared for its uncertainty and apparent power. Medieval European Christianity saw women as primitive creatures of nature, the carriers of corruption, pollution and death against whom the church had to stand as a bulwark of purity and civilisation. In modern times, medical science has tried to demystify and take control of women's biology; through their dominance in gynaecology, men have been able to participate in and take charge of this ultimate mystery. For other men it remains a totally magical and even enviable aspect of womanhood.

Men may fear the apparent otherness of women, their unfathomable morality, their inaccessible thoughts, the whole secret structure of their femininity. They fear women's sexuality, which, once released, may prove insatiable. They fear the iron grip of domesticity and fatherhood as their fate, for which biology baits the trap.

Such fears are increasingly arcane and meaningless to each new generation. Co-education, mass culture, changing sexual mores, egalitarian marriage and the integration of women into the labour force have all worked to undermine the separation of women and men which fed the ignorance and prejudice of the past. In so far as the fear of women is based on fantasy it will eventually fade away; but like all potent myths it will be a long time dying. In the meantime women who challenge the power of men will meet with an anger which has sources far deeper than the rational defence of male interests.

Some tendencies in the feminist movement have directly and deliberately stimulated men's fear of women. If, for example, revolutionary feminists define all men as monsters and threaten to kill or castrate them, fear and anger are the only possible responses. Even some of the less extreme rhetoric of feminism, just because points must be strongly made in order to be heard at all, tends to stereotype men in wholly negative terms. To argue that men never take women seriously because they are not physically afraid of women, that men cannot express real tenderness towards women, that men are constantly obsessed with sex, and that all men are violent, reduces the male part of the human race to something less than human.[6] Such statements, like those which attribute a maternal instinct or a lack of aggression to all women, are simply false. Their political *purpose* is to jolt men into recognising that a problem exists and to bring hidden conflicts into the open. In radical politics, sweeping statements are unavoidable, but they carry penalties in terms of credibility and public antagonism which have to be balanced against the new awareness which their shock value may create.

In its strongest most Manichean form, the stereotyping argument suggests that, if all men are evil, all women must be good: or, more abstractly, if all things associated with maleness are evil, all things associated with femaleness must be good. Men in general are quick to react against both the moral and the practical implications of this line. A liberal male might readily admit that a whole group or class of people had been unjustly discriminated against. The sticking-point for most would be the further claim that every member of that group could claim moral superiority over every member of the group which had historically been responsible for that discrimination.

The feminist movement sparked off another and more devious male response. A minority of men have turned feminism on its head by claiming that it is the *women* who have special social privileges and the *men* who are oppressed by traditional sex roles. In its crudest bar-room form, this is the argument that 'women have it easy' because the exhausting competition of the labour market is for them a matter of choice. They lose no status by failing in the competition, and without penalty they may choose not to compete at all.

This particular form of aggression comes out in more subtle ways in the so-called 'men's movement', which claims not to be in opposition to feminism. This is more an American than a British phenomenon, some 200 American groups being organised as the Coalition of Free Men. These groups must be distinguished from the explicitly pro-feminist, anti-sexist male organisations which fully support the women's movement. Free Men, and groups like them, are advocates of more rights for men in the spheres usually assigned to women. They are especially concerned with the limitations of the father role, and the excessive power which they believe women have to hold and to control children. Emotionally, they feel that men are cramped by the bottled-up emotional lives which their roles force them to lead at home and at work. Mental and physical health suffer from the compulsion to be tough, competitive and to make money. Their complaint is a sophisticated version of the 'women have it easy' argument. The kind of convergence they want is one where men are allowed and encouraged to become more feminine emotionally and to build stronger relationships with their children. It is probably true to say that this part of the men's movement is more pro-man than anti-women, but it is a magnet for anti-feminist sentiment. Men have as much right as women to challenge their traditional roles, but the logic of the Free Men line is that all the claims of feminism beyond equal opportunity are misguided and false, because women already have the easier role.

Men in the left-libertarian political sub-culture have had particular difficulty in coming to terms with feminism. While men in general may find many reasons to dismiss women's claims, male radicals are forced to admit their justice. Yet the costs for them are no less than for other men, and their responses have been deeply ambivalent. The socialist sections of the women's movement have consistently called on their male allies to 'recognise their own sexism' and have as consistently been disappointed. The reasons are fairly obvious. The identity of a radical activist is linked to a certain sense of self-righteousness, of being on the side of good against evil. The suggestion that he may in one respect be on the side of evil is therefore very painful. Just as the American black power movement in the 1960s managed to paralyse white radicals with a sense of guilt over black oppression,[7] so some tendencies in women's liberation demanded that individual men take responsibility for the whole history of women's oppression. Guilt is part of the dynamic of any liberation struggle, and arousing guilt in the oppressor is a well-tried political tactic. Trying to lay collective guilt on a whole group or class of people regardless of their specific behaviour is a more double-edged weapon. Men who approached feminism in a fairly positive and egalitarian spirit tended to back away when confronted with the demand that they shoulder the burden of the sins of all mankind.

Radical groups, especially radical separatists, are concerned with women, and do not want to waste time or energy on making fine distinctions between men. Their strong anti-male line, being the most dramatic expression of feminist feeling, has often been wrongly taken to represent feminism as a whole. But for very many feminists, men, their power and their culture are a primary concern, and the question of how the movement should relate to them has been hotly debated from the beginning. Anne Koedt wrote in 1971 that ' "Man is the enemy" is only true insofar as the man adopts the male supremacy role',[8] and many feminists would agree that some men may be treated as allies.

So far, however, the record of men as active allies of feminism has been a dismal one. In 1980 a conference was held in Britain on the theme of the 'Women's Liberation Movement and Men'. What emerged was that 'male feminists' (mainly socialists) had had a divisive rather than a supportive influence. As academics they had aggressively entered the field of women's studies, trying to appropriate it to themselves. In politics, feminist men had taken over women's issues, challenged the right of women to a fully autonomous movement and to exclusive female groups, conferences, meeting-places and journals and had tried to open up divisions between women along class lines rather than accepting the feminist position that women were united by common oppressions.[9] In America, self-defined male feminists have recently been going to court to challenge women-only commissions, enterprises and organisations on grounds of sex discrimination.

It was never likely that most men would be allies of women's liberation. Nor is it possible for a strong women's movement to exist without alienating men. Liberal equal rights groups have been able to claim some powerful men as allies, and have made immense gains by doing so. Feminist demands of a more far-reaching kind do not attract the support of male elites, and many feminists would prefer to insulate themselves altogether from the male world of politics and power. A movement for and about women, they argue, should be a movement *of* women.

Opposition from Women

Unlike blacks, unlike even the industrial working class, women form the majority of the populations of Britain and America. In theory at least, a united movement of women could realise its goals against any conceivable coalition of opponents. But recent opinion polls in America have indicated that about 90 per cent of all adult women are indifferent to the women's liberation movement, and that around 70 per cent believe that they get as good a chance in life as men.[10] No comparable surveys have been done in Britain, but the indirect evidence of participation rates in feminist groups and the readership of feminist journals gives us no reason to suppose that British women are more enthusiastic about the movement than their American sisters.

People do not easily become involved in radical causes, and this widespread indifference only tells us that most women, like most men, accept the status quo. More important is the extent of actual opposition among women. For those who have chosen or would like to choose traditional female roles the movement is not just an irrelevance, it is a threat. Older women with families and younger ones with poor education or training fear that feminism may sweep away the foundations of their future lives as wives and mothers, offering nothing in return but a lifetime of low-paid, unskilled work, or unemployment and poverty. Such women form the hard core of the female opposition to feminism, a deep, passive hostility which the movement has been unable to overcome. They cannot see that the movement offers *them* a real choice, though they grant that it may be good for young career women. It seems that they are being asked to tear their lives to pieces and go it alone in quest of an abstract idea of social justice. But movements only attract mass support when they can hold out the promise of immediate and tangible benefits.

Feminism is also blamed bitterly, and certainly unjustly, for the decline of the traditional family which formed the stable framework of most women's lives. Yet the feminist movement was one *result* of a long process of change in sex roles which had been undermining the family for decades. This process was consolidated in the permissive and libertarian years of the

1960s, and men took full advantage of it to redefine the male role to their own advantage. Monogamy and a man's lifetime responsibility to his wife and children were suddenly *passé*, divorce rates soared, and women, left with children and without support, looked around for someone to blame. The feminist movement, with its anti-family rhetoric, was the obvious target and, for women's future, it seemed to offer more of the same, and worse. Women's liberation was accused of offering a *carte blanche* for men to shirk their family duties (although men have always been able to do this), and of destroying an imaginary golden age of family stability and harmony. For the most part the media were happy to go along with this interpretation of events.

Since the earliest beginnings of feminist consciousness in the 1830s, it has been recognised that women would be hard to mobilise. Separated from one another in the households of men, locked into a set of intimate and dependent arrangements with those men, it was uniquely difficult for them to achieve a common sense of identity and purpose. In the twentieth century women's work outside the home has loosened these tight bonds, but for many of them their lives, their only hope of security (however fragile) and their only sphere of authority, are bound still to home and family.

Even for those best qualified to escape into a wider sphere, the feminist challenge was frightening. It substituted choice for destiny and freedom for security, and it said that women could have it all. The image in the early 1970s was of 'superwoman', juggling career and home and family, gaining everything and losing nothing in her new liberation. More recently, the popular success of books like Collette Dowling's *The Cinderella Complex*,[11] which encouraged women to throw off their dependency and their fears of success and competition, suggested that the superwoman image was still very much alive. Yet cracks were beginning to appear in the façade, as we shall see in the next chapter. Many of the fears about what women were being asked to do turned out to be well grounded.

But feminine opposition to feminism was not based only on concern about changing traditional roles. Many, if not most, women found aspects of socialist and radical feminist programmes morally or personally repugnant. One need not labour the point that rejection of men, political lesbianism or socialist revolution, for example, are unlikely to attract mass support within the present cultures of Britain or the USA. Politically aware and active women who supported the movement's egalitarian aims could involve themselves with the liberal wing of the movement in the USA or with the Labour Party and trade-union sectors in Britain. But many tentative sympathisers were offended by some expressions of radical feminism, notably by the conformity of ideas and personal style which this element demanded and by the recent attempt to blame non-lesbian women for their heterosexuality. Over the years, *Spare Rib* has regularly published letters from women who wanted to be active feminists but could find no comfortable place in the movement.[12]

One expression of the general female response to feminism was a renewed emphasis on femininity as a source of women's traditional power. In the USA Marabel Morgan's *The Total Woman* (1973) sold over a million copies and spawned a host of imitators, some of which stayed on the national best-seller lists for months at a time. Their message was attractive, because they allowed and encouraged women to be beautiful and to love men but claimed that, in the modern, post-civil rights age, they could still be free to fulfil their lives in other ways. Feminism, they claimed, had done its job and was now redundant.

Until very recently the arguments of anti-feminist women have been paid almost as little attention in the movement as those of men. They have been dismissed as a male-identified fifth column or, more devastatingly, with the well-worn Marxist phrase 'false consciousness'. This implies that the ideas of most women are not their own and are, indeed, against their best interests, but that the overwhelming power of culture and training has brainwashed them into thinking that way. Not all feminists accept this negative interpretation because it can be read as an attack on the intelligence of women; the Redstocking's pro-woman line explicitly rejects it, saying that women have their own subversive thoughts but are coerced by the power of men into pretending that they do not.

There is no mystery about the origins of the anti-feminist attitudes among women (and men) which I have outlined. They reflect a life-long conditioning in traditional male/female sex roles, constantly reinforced by the immediate and tangible ways in which society rewards 'correct' sex role behaviour and punishes 'incorrect' behaviour. Knowing this, however, does not make it go away. Breaking these cultural codes will be the work of generations, but the very existence of a feminist movement shows that their disappearance can be conceived. Women and men now alive have watched the sexual rules of the game change in their lifetimes, and adjustment for them is particularly hard. Many cling fearfully to what is familiar. To them, the women's liberation movement appears in the guise of an agent of chaos, destroying secure worlds and familiar roles for no very obvious reason. But feminism is the carrier of ideas and changes which are deeply rooted in the culture. Barring some major reversal, each new generation will find its message a little less threatening and sociologists of the future may look back on the rigid masculine/feminine roles of the twentieth century as a historical curiosity.

The Organised Opposition

Anti-feminist sentiments have found their clearest expression in a number of more or less organised opposition movements. In America semi-serious groups like the Pussycat League, Protect Our Women (POW) and the League of Housewives sprang to the defence of the family and the rights of women to their femininity. The only traceable imitator in Britain was something called the Campaign for the Feminine Woman. With the possible exception of Marabel Morgan's successful courses on Total Womanhood and similar American undertakings, these pro-femininity groups attracted little support and were taken seriously by almost nobody.

Far more threatening were the campaigns which harnessed the conservatism of the late 1970s to attack some of the most essential demands of the women's movement, in particular the campaign against abortion and (in America) against the Equal Rights Amendment. Both campaigns depended substantially on women for their support.

The British Abortion Act of 1967 had, as we have seen, been under attack since 1975. The impetus came from the Catholic

Church, supported by High Anglican churchmen and conservative politicians. The most powerful single organisation against abortion rights, the Society for the Protection of the Unborn Child (SPUC), had branches throughout the country by 1980. Life Groups, the Festival of Light and many smaller associations backed the campaign, with slogans like 'A woman's right to kill' and 'Would you be alive today if abortion had been legal then?'

The anti-abortion forces were better funded and, it must be conceded, better organised than the women's liberation movement. They also had powerful friends and were able to arrange a great deal of favourable publicity for themselves. Anti-abortionists had ready-made platforms for their views in churches, schools and in the conservative press, none of which was available to feminists. The opposition's line was simple: abortion was murder, it destroyed the family, and (an important undercurrent) it took away one of the main incentives to sexual morality. Given the strength of these groups and the emotive appeal of their message, it was a remarkable achievement of the women's movement with its allies in the unions and the Labour Party to defeat the first three parliamentary challenges. Despite a degree of political disarray in the abortion rights campaign and despite the confusion caused by groups like Women for Life which claimed to be pro-feminist but anti-abortion, the British women's liberation movement was able to win through because anti-abortion was a limited, elite issue, not backed by the government and not supported by popular sentiment. The intervention of the TUC in 1976 was also crucial. But SPUC and the rest do not believe that they have lost the war, and the limited abortion rights provided by the 1967 Act will have to be continuously defended.

In America the line-up of anti-abortion forces has been different, for there is a fundamentalist religious strain absent in Britain. The National Right to Life Committee, with hundreds of associated branches and coalitions, is a major phenomenon of the rise of the so-called 'Moral Majority' in the heart of American political life.[13] Dozens of reasons have been suggested why Americans in the 1980s should embrace the simplicities of a nineteenth-century moral crusade: the economic crisis, the disillusionments of Vietnam and Watergate, the fear of total war, a general backlash against the rising powers of women, blacks and youth. What matters here is the pervasive power of a neo-conservative political culture which has as one of its major aims to put women back in their place.

So far, the American feminists have been almost as successful as the British in fighting off this challenge. Their main failures have been the repeated decisions of Congress since 1977 to deny financial aid (Medicaid) to poor women seeking abortions. But the combined weight of Catholic and fundamentalist Protestant churches supported by the neo-conservative political establishment adds up to a far more formidable anti-abortion force than exists in Britain. Unless the political and religious climate changes, it would not be surprising if, in the teeth of all feminist opposition, abortion rights were cut back in the USA during the 1980s. At the beginning of 1981 a Human Life Amendment was introduced into Congress which would have outlawed abortion entirely.

On 30 June 1982 the Moral Majority won a great victory against the American feminist movement and against American women. The Equal Rights Amendment failed to secure ratification in the required number of states, and was defeated. In effect, this gave constitutional sanction for the continuation of many kinds of discriminatory practices, and was a major step in the Moral Majority's campaign to put a stop to the movement for sexual equality once and for all. It was also a deadly blow to the morale of the women's movement.

The ERA had been opposed since it was first put forward in 1923, but the most recent wave of opposition dated from 1973 when it seemed possible that the Amendment (passed by Congress) would be ratified by the states. Conservative and ultra-conservative groups, including the John Birch Society, the American Nazi Party and the Daughters of the American Revolution, mobilised all their forces against it, denouncing the ERA as a 'communist plot'. A mixed coalition called STOP–ERA was put together to carry the message to the states, especially the rural and conservative states of the south and mid-west. The message, aimed mainly at middle-class white 'home-makers', was that women would lose their homes and families if the ERA was passed. With no laws to protect them, they would certainly be abandoned by their husbands and probably drafted into military service. It is worth remarking that these conservatives demonstrated almost as jaundiced a view of men as their radical sisters.

The presiding genius and chairperson of STOP–ERA was Phyllis Schafley, a lawyer, mother, inspired organiser and ex-member of the anti-communist John Birch Society. Her ideas were spread through public and television appearances, a newspaper column syndicated in over a hundred papers, and a newsletter which circulated 350,000 copies. Like the anti-abortion forces of which they were a part, the anti-ERA campaigners were well funded and had many powerful friends.

Liberal and radical feminist groups in America did their best to contain the damage done by this conservative/fundamentalist onslaught. Their campaign for the ERA was conducted with tremendous energy; in one demonstration alone, on Mother's Day 1980, 100,000 women marched for ratification in Illinois. Traditional forms of political action were combined with inventive guerrilla theatre actions which recalled the early days of the movement. Phyllis Schafley's speaking tours, for example, were dogged by a group calling themselves 'Ladies Against Women'. Dressed in hats and gloves, they carried signs which read 'Sperm are People Too' and 'You're Nobody Till You're Mrs Somebody'. However, support for the ERA was still strong. In a 1981 opinion poll 63 per cent of women supported the Amendment and only 32 per cent opposed it, the rest being undecided. Among non-white women, only 16 per cent were opposed. Men on the whole were slightly less likely to be against the ERA than women [14] But this was no longer a contest of majorities but one of power and influence. In America in 1982 the feminist movement was not powerful enough to contain the well-funded and well-organised forces of the new religious right.

The British government has not been so openly an enemy of women's liberation. In recent years it has remained officially neutral on issues like abortion, divorce and homosexuality, and the pro-family rhetoric of the Thatcher administration has been largely a matter of expediency. The rundown of the welfare state can be argued on the grounds that many of its supportive functions can and should be taken back by the family (which means in effect by women).

In America, by contrast, the Reagan government's pro-family line has been far more aggressive and involved a direct attack on women's rights.[15] The administration cut back sharply on senior government appointments for women and has been accused by NOW and other groups of failing to enforce the anti-discrimination laws and of encouraging private companies to evade affirmative action guidelines. The Family Protection Bill, introduced in 1981, included clauses to prohibit funding for pro-feminist organisations or educational courses and to deny protection against discrimination to homosexuals. President Reagan's budget proposals for 1983 included cuts in food programmes, medical care, education, aid for dependent children, social security and job training, all of which would seriously worsen the situation of poor women.[16] Government support for such policies suggests that the American movement in the coming decade may face a bitter struggle to defend existing rights rather than moving forward on the basis of rights already won.

The new religious right shows no signs of slackening its campaign to roll back the progress which women have made in the past decade.[17] Phyllis Schaffley's organisation, the Eagle Forum, has turned its attention to the abolition of sex education and an effort to rid school textbooks of 'feminist influences'. The Moral Majority is pushing hard to ban feminist health books like *Our Bodies, Ourselves* from public libraries and has launched a massive pro-family propaganda campaign. On the lunatic fringe, violence and at least one bombing have been directed against local women's centres.

Ironically, perhaps, this level of opposition may be a measure of the movement's success. Fringe groups only irritate the powerful, and attract little more than ridicule. It is only when a movement is seen as a substantial threat to the established order that significant forces of repression are mobilised against it. Using this yardstick, we may judge that the women's movement in America is taken far more seriously by those in power than the movement in Britain.

Hostility to Feminism in the Mass Media and Commercial Culture

From the very beginning an antagonistic relationship existed between the women's movement and the mass media. We saw in Chapter 4 how the movement's first actions were treated with ridicule and its supporters labelled as deviants. Every device, from the bra-burning myth to the sneering diminutive 'women's lib' was mobilised to reduce feminism to the status of an amusing and sometimes titillating sideshow. As two historians of the movement wrote, 'Rage would not be too strong a word to describe the emotion felt by large numbers of feminists about the media's coverage of the women's movement.'[18]

The response of most feminist groups was to boycott the press altogether, or to give information and interviews only under strictly controlled conditions. This cut down the flow of negative and divisive stories and, for a while, it intrigued journalists enough for them to take the movement somewhat more seriously. After all, most groups go out begging for publicity, and it was a new experience for the press corps to be treated with such contempt. But the novelty value of secrecy soon wore off, and bad press relations have since been reflected in the patchy, irritable and often hostile treatment of feminism in almost every medium.

The importance of this can scarcely be exaggerated. In the modern world the media hold the key to political and cultural change; anyone who doubts this should consider the iron censorship which all authoritarian regimes find necessary. The great majority of people will have no direct knowledge of feminism, or any other movement for change, unless they learn of it through newspapers, magazines, radio or television. Journalists have become, by default, the gatekeepers of social knowledge, and they can exercise that power in numerous ways, virtually without constraint.[19] And most journalists serve male masters whose fundamental interest is in the maintenance of the status quo.

Among the powers of the press is the ability to reduce any movement or interest group to insignificance by choosing *not* to report it or reporting it in such a way that it appears ridiculous. If journalists do decide that the movement is interesting, they may do as much damage by picking up issues and ideas out of context, simplifying and stereotyping complicated theoretical issues ('all feminists hate men') and defining the nature of the protest on behalf of the protesters ('what the feminists want is . . .'). Hardly ever is a radical group allowed space in the mass media to speak clearly and with its own voice.

More overtly hostile tactics include trying to weaken the movement by publishing inflated accounts of its internal divisions and setting one group against another, exaggerating the rhetoric and militancy so that politicians define the movement as extremist, and simply using media expertise and public access to put forward hostile arguments to which the movement has no chance of reply. All these devices have been used from time to time against feminism.

A more subtle route has been to co-opt sections of the movement and try to render them harmless, and this tactic has been consistently used against American liberal feminism. The media willingly embrace social movements which pay the price of staying within a legitimate frame of values, and which provide accessible, respectable and reliable spokespersons to comment on the issues of the day. It makes the journalist's job easier, and it helps reinforce the ideology of a dynamic and democratic society where many interests are heard. Co-optation is double-edged, however, and many of the successes of the American liberals have precisely been due to their skilful playing of the publicity game, enrolling journalists in their cause or using the media to turn otherwise invisible problems into public issues.

Many feminists, not all of them liberals, believe that this is the way to win the battle of the media – by slowly infiltrating feminist ideas and issues until they become a part of everyday public consciousness. The more revolutionary tendencies counter that this strategy works only for reformist demands, and that the result will be to associate feminism in the public mind with nothing but civil rights issues, leaving radicals and socialists out in the cold. Even to introduce serious feminist issues into the mass media is a contradiction, they argue, because the media continue to spread oppressive images of women through their advertising and editorial matter. A not too far-fetched analogy would be for the *Financial Times* to include serious Marxist analyses of the evils of capitalism among its stock market reports. Nothing can be dangerous which appears in such company.

Negative media coverage not only poisons public opinion, but reflects back directly on the movement itself through its influence on supporters. A hundred years ago a movement like socialism or populism might expect that the majority of its followers would read little or nothing but the movement's own papers and newsletters (and, of course, would hear no radio and see no television). Now, a movement is lucky if its followers spend more than a fraction of their time on such reinforcing material; the rest of the time they are immersed in the same media images received by everyone else, including images of *themselves* as socialists, feminists or whatever. Some women who define themselves as feminists have left the movement (often with loud publicity) because they cannot bear to be associated with the images which they, their family and their friends receive through the media.

The definition of news ensures that women in general, not just the women's liberation movement, will occupy a minor and closely defined place. A glance at any newspaper or television news programme will show that individual women feature hardly at all. Female politicians, royalty and actresses appear as news-makers, but the overwhelming majority of what journalists define as news is made by men. A randomly chosen sample of the home news pages in one issue of *The Guardian* daily newspaper in December 1982 contained 96 male names and 5 female names. The females named were: the Queen, the Prime Minister, Dr Shirley Summerskill, the Princess of Wales and Elizabeth Taylor.[20]

If women are invisible or caricatured in the news, they are everywhere in advertising. Feminist scholars regard most advertising as profoundly hostile and damaging to women. After a brief retreat in the early 1970s, the sexism and sex fantasies of the advertising world have returned full force. Adding insult to injury, some advertisers have set out to exploit what they see as the 'liberated woman' market using the same techniques. Protests to controlling bodies like the Advertising Standards Authority have been largely futile, but some groups have kept up the tactic of pasting stickers saying 'This exploits women' on publicly displayed offensive advertisements. Television advertising has been more discreet in its sexual imagery, but worse in portraying women invariably in traditional housewife/mother roles.[21]

In the wider commercial culture, feminists have found the channels of communication equally controlled by an indifferent or hostile establishment. Commercial publishers were quick to exploit the more harmless aspects of feminism (theory and history, for example) while rejecting more overtly political statements. The feminist publishing houses had too few resources to keep the balance and, in any case, they too were subject to the forces of the market – among them the unwillingness of most major bookselling chains to sell radical or unorthodox material.

Only in the USA have strongly feminist books sometimes broken through to best-seller status in the commercial market, Marilyn French's *The Women's Room* being probably the best example. When issued in Britain it was attacked by almost every serious critic as the work of a psychologically disturbed and neurotic person and touted by bookshops as a sensational look into the bizarre lives of middle-class American women.

It is clearly understood that the mass media and the whole commercial culture are part of a market system, not neutral channels of communication. The aims and values of both socialist and radical feminism are fundamentally opposed to the interests of the market's controllers, who can hardly be expected to give a platform to their enemies. There are few ways in which the movement can effectively answer the hostile messages which pour out of the communications industry.

But there are some hopeful signs that the hostility can be overcome. Sympathetic journalists and editors, usually but not always women, have transformed the reporting of women's issues beyond recognition over the past fifteen years. Witness, for example, the thorough and sympathetic reporting of the ERA campaign by almost every major American newspaper, news magazine and television network, and the in-depth analysis of feminist issues like sexual harassment, rape and domestic violence recently seen in sections of the British media. Television images of women are immensely important because they are so pervasive. The advertisements and soap operas have not changed, but most television channels have now introduced female presenters who are not just decorative but who handle hard news, interviews, science and economics. These changes may be, as some feminists claim, mere tokenism; but tokenism, like reform, can offer real footholds for the movement to exploit.

Intellectuals and Renegades

The movement was first organised by university-educated women; some of the earliest groups were formed within the universities themselves. Feminism stood out from the chorus of voices of protest in the late 1960s as a new and exciting cause. Young intellectuals, men as well as women, were attracted by the promise of feminism, which was to open up a new era of honesty and equality in *human* relations.

Somewhere along the way that vision got lost. Male intellectuals and radicals were too slow to respond, or responded in confused and partial ways. As significant parts of the movement hardened their anti-male rhetoric, erstwhile male supporters began to retreat from it. Like the white liberal supporters rejected by the ideologies of black power, they simply walked away, leaving the women's movement with no strong voices in the enemy camp. Some potential advocates had been turned into wary neutrals; some feminists welcomed their silence.

The significance of this becomes clearer when we realise that the interwoven worlds of radical politics, intellectual life and university work are small but crucial as the sources of *avant-garde* social thought. In Chapter 3 it was argued that the problems of social change have now become so complex that the theoretical work of many intellectuals is necessary to determine the what, why and how of any vision of the new and better society. Only when a substantial number of intellectuals in positions of power and influence (teaching, research, publishing, policy-making) become committed to a particular vision will the necessary work be done.

The influence of intellectuals in social change movements is more apparent in countries like the USA and France than in

Britain, where they have always occupied a marginal position. Nowhere do universities and intellectuals convey ideas *directly* to the people, for this is the role of the mass media. But many ideas which take shape in academic conferences, seminars and obscure research journals are conveyed in a diluted form to political and cultural elites (administrators, politicians, writers, film-makers, and so on) and eventually find their way, even more diluted, into the mass media. In this way the frontiers of research for one generation tend to become conventional wisdoms for the next.

What goes on in universities and other educational institutions is therefore not merely intellectual exercise but the creation of a long-term social resource which may be particularly significant for social movements, including feminism. And, to be sure, the academic world has taken an interest in feminism. Hundreds of books and thousands of articles testify to the fact that women have now become a legitimate field of study. This might be taken as a positive sign, implying as it does that long-hidden issues are being taken seriously by people whose business it is to define what is and what is not significant knowledge. But the response from feminists outside the universities, especially in Britain, has been mixed. Academic interest in feminism, particularly on the part of men, has been attacked as a form of exploitation. The present book, for example, was so labelled before a word was written, the debate surrounding its publication reflecting a current of anti-intellectualism which argues that on such highly charged issues as feminism only the voice of the partisan should be heard. Unwilling to start a fight, many university teachers, intellectuals and other social commentators have assented to this with their silence.

Inevitably, then, intellectual debates about feminism became restricted to a limited range of orthodox questions and certified theoretical positions. Women's studies became a feature of the academic scene, another discipline among many with its own special language and special interests. These programmes established themselves against considerable prejudice and hostility within the academic community. They contend with the fact that the status of women in the universities remains low, only a tiny number holding top positions in the most prestigious departments. By definition, anything labelled 'women's studies' will share this low status, and those teaching it tend to find themselves relegated to insecure, untenured positions with poor prospects for promotion.

It should not be denied that women's studies programmes have been enormously important in supporting and informing female students of things which they would never have learned in the traditional university curriculum, and therefore raise the consciousness of a critical sector of the population. Young men who participate also get a new view of the world. But the isolation of women's issues in the intellectual community today looks increasingly like the isolation of black issues in America a decade ago, a recipe for disengagement.

It is hard to see how this could have been avoided. At the start the only hope of survival for women's studies was separation, carving out a special niche for the new discipline and defending it against the interference of the male educational establishment. Yet this same separation allowed the universities to contain the challenge of feminist thought even while appearing to accept it. The movement among feminist intellectuals today is towards a measured integration of women's studies into the mainstream of the humanistic disciplines. Thus women's studies become gender studies and eventually become diffused through the curriculum, appearing as part of the study of inequality, of political power, of economics and the labour market, of literature, of history and of art. The ideal is for knowledge about women to become part of what is accepted as knowledge in general, not a special enclave, and for women's studies to become as redundant as the idea of 'men's studies'. Yet this development would also bring more women into male spheres of power and influence; the passive hostility of university elites might turn into something more open and, perhaps for that reason, easier to fight.

A few intellectuals in the USA have already chosen to mount a direct attack on the assumptions and practices of feminism – especially radical feminism. They can be counted as part of the neo-conservative revival, of which the Moral Majority is the anti-intellectual counterpart.

The most direct of these assaults so far has been Steven

Goldberg's *The Inevitability of Patriarchy*. Goldberg turns his argument against those who believe in the possibility of a past or future matriarchal society, using anthropological and biological research in support. In studying the evidence of anthropology, he claims to find that in *no* society, past or present, has power or authority been invested in women. Even in those few tribes where feminist writers have claimed to find female dominance, his review of the original studies argues the reverse. Patriarchy is truly universal, says Goldberg, as is the subjective perception in all societies that men dominate women. A single exception would destroy his thesis, but there are no exceptions.

The power of males, according to Goldberg, is rooted in their superior power of aggression, not merely in the sense of physical violence but in an innate drive to dominate their environment. Turning to animal and human biological studies, Goldberg argues that the interaction of hormonal differences with male testosterone levels produces higher levels of male aggressivity in all but a tiny number of species, and definitely in the human species. He avoids the nonsensical proposition that all men are more aggressive than all women, preferring to say that the aggregate difference gives men as a group 'a head start that enables them to better deal with those elements of the societal environment for which aggression leads to success'.[22] These elements include all the powerful institutions of society.

Women, he claims, have complementary biological qualities which have led historically to their being assigned different social roles, especially the care of children. The mistake the feminists have made is to assume that these different roles are inferior and, indeed, their proclaiming the fact has made it so. While Goldberg says that biology cannot justify refusing any particular role option to women, he adds that it is socially destructive to socialise them towards endeavours which require male aggression and in which most of them will therefore fail. The existing social and economic arrangements do not cause women to be subordinate to men, they simply conform to the biological fact that women have different human capacities which have been socially defined as inferior. Women have their own sources and spheres of power, which feminism asks them to abandon for a hopeless assault on the powers of men.

Goldberg's general thesis has been supported by male socio-biologists like Edward O. Wilson.[23] But biological arguments are always suspect in politics. Between fact and interpretation, is and ought, there is a huge gap. Feminist responses to such arguments have in the past concentrated more on the interpretations than on the data; the data on biological sex differences are formidable and can only be evaluated by experts. Biology and sociobiology can indeed be used as a red herring to conceal moral and political issues about *how* men use their power, and to persuade women that they have no choice but to resign themselves happily to their destined roles. But feminists also could not ignore the substance of the scientific debate over innate sex differences, and counter-arguments of a scientific form are now beginning to appear.[24] As yet there is no scientific consensus, but the ideological power of science is such that if a consensus unfavourable to women does emerge it will be difficult for non-scientists to challenge. Once cultural habits and popular prejudices are validated by science, they become almost impossible to change.

Compared with Goldberg's work, most other intellectual attacks on feminism have been lightweight, concerned with social and family issues and the protection of traditional values. George F. Gilder's popular *Sexual Suicide*[25] assumes that biological differences exist for a social purpose. The suicide of the title is the fate which he believes will overtake any society which encourages women to abandon their role as mothers. Women socialise and humanise men, transmitting qualities which limit male aggression and make civilisation possible. Once reproduction is turned into just another form of industrial production, Gilder argues, these feminine qualities will atrophy, leaving a society of atomised, competitive individuals without families and without the experience of love. Gilder has since become a minor prophet of the American new right with a book called *Wealth and Poverty*,[26] in which he mounts a fierce attack on the entry of women into the labour market, blaming feminism for many of the current ills of capitalism. Not only do they take away men's jobs, he argues with dubious logic, but they do those jobs far less efficiently. The book would be unimportant if it were not that it was taken very seriously by highly placed members of the Reagan administration.

Among the female conservative intellectuals who have taken up their pens against feminism, Midge Decter is probably the best known and the most widely read. Her point, first put forward in *The New Chastity and Other Arguments Against Women's Liberation*, and repeated in her later writings, is essentially a simple one. The vanguard of the new feminism were spoiled and sheltered children of the upper middle class. Brought up to believe that their lives would be effortlessly perfect, they were stunned and angered to discover that adulthood was really very difficult.

Decter's central theme is choice. Modern women, she asserts, do not lack freedom; on the contrary, they suffer from too much. She sees the whole feminist movement as an effort by frightened women to escape the bitter pills of choice and self-responsibility in their lives by claiming that they have none. The choices women want to escape, according to Decter, are those related to the adult role: being responsible for the welfare of others, handling the complexities of a liberated sexuality, taking risks, and paying the price for one's own mistakes. Adulthood, marriage and above all motherhood do exact a high price from women but, in Decter's eyes, by refusing to pay this price the feminists are signalling their refusal to grow up. Similarly, their realisation that the competitive world of work and professions could lead not only to power and glory but to failure and humiliation led many feminists to reject that world also:

> Terror lies behind Women's Liberation's discussions of work; it is a response not to the experience of exclusion but to the discovery that the pursuit of career is but another form – in some ways more gratifying, in many ways far more bruising – of adult anguish. The equality demanded by the self-proclaimed victim is . . . to be *deemed* equal, no matter what.[27]

In short, Decter charges that the liberation desired by feminists is liberation from the ordinary constraints, demands and obligations of society into a free-floating state of painless equality, and that the purpose of the movement is to allow women to escape from the abrasive experiences of competitive life into a safe, secure, all-female space.

The victim-psychology of the movement has been attacked by many other writers, among them Joan Didion,[28] who, like Decter, see it as little more than a symptom of a post-war society which promised too much too easily. In Britain there has been no similar vein of intellectual criticism, in part because radical feminism has been less visible, and in part because some of the more elitist fantasies of affluent American feminists have been absent. Here, as we shall see in the next chapter, the challenge to utopian feminism has come mainly from within the movement.

Conclusion

Significant sections of the feminist movement have organised themselves as a female counter-culture within patriarchal society rather than as a political crusade for social change. For them, the kinds of opposition described may be tolerable and even useful so long as they do not turn into the outright suppression of life-style choices. The enemies of women's liberation simply validate the distinction between mainstream culture and the feminist alternative.

Groups which do work for specific social changes – reformist or revolutionary – need allies. Practical politics suggests that support may most easily be found in other oppositional groups which have egalitarian aims and ideals compatible with feminist theory, and which already have some measure of political power. Here, the alliances being forged by British socialist feminists with the trade unions and the Labour Party may be crucial in future political struggles.

In the USA economic conditions have undermined the possibility of a potentially powerful coalition between women and ethnic minorities. Blacks, Indians and Chicanos have observed that civil rights and affirmative action programmes have benefited white women at their expense, and the relationship between these minorities and the women's movement has turned sour.

Such conflicts are especially costly because the women's

liberation movement has so few friends and so many powerful enemies. Opposition is not always and entirely a negative force in social movements. It can create a sense of solidarity and significance, which is better than the empty sensation of being ignored. But when opposition comes from so many directions in so many different forms, and the movement is not organised to make any effective response, a siege mentality is likely to appear. The low profile of the British movement has somewhat protected it from the public attacks which have shaken feminists in America. But a low profile, in politics as in war, is a defensive position.

7. Testing Times: the Women's Movement Today

Feminism today is a universal movement touching every aspect of politics and daily life. In its broadest definition, feminism includes women and men who advocate pro-woman issues in governments, political parties, trade unions, schools, universities and the mass media, as well as socialist groups, radical separatists, consciousness-raising groups, peace campaigners and women's centre volunteers.

This protean character makes it difficult to draw an adequate picture of 'the movement', especially as there is no consensus about who can and cannot be counted a feminist. The practice in this book has been to include any group or organisation which so defines itself, though this clearly excludes many people who support some or all of the aims of women's liberation. But within the narrower definition how many women in how many groups are involved in the actions which have been described? The only comprehensive listings of groups are kept by women's information services, which are understandably reluctant to reveal total numbers, and the groups themselves often keep no formal membership lists.

If we confine our attention to *activists*, those who subscribe to journals and newsletters, go on marches and attend conferences, an educated guess is possible. In Britain there are roughly 300 feminist groups of all types, and the total number of women actively and regularly involved probably does not exceed 10,000, with perhaps twice that number marginally or occasionally active. At the core of the active group are the super-activists, perhaps 2,000 radical/revolutionary feminists and an approximately equal number of socialists and Marxist feminists. These are the people who do the work of the movement, and who devote almost their whole lives to it.

Such modest numbers do not add up to a mass movement, though they compare favourably with the support base of most radical organisations. The most generous estimate of sometimes active participants (20,000) would comprise only one-tenth of 1 per cent of the adult female population, or one woman in a thousand. By contrast, the Women's Institute (WIs) and other associations for housewives have combined memberships in excess of half a million. Yet on special issues like abortion up to 60,000 women have turned out for demonstrations, and over 30,000 joined an anti-nuclear protest at Greenham Common in Berkshire in December 1982. Whether or not all these are 'feminists' in the narrow sense, their numbers certainly indicate a growing potential base of support for the British women's liberation movement.

But sheer size is not the most significant attribute of a social movement and, as women's liberation has already clearly demonstrated, a small but determined group can have an impact out of all proportion to its numbers. Activism and commitment are potent weapons in a passive political culture, and these are the greatest strengths of the contemporary women's movement.

Activity is heavily concentrated in large urban areas, and especially in certain strongholds like London, Bristol, Leeds, Nottingham and Sheffield. The movement has gained strength in Scotland since 1977, with a wide range of activities in Aberdeen, Dundee, Edinburgh and Glasgow and smaller groups scattered in half a dozen towns. Scottish women's liberation seems to attract a higher proportion of working-class women, and male violence in this strongly patriarchal society is a central issue for them. There are also nationalist overtones in the Scottish movement, and it has developed its own journals (*Scottish Women's Liberation Journal*, *Ms Print*, *Nessie*) to combat what is seen as the domination of feminism by English women. In the hostile atmosphere of Wales and Northern Ireland, the movement has been still slower to develop, though groups and campaigns exist in the cities. Though small, women's liberation is nationwide in its scope.

The movement remains resolutely unstructured. Local

organisation is based on the women's centre, and these now exist in about forty British cities. The centres act as information sources, often carrying substantial libraries of legal and welfare books and pamphlets; they may offer personal counselling, advice on housing, health, contraception and abortion, referral services and social events. The growth of women's centres was indicated by the calling of a National Women's Centre Conference in 1981. Along with their more practical aims, the centres have proved to be an effective way of attracting working-class women to the movement. The consciousness-raising groups of the early days have not vanished from the scene – a current issue of *Spare Rib* lists forty open to new members throughout the country – but they are now valued more as a stage in the development of a feminist group than as an end in themselves.

A typical provincial city in England will have one or more active consciousness-raising groups; a women's centre; a shelter for battered women; a rape crisis centre; a branch of the National Abortion Campaign; a nursery campaign or co-operative; a lesbian group or nightline; a health group; one or several arts or writing groups; one or more groups for socialist women; a revolutionary feminist group; a bookshop; one or more newsletters. In addition, depending on local interests, a number of still more specialised small groups may emerge from time to time (Rock Against Sexism, Women Against Racism and Fascism, Girls Against Sexism, Working Class Women, Women Opposed to the Nuclear Threat). The memberships of these groups are often overlapping and interlocking, and the women's centre will act as a clearing-house for contacts and information in the city. Some women will be into alternative lifestyles, some into single-issue campaigns, some are full- or part-time workers in social services functions like refuges, and some are writers and theorists.

This fruitful chaos defies all the conventional wisdoms about the development and survival of social movements. Historically, movements have had a common tendency to become more centralised, more bureaucratic, more professional and less radical as they get older. If anything, the British women's movement has moved in the opposite direction, though there are a very few women who may be regarded as 'professional feminists' in journalism, the academic world and trade unions.

In America the women's movement has come closer to the conventional pattern of development. Liberal feminism is part of the political mainstream, and attracts a vastly greater following among women and men than the political sub-culture which is the base of the British movement. A poll taken in 1981 indicated that 4 per cent of women and 2 per cent of men were either members of or contributors to an organisation promoting women's rights;[1] in crude numbers this means about 3 million women and $1\frac{1}{2}$ million men. In terms of resources alone this makes the American feminist movement richer than any in the world. The National Organisation for Women (NOW) claims 175,000 members, Women's Equity Action League (WEAL) 10,000 members, Women's Political Caucus 35,000 members. In all, the large liberal feminist organisations can probably claim the active support of around 300,000 (mostly middle-class) women and men. Half a million read the magazine *Ms*. For comparison, traditional women's groups have combined memberships of nearly three million, but nevertheless the American liberal feminist organisations have a mass character which does not appear in the British movement.

Along with such levels of support and funding comes a certain professionalisation. Far more than in Britain, the American movement now provides attractive career opportunities in everything from journalism and publishing to office management, lobbying, law, accountancy, health and counselling. Many women also give their time and energy for nothing but, at the core of the movement, there is a substantial group of highly trained professionals for whom feminism is a rewarding career, and their interests define the tone and temper of liberal feminism in America.

On the periphery, however, are the still active radicals. Every town and city has one or more radical feminist groups, and estimating their numbers is difficult. The groups are not as fluid and changeable as they were in the early years, but they have no central co-ordinating agency and no membership lists. Using similar evidence from the circulation of journals, attendance at conferences and related measures, it is possible to guess that a total of some 50,000 women are actively involved in radical and/or socialist feminist groups all over America. This figure is more closely comparable with the involvement of British women, and represents a slightly smaller proportion of the adult female population. But if we include the liberal feminist organisations, about one American woman in 300 has contact with a feminist group of some kind.

Numbers aside, the patterns of activity outside the liberal mainstream are similar to those described for Britain. Any city will provide a listing of women's groups concerned with violence, rape, pornography, abortion, lesbian rights, health, nurseries, and so on. Most will also have special groups for black, chicano and native American women. While the campaign for the ERA continued, radical and liberal feminists submerged their differences in united efforts to influence the legislators in their local areas, especially in those states where the ERA was still to be ratified. Even in times of economic recession and political conservatism, the women's movement in America remains a visible and formidable force.

By the early 1970s every Western country had developed a feminist movement adapted to the history, culture and politics of its own society. The one common factor has been the diversity and decentralisation practised within those movements and the wide variety of groups, theories and tactics which have found expression under the banner of each national form of women's liberation. In Europe the pattern of development has tended to reinforce the thesis that, in modern societies, social movements do best in political cultures which already have strong egalitarian and liberal commitments. Thus the largest and most integrated feminist organisations are to be found in the Scandinavian countries and in Holland (where, in 1981, feminists were able to organise a million women out of six million in a strike against restrictive abortion laws).

Countries with more traditional or authoritarian cultures, like France, Germany, Italy, Spain, Belgium and Greece, have presented feminists with more difficult challenges, but there have still been some remarkable successes. In conservative and Catholic Italy, for example, women have gained rights to divorce, equal pay and limited abortion which would have been inconceivable ten years ago. French feminists pushed through equal pay laws in 1972 and a legalised abortion law in 1975, and France has a government minister for women's rights. Abortion remains the major issue in countries where it is still illegal or strictly limited, like Spain, Germany and Belgium.

Where national movements have succeeded in their basic civil rights aims there has, as in Britain, been a tendency for feminism to fragment into confused factions, uncertain how to attack the broader ideological and cultural forces which oppress women. The French feminist movement has turned into a battleground of sects, with one small and powerful group called *Des Femmes/Psyche & Po* aiming to take control of all feminist publishing and even appropriating to itself the exclusive use of the title *Mouvement de libération des femmes* (women's liberation movement).

The cause of women's equality has been taken up by the European Economic Community (EEC), which in 1981 published a 16-point plan for a Community-wide campaign against discrimination. Many cases of employment discrimination have already been heard in the European Court of Justice, but such initiatives do not appear to be supported by any great groundswell of public opinion. The court has been unwilling to touch issues on which public opinion is much stronger, like abortion rights.

Worldwide, the feminist movement is so diverse as to defy proper description. An international meeting of feminists at Haifa, Israel, in 1981 brought together scholars and activists from Europe, India, Africa, the Middle East, Japan, Latin America and North America. Their common concerns with family, childbirth, child care and economic independence provided a basis for discussion and the sharing of knowledge; but the vastly different cultural contexts in which those concerns had to be turned into practical politics were reflected in the unique nature of each national feminist movement. International contacts are managed mainly through the International Feminist Network and its information service, ISIS, based in Italy and Switzerland.

In the communist world there are no open movements for women's liberation. During the late 1960s some feminists had an image of China as a nation where the differences and disadvantages of sex had been wiped out in an androgynous uniformity of work, dress and education. This image has dissolved as China has been more fully observed by Western journalists, who have noted not only the absence of women in positions of power but a concerted effort by the Chinese hierarchy to reimpose traditional family patterns and sex roles after the upheavals of the Cultural Revolution. In the Soviet Union a tiny underground feminist movement appeared in 1979, attracted the attention of the KGB and has since been repressed, with a number of its leaders arrested. Many Russian feminists, like other dissenters, have been forced into exile.

In the late twentieth century there has been a near universal upsurge of feminist consciousness, almost certainly due to the ease with which ideas, values and aspirations can be transmitted from one culture to another. Even in those places where it has been most brutally suppressed, like post-revolutionary Iran, the idea of women's liberation has managed to survive as a secret vision.

Balance-Sheet: The State of the Campaigns in Britain

The seven demands of the British women's liberation movement have been a curious and not entirely satisfactory framework for campaigning. Over the years they have entered the agenda of the movement in a variety of ways, none of which can be said to reflect a democratic consensus of all the women in the movement. The result is an odd mixture of socialist, civil rights and welfare issues with revolutionary cultural demands. There is a continuing debate over the relevance of the seven demands, but in the absence of national conferences since 1978 there is no agreed way of changing them. On the other hand, the demands have no policy-defining power, and no particular women's group need pay any attention to them at all. The purpose of the demands is therefore unclear, yet, by virtue of their existence, they exercise a kind of constraint on British feminists, and the most important campaigns have been built around them. In reviewing the state of the British movement it is therefore appropriate to use the seven demands as an organising principle to show what has been accomplished, and what remains to be done.

The demands are preceded by the sentence: 'We assert a woman's right to define her own sexuality and demand':

1. 'Equal Pay for Equal Work'

This demand, as a statement of a basic principle of fairness, has won almost universal public and political assent and was written into law by the Equal Pay Act of 1975. Yet between 1977 and 1982 the wage gap between women and men actually grew wider; by 1982 a working woman could expect to earn less than two-thirds of a working man's hourly wage.[2] The fatal flaw in the equal pay legislation, from the point of view of improving the market situation of women, was that equality was only guaranteed for 'the same or mainly similar work'. This phrase not only gave employers endless opportunities for avoiding the law by redefining jobs and restricting women to all-female tasks, but it entirely avoided issues like the quality of women's work lives, insecurity and exploitation.

For those women not already protected by trade unions, the feminist movement has been able to do very little; as we have already argued, it is not organised to deal with such issues and does not really aim to do so. The industrial tribunals have dealt with a steadily diminishing number of equal pay cases, and many trade unions have also been unenthusiastic about getting involved, given the resistance from their male members.

It is therefore not clear exactly where equal pay now stands as a *campaign* issue. Some sectors of the movement hold that equal pay for equal *work* is a demand which distracts attention from the plight of the non-waged, including housewives, and should therefore be changed to a demand for a universal social wage or dropped altogether. The Working Women's Charter, which was the campaign most fully involved with equal pay, was moribund by 1979. Socialist feminist groups have continued to protest against working conditions, low pay and redundancy, and to intervene in some industrial disputes, and a Women's Right to Work Campaign was launched in 1981. Women's unemployment, always chronic, has become acute in the 1980s, and industrial actions increasingly fail. The problem seems to be a structural one – the existence of a large pool of unskilled female workers at the bottom of the labour market whose conditions are made more precarious by economic depression. Only a dramatic change in the whole structure of the market would alleviate this condition in the long term; meanwhile the movement can only campaign to protect women from its worst effects.

2. 'Equal Opportunity and Equal Education'

The great influx of women into paid employment after the Second World War was a revolutionary change in the labour market. But, like immigrants or any new group entering the labour force, women started at the bottom. The campaigns around the second demand are designed to change the practices and prejudices that operate to keep them there.

In broad outline the disadvantages affecting working women are well known, and are very well documented elsewhere.[3] Despite the enthusiasm of newspapers for citing 'firsts' – the first fire fighter, bus driver, brain surgeon, deep sea diver, etc. – the broader pattern has been depressingly slow to change. An Equal Opportunities Commission Study report showed the familiar picture of women concentrated in unskilled manual, junior non-manual and service jobs, while men made up 95 per cent of foremen and supervisors, 91 per cent of skilled manual workers, 89 per cent of professional and managerial staff and 87 per cent of employers and managers.[4] Although the same study suggested that employers had become somewhat less prejudiced against women at the top in the past five years, many still resisted giving women promotion because of beliefs about female psychology and/or the pressures of family life. Even for women who achieve professional status, strong barriers against promotion still operate. In Britain, for example, some 25 per cent of doctors are women but only 9 per cent of consultants, half of all law students but only 10 per cent of practising barristers and solicitors and less than 3 per cent of high court judges, 10 per cent of university teachers but only 1 per cent of full professors.

In part this is simply a factor of the late and restricted entry of women into many fields of work, but it provides a strong campaigning issue. However, only liberal and moderate social-ist feminists are in a position to take advantage of it, since it makes little sense for revolutionary socialists to claim a better share in the capitalist system or for radicals to join in the power struggles of patriarchal organisations. As a result, the struggle for equal opportunities goes on at the margins of the women's liberation movement. The affirmative action programmes which have been successful for trained women in America form the basis of a campaign on Positive Action for Women launched in 1981 by the National Council for Civil Liberties with support from *Spare Rib* magazine and the Rights of Women collective. A journal, *Equal Opportunities International*, was launched in the same year to co-ordinate information in this area.

Another American idea which has recently taken hold in Britain is the women's network: the feminine equivalent of the traditional and powerful 'old-boy' networks. Women, mainly professionals concerned to improve opportunities for themselves and others like them, have begun to organise as informal support groups and information exchanges, unconnected with the existing feminist organisations. Because of their separate, highly individualist ethic and because they draw off talented and energetic women, their style of 'emancipationist' or self-help feminism has been treated by some British feminists as a possibly damaging tendency.[5]

Equal education, like equal job opportunity, is enshrined in the Sex Discrimination Act but has not been the object of much positive government action. Many detailed studies have been made of sex differences in learning, and the major problems are generally understood.[6] At the family level there is the need to make parents conscious of sexist child-rearing practices and – more difficult – to persuade them to change. In the schools, despite some recent improvements, a strong trend remains to teach boys and girls differently and to encourage them towards different subject areas, the boys taking by a three to one ratio the science and technical subjects which lead to economic success. This bias carries over into job training, where boys get nearly 90 per cent of skilled and technical apprenticeships, and into higher education, where few girls enter the most prestigious scientific and professional fields. It is well established that girls attending single-sex schools are more likely to choose professionally and economically rewarding subjects, and to follow through into more successful university and work careers. In part this must be a result of the generally superior quality of single-sex schools, but there has been much debate over the singularly difficult question whether sex equality in education might best be achieved by sex segregation, with all its echoes of 'separate but equal'.[7]

Initiatives in education and job training are not within the scope of a small, poorly funded social movement. Research and policy have been mainly in the hands of the Equal Opportunities Commission and the Manpower Services Commission, both of which have promoted better training and positive action for new and returning women workers. Funding for such agencies has come under pressure from public expenditure cuts in the 1980s, but the feminist movement has no alternative strategy or resource adequate to the scope of the second demand.

3. 'Free Contraception and Abortion on Demand'

In practice, the campaigns around this demand have been almost entirely concerned with defending the limited rights to abortion already conceded under the 1967 Act. As it stands, and in the present political climate, the full demand is utopian, at best a consciousness-raising device. Despite support from the Labour Party through the Labour Abortion Rights Campaign (LARC), and even a small conference grant from the EOC, the women's movement appears to be losing ground on this issue. Economic cutbacks have also affected the ability of Area Health Authorities to provide contraception under the 1975 legislation.

In March 1981 the Department of Health and Social Security used its powers to alter the grounds on which a doctor could legally perform an abortion. Instead of a choice between medical and social grounds, doctors were now required to state medical grounds only. Those who refused to conform may be subjected to police investigation. Potentially, this is a drastic curtailment of the right to abortion; over a million abortions have been performed on social grounds since 1967, and these would presumably now be illegal. The NAC, LARC and ALRA, already taxed by the year-long campaign against the Corrie anti-abortion bill, mobilised again against the new regulation. So far it has not been rigidly applied, since the government is unwilling to enter a major confrontation on this issue, particularly as this would bring them into conflict with a medical establishment chronically jealous of its professional autonomy. But the undermining of the abortion rights principle is part of a conservative backlash which, in Britain as much as in the USA, aims to stop the movement for women's liberation in its tracks. In 1982 another attempt to tighten the Abortion Act was made by Lord Robertson, and MP John Corrie has been under pressure to reintroduce his ill-fated 1979 bill.

The disagreement previously described between women who argue that abortion is purely a women's liberation issue and those in the National Abortion Campaign who would prefer to treat it as a class issue still continues. Trade-union and Labour Party support has been essential in holding off the threat to abortion rights, but it has also been divisive and creates a sharp point of conflict between separatists and socialists which emerges whenever large demonstrations are organised which include men.

4. 'Free Community Controlled Child Care'

In Chapter 4, the significance and the difficulty of the fourth demand were explained. Child care does not arouse the religious and emotive opposition which the abortion campaign must face; it is far more directly an economic issue. The 1960s' faith that the state could be coerced into unlimited welfare expenditures has taken a hard knock in recent years, and the full cost of free 24-hour child care is almost incalculable. By 1982, despite modest support from the TUC and some unions, the desperate need of working mothers for free or cheap child care was as far as ever from being fulfilled. There has been an increase in the absolute numbers of nursery places available for under-5s, from 261,000 in 1970 to 429,000 in 1980, but this does not begin to cover the need, nor do the limited hours of nurseries cover the working hours of many mothers.

Here again, as long as the present cuts in public expenditure continue, the women's movement seems powerless to act effectively. An alternative strategy to the existing demand would be to campaign for flexible working hours for both men and women, to enable child care to be more easily managed by families. But this would fall far short of the liberating potential of the existing fourth demand. Meanwhile the self-help tactic of organising child-care centres staffed by volunteers at the local level remains the most practical use of resources in this area.

5. 'Legal and Financial Independence for All Women'

With the fifth demand we are back in the traditional realm of civil rights. Legal and financial independence is a campaign for equality and justice rather than a claim on the state for special benefits for women. The concessions gained by the campaign up until 1978 were outlined in Chapter 4. Changes in social security and taxation rules had by then partially undermined the conventional government approach to the 'family wage', i.e. the treatment of wives and husbands as a single economic unit in which the wife (or cohabiting woman) was treated as an absolute dependant.

Two groups have quietly pressed ahead with the hard and detailed work of exposing the remaining areas of legal and financial discrimination. One is the Campaign for Financial and Legal Independence, already described (pp. 109–10), and the other is an organisation of women legal workers called Rights of Women (ROW). Their common aim is to have every adult treated as an independent individual for legal and social security purposes.

Under pressure from these groups, together with the NCCL, the EOC and the EEC Commission, the government has reluctantly sustained a low-key debate on the issues, with a review of supplementary benefits in 1978 and a Green Paper on taxation in 1982. But none of the proposals has come close to satisfying the demands of the campaign, and the current combination of public spending cuts and conservative family policies offer little hope of immediate change. Given the undisputed justice of the demand, however, it seems probable that a series of small incremental improvements spread over a number of years will eventually have the desired result as successive governments reluctantly accept the precedents set by previous legislation.

6. *'An End to All Discrimination Against Lesbians'*

This is a difficult issue on which to campaign, since there is no law which supports discrimination against lesbians. Between 1974, when the demand was first added to the agenda, and 1981 it existed more as a statement of principle than a campaign. Yet numerous cases of informal discrimination against lesbians, particularly in employment, were known to exist, and in 1981 a campaign was started to add a clause to the Sex Discrimination Act making it illegal to treat someone less favourably on the grounds of their known or suspected sexual preference. With the National Lesbian Conference and the NCCL behind it, the campaign immediately attracted wide support in the movement but, at the time of writing, it is too early to say whether enough pressure can be brought to introduce a parliamentary bill on these lines or what its fate would be.

In the past two or three years there has also been far more discussion within the women's movement of the problems of lesbian mothers, and it is likely that this will develop into a distinct campaign during the 1980s.

7. *'Freedom for all women from intimidation by the threat or use of violence or sexual coercion, regardless of marital status. An end to all laws, assumptions and institutions that perpetuate male dominance and men's aggression towards women.'*

The seventh demand introduced in 1978 is, like the sixth, more a statement of principles than a specific campaigning issue. It implies not merely changes in the law but a revolution in culture and attitudes, particularly male attitudes. The feminist movement has not yet developed a theory of cultural change adequate to the challenge presented by this demand. Instead, the focus on male violence has given rise to a number of specific issue campaigns (described in Chapter 5) which seem certain to continue and grow in the 1980s.

The deepening economic recession has brought with it an increase in all forms of male violence against women. Idle men on the streets or at home have an increased potential for violence, and women are left with fewer opportunities for economic independence which, in better times, might provide an escape route. In response the campaigns against violence have increased in intensity.

Women Against Violence Against Women held their first national conference in 1981, with 800 participants, and have been highly active in publicising the problem. A campaign against rape in marriage was successfully launched in the same year, and the Women Against Rape group have continued to press for improvements in the treatment of rape victims, including automatic compensation from the Criminal Injuries Compensation Board. Although no further improvements in the law have been achieved, there is evidence that the mass media and some MPs have begun to take rape more seriously, though this attitude has yet to filter up to the judiciary.

The most visible actions in support of the seventh demand have been the 'reclaim the night' marches, now a regular event in many cities, and the continuing series of protests, pickets and physical attacks against sex shops and pornographic cinemas. The violence which has sometimes accompanied these actions poses a moral problem for a movement deeply opposed to violence, and raises again all the old debates about the value of civil disobedience. In a few cases, (empty) sex shops have been attacked with petrol bombs, and some women have expressed disquiet at the implications of the use of such potentially lethal weapons.

Although these campaigns are simply guerrilla tactics against a hostile culture, and do not pretend to attack its foundations, they have been very successful in raising the general level of consciousness about male violence against women. For the victims of violence, the Women's Aid movement for battered women, rape crisis centres and similar support services continue to expand in response to an apparently unlimited demand.

Beyond the Seven Demands

The seven demands are far from being a full statement of the politics of the women's liberation movement. Not all feminists agree with all of them, not all believe they are achievable short of revolution. And work goes on in many areas of interest to women but which are not covered by the existing demands. Wages for Housework is an obvious example, rejected by national conferences but still the centre of an energetic campaign. Perhaps the three issues most conspicuous by their absence from the formal programme are health, racism and peace.

The nature and quality of health care available to women has increasingly been a matter for concern. The attitudes of the medical profession, especially in areas like gynaecology and obstetrics, are experienced by many women as patronising and humiliating, and provoke feelings of helplessness and anger. The poor quality of care for women and children generally and the prohibitive cost of private treatment are also substantial issues. Medical school admission discriminates against women, and the male power structure of the profession continues to discriminate against those who do qualify. A partial solution, favoured by some American feminist groups, is to set up collective health care centres with volunteer help; another tactic is to publish medical information which concerns women in an accessible form in order to demystify the knowledge which doctors like to keep to themselves.

Local campaigns for medical treatment more responsive to women's needs – 'well woman clinics' – have begun to gather support, and a movement for woman-controlled childbirth seems likely to become one of the major feminist issues of the 1980s, along with a campaign for safer contraception techniques.

Other health issues are only just beginning to emerge. Cigarette smoking among women is on the increase, though men now smoke much less. Bobbie Jackson's *The Ladykillers* pointed out the hazards for the physical and mental health of women, already well known, and argued that smoking is a feminist issue, since male-run companies and male-inspired advertising were exploiting women for profit.[8] Weight has become an issue:[9] both the social stigma of overweight and the associated risks of dieting and anorexia. And alcoholism, like smoking, has risen sharply among young women during the past decade. The most recent research suggests that high alcohol consumption may be much more physically dangerous for women than for men, as well as being more highly stigmatised by society.

Racism, debated in the American movement for years, has only become prominent in the British movement very recently. Prompted by the treatment of immigrant women and by racial violence in British cities, left groups like Women Against Racism and Fascism (WARF) and Women Against Imperialism (WAI) have begun to campaign for a specific anti-racist statement in the platform of the women's liberation movement.

The awareness of racism as an issue stimulated questions from black women about racism *within* the women's movement. The proposition that all men should take responsibility for sexism because all men benefit from male power has been turned against the mainly white women's liberation movement. Black women have argued that, by the same logic, white feminists should share responsibility for racism since whites as a group are the oppressors of blacks as a group, and benefit from this oppression. Since about 1980 this painful question has been raised several times and widely debated in the British movement.[10]

The election of hawkish, right-wing leaders in Britain and America and the sharp escalation of the arms race gave rise to a renewed concern about nuclear war and a revival of the peace movement. If war is the ultimate form of male violence, then disarmament is *par excellence* a women's movement issue, well illustrated by the slogan 'Take the toys from the boys.' Groups like Women Opposed to Nuclear Threat (WONT) sprang up and, in August 1982, a group of women set up a peace camp at an American base at Greenham Common in Berkshire, and remained there. In December 1982 women were invited to encircle the nine-mile perimeter of the base, and the outcome was an unprecedented *coup de théâtre*. Some 30,000 women came to join the protest, covering the perimeter fence with banners, children's pictures, toys and clothes. Partly because it was an all-women protest (men being assigned a service role in a restricted area), it attracted huge and mainly sympathetic press coverage. Other camps were established at other bases, some all-female and some mixed. Although the women's peace movement is not feminist in the narrow sense, it clearly has the potential to become a true mass movement of women and a uniquely powerful campaign for raising consciousness about violence.

Many women have also seen a natural link between nuclear concerns and the ecological movement, and a unifying network called Women for Life on Earth exists to develop this theme.

While health, racism and peace are therefore clear and natural issues for the women's liberation movement in the next decade, two topics are still so fundamentally disputed that they are unlikely to find their way into a national feminist platform in Britain: the role of women in politics, and the role of women in the family.

More Issues for the 1980s: Women in Politics

Women have no shared interests *as women* which cut across all other divisions of race, class, status and age, with the possible exception of male violence. Wealthy women have no personal interest in free abortion or social security, powerful and successful women have no personal interest in equal opportunity or equal pay. The politics of women's liberation have been intrinsically the politics of women who are powerless, excluded or otherwise vulnerable; in the British political spectrum their natural alignment has been to the left.

Yet the movement has been slow to seek a power base in the mainstream of left-wing politics, where women's votes might be drawn in support of women's issues. Both radical and socialist feminist theories entail a profound mistrust of the existing structures of power, and present feminist women who seek power with a painful dilemma: is the end worth the means? Indeed, is it even possible for a committed feminist to enter the world of power without abandoning and selling out other women? The records of many female politicians hardly support the notion that women with power are *ipso facto* supporters of women's interests: 'One prime minister doesn't make a matriarchy', as *Spare Rib* remarked on Mrs Thatcher's election; and indeed the records of highly placed parliamentarians like Jill Knight and Sally Oppenheim do not give cause for much optimism.

The women's liberation movement has two options in mainstream politics: to work for the election of candidates within the liberal-left spectrum who are committed to support the movement's main demands; or to field candidates of its own on behalf of a separate 'women's party'. The latter option has not been seriously considered. There seems an argument to be made that, almost regardless of their politics, a greater number of women in power would be good for women's liberation. As more and more women enter the labour market, it may be expected that their political awareness and participation will increase. Once the isolation of the family is broken, women perceive how the political process may serve their interests. They want a voice in the future, in the choice between peace and nuclear war, between corporate profits and social security, and all the other issues that affect their lives. In the past women have been under-registered as voters; this is changing. They have been stereotyped as incurably conservative, a 'fact' which is merely a product of age distribution – more older women are alive to vote, and older people tend to vote conservative for generational reasons.[11] Moreover, the most recent evidence suggests that the traditional gender gap in voting patterns is quickly vanishing, and that women are likely to be less conservative than men on issues concerning peace and social services.[12] To dismiss the potential participation of women in politics as a waste of time therefore seems shortsighted. Many of the movement's demands are achievable through normal political processes, if only enough women are involved.

There is a long way to go. With only 19 seats gained in the 1979 election (11 Labour) and a success rate of about 12 per cent in local government campaigns, women are hardly sweeping to power through the democratic process. But attention is being focused on the barriers which the electoral and party systems raise against them. The procedure by which candidates are adopted is private, and both parties have played the game of adopting more and more female candidates ('we believe in equality, you see') but placing them in unwinnable seats ('how unfortunate').[13] This is a tactic which can be and is challenged from within the parties. More difficult to handle are the stresses of candidacy and public office which fall more oppressively on women than on men. Most women politicians have family responsibilities which bear heavily on them: many are single parents with the double burden of domestic duties and the searching scrutiny which public office brings to bear on their personal lives. But these are defects of the system, not facts of nature. If more women candidates are selected for good seats, and better support systems provided for women in politics at every level, there is not the slightest reason to suppose that women cannot achieve their due share of political power.

In 1980 Women in Media and the Fawcett Society brought together delegates from some fifty organisations and groups for a Women's Day of Action to draw up an agenda for placing more women in positions of power.

In pursuit of this goal the '300 Group' was formed. This national, multi-party group aims to train and organise women for successful political candidacy. It has quickly attracted 1,500 members, and plans to set up fifty regional groups. The title refers to the number of women MPs necessary to bring a near-equal representation of women in the (at present) 635-seat House of Commons.

By the end of 1982 by-elections had brought the number of women MPs up to 24, three of the five new members being from the Labour Party. Nevertheless, while the female half of the population continues to elect parliaments which are 96 per cent male, it is clear that organisations like the 300 Group have a wider problem than just promoting suitable female candidates; they must also convince women to vote for women.

Within the Labour Party feminist activists have begun to make an impact in the constituencies, and the Labour Party Women's Conference and the Women's Action Committee of the Campaign for Labour Party Democracy have become forums for pro-women policies. In the trade unions, while women are still largely excluded from the top leadership positions,[14] similar pressure tactics by women's caucuses are beginning to show results, the most dramatic being the TUC's decision to support abortion rights.

Radical and revolutionary feminists may despise these manoeuvres, but the socialist feminist political elite believe that real progress will only come if power is wrested from men through the political process: 'We must seek to wield power ourselves – *as feminists*. That is, unless we are content to ask favours of powerful men for the rest of our days.'[15]

More Issues for the 1980s: Women, Motherhood and the Family

The debate on the family has been inhibited for much the same reasons as the debate on women in power: it demands a reconciliation between contradictory principles which lie at the very heart of the movement. When the new feminism first emerged, the existing patterns of motherhood and family life were recognised as crucial aspects of women's subordination. Socialist feminists theorised that the family was a device for the exploitation of women as unpaid houseworkers and child-minders. Thus the family served the purposes of the capitalist state, a fact demonstrated by the many ways in which state policy was and is used to reinforce traditional family patterns. Radical feminists identified the family, and the biological function of motherhood, as the central institutions of male power, serving to enslave women in the interests of men.

In the late 1960s and early 1970s, therefore, significant numbers of young feminists rejected the whole package – monogamous marriage, motherhood and family life – as a bad life-choice for any woman. Their rejection was made easier by the facts that, technically speaking, maternity was now a choice rather than an inescapable destiny and careers more readily available. The whole social atmosphere from which the women's movement emerged was one which exalted personal freedom and self-development, an atmosphere entirely alien to the restrictions and responsibilities of family. Some radicals envisaged a utopian future where childbirth would, through science, be removed from the domain of women's bodies altogether.

As the decade moved on, these attitudes became harder to maintain, in part because of the deep hostility of many women outside the movement, but in part also because they were very difficult to live out in practice. The apparently simple matter of housing is one instance. Housing (in Britain especially) is almost entirely designed for the family, not for single or communal life. The many communal alternatives which were tried proved unexpectedly difficult, for both practical and psychological reasons.

But, at bottom, the problem with the original critiques of the nuclear family was that so many women continued to want children, and indeed to want marriage. Despite the soaring divorce rate, marriage (and remarriage) continued to be almost universally popular. A 1980 poll asked women to name their ideal life-style choice: 74 per cent chose marriage with children, 10 per cent marriage without children and only 8 per cent looked forward to single life (the balance were undecided).[16] In the past five years a clear trend has emerged among working women towards starting families in their mid-30s, and the mid-1970s' slump in the birthrate has given way to a minor baby boom. Women who grew to maturity in the anti-family ethos of the late 1960s are changing their minds.

What are feminists to make of this? The objective conditions of marriage and motherhood have not changed. Feminism is up against a biological force, or an unbreakable ideology, or both, and a new political analysis of marriage and motherhood has become a matter of the most urgent necessity.

One such analysis comes out of the radical pro-woman line, and argues that women's most special and unique quality is their ability to bear children. A theoretical separation therefore has to be made between motherhood (which is good for women, if they desire it) and the heterosexual, nuclear family (which is bad for women). Thus some sections of the radical movement have stopped denigrating the maternal role, and have begun to idealise it as an essential stage in feminine self-fulfilment. In this vision, maternity is freed from the domination of men and the resulting families consist of and are controlled entirely by women, which is to say that they are pure *matriarchal* families. Fertility, in the matriarchal family, is to be controlled by women through artificial self-insemination.

A second approach to feminist motherhood, coming out of the liberal tradition, takes a totally different line. The spokeswoman for this new idea is Betty Friedan, whose 1981 book *The Second Stage* has caused something of an uproar in feminist circles in America and in Britain. Friedan proposed that the cost of the first stage of feminism for women had been too high.

Many of the civil rights gains had proved to be illusory (no news there for radicals), and women had been lured by the promise of equality into a whole new set of traps. Some tried to be superwomen, wearing themselves out in a hopeless effort to manage career and family together, and often failing at both. Others, accepting the anti-family rhetoric of the first stage, have gone too far in the opposite direction. They found themselves isolated in what Friedan called a 'half-life of reaction', having rejected both family and career to pursue an ideology which could offer them nothing in exchange but an abstract concept of justice.

In place of the feminine mystique which she herself exposed in the early 1960s Friedan argued that a 'feminist mystique' had grown up which was equally stereotyped, rigid and restrictive. Feminists escaped from one set of orthodoxies only to lock themselves into another in which opinions, appearance, politics and sexuality were all prescribed.

From this argument grew the concept of a second stage of feminism which would embrace all women, not just the committed few, and which would have the family as its focus. In the second stage men would be equally involved with women in reshaping the relationships between home and work and between mothers, fathers and children. What were now women's politics, said Friedan, would become human politics, reshaping the whole sexual division of labour so that work would no longer be the primary source of male identity, nor home of female identity. A revolution in work organisation would be needed as much as a revolution in attitudes, but Friedan saw both as possible in a world where so many women and men were unhappy with their existing choices.

The book struck a responsive chord, in part because it revived the familiar and popular idea of the companionate family as a structure for sharing life. In the USA at least the image of the domestic or 'nurturing' father was received with remarkable enthusiasm. A whole issue of *Ms* magazine (February 1982) was devoted to the theme, and fathers with children suddenly began to appear in advertising.

As she had done in the 1960s, Friedan was picking up on a current of change already in progress. The *dual-career family* with shared responsibilities had been an emerging pattern in

America and Britain for years. In New York a career and family centre called Catalyst had been functioning since 1962 to provide advice and information for such families, and the service was greatly expanded in the late 1970s. Friedan's point was that, if this is the wave of the future, feminists should consider how to assimilate it and how to ensure that the new family form develops along feminist lines.

Many critics saw *The Second Stage* as a dangerous book which threatened to undercut all the progress which women had made towards emancipation. Others welcomed it as a fresh breeze of common sense which cut through the stale rhetoric of the past decade. Since most women expect to work, most expect to marry and most expect to have children, Friedan's supporters argued that feminism should concern itself with how things should best be organised for the benefit of women, not with attacking women for making the wrong choices.

Friedan's detractors argued that the kinds of choices which she offered were in any case available only to highly educated middle-class white women. The dilemma of superwoman was hardly relevant to working-class housewives, unemployed single mothers or poor blacks who never had the option of fulfilling and satisfying careers or, for that matter, of comfortable suburban family lives. In Britain especially, although the book was widely reviewed and discussed, it was seen mainly as a product of American elitist feminism.

On the socialist side of the movement, the family debate continued to evolve beyond the economic critiques described in Chapter 3, though women's low-paid and unpaid work has remained a central theme.

The claustrophobic, excessively private nature of family life was attacked by Sir Edmund Leach in the 1967 Reith Lectures, when he remarked that 'The family, with its tawdry secrets, is the source of all our discontents.' In 1982 Michèle Barrett and Mary McIntosh published a book called *The Anti-Social Family* which elaborated this criticism from a Marxist perspective.[17] They argued that the overwhelming strength of the individualistic, private family ideology had the broader effect of devaluing values like sharing, co-operation and social responsibility in the wider society:

It is as if the family had drawn comfort and security into itself and left the outside world bereft. As a bastion against a bleak society, it has made that society bleak . . . Caring, sharing and loving would be more widespread if the family did not claim them for its own.[18]

Other themes being explored and debated are single motherhood, lesbian motherhood and childlessness as options for women.[19] In part, the range of the debate reflects the rapidity of social changes which have made the traditional family problematic but which do not yet suggest any better alternative way of raising children or maintaining close personal and sexual ties in the new society. Only about a quarter of all households now consist of a couple with one or two children, and far fewer conform to the stereotype in which the husband goes out to work and the wife stays at home. Over the past twenty years clear and consistent trends have emerged towards smaller households, divorced and re-formed families, cohabitation, single life and single parenthood.[20] Attitudes are changing along with the family itself,[21] and it would be unrealistic to imagine that the women's liberation movement could yet propose a clear and consistent policy on family matters.

The one unarguable fact to emerge from the whole family/motherhood debate is that child care remains an absolutely central issue for the women's movement. Whether women choose single motherhood or dual careers, the quality of their lives will depend fundamentally on the availability of child care; in the 1980s this may be the single issue most likely to mobilise more women in support of feminism.

Balance-Sheet: The American Campaigns Today

Only a very brief review is possible here of the enormously varied and intricate activities of feminist groups working in America today. Since there are no 'seven demands' to serve as a framework (the NOW Declaration of Aims and Sexual Determination Resolution amount to almost the same thing) the state of the campaigns will be summarised under five headings:

equal opportunity; the fight for the ERA; political power; abortion and family policies; sexual politics.

Equal opportunity

For middle-class and professional women the fight for equal opportunity has been the greatest success story in American feminism. The campaigns for better access to graduate and professional training, which began in the early 1970s, have paid off handsomely, and the constitutional sanction for affirmative action has worked most strongly in favour of educated white women. Between 1973 and 1978 the number of women applying to medical schools increased by 87 per cent; in the legal profession only 3 per cent of qualified lawyers were women, but by 1981 the figure had risen to 12 per cent and is expected to reach 30 per cent by the turn of the century. The number of women holding seats on the boards of major corporations has doubled since 1975. More women than men now go on to college, and increasingly the women are studying in traditionally male fields like science, technology, economics and management.

The professional phenomenon of the 1980s is 'networking'. Informally, and through hundreds of specialised organisations, professional women are making contact with one another to break down the remaining barriers. Some of these barriers are formidable. While corporations and universities (prodded by the EEOC and liberal feminist organisations) have found that trained women make good middle-managers and teachers, they are far less willing to tolerate a female presence at the real centre of power.

But below these exalted levels, the picture is grimmer. Since 1975 the gap between overall male and female earnings has actually increased, so that a man will take home $1.75 for every $1.00 earned by a woman. This reflects a job segregation as sharp as that in Britain. As the recession closes in, women are also 50 per cent more likely to find themselves unemployed than men. However, there have been some big successes in the equality fight for ordinary working women; in 1978 a judgement against the giant American Telephone & Telegraph Corporation cost the company $35 million in compensatory payments to its female employees. But weak unions and a declining economy do not provide a good climate for such struggles, and the relative situation of women in unskilled jobs continues to worsen. In a 1982 Gallup Poll 54 per cent of women felt that they did not have equal employment opportunities.

In spite of many sincere efforts, most feminist organisations in America have been unable to engage with this problem. Their efforts are not geared to redressing the injuries of class and race inflicted in the past. Some socialist and radical groups play a marginal role in organising working-class and black protests; but liberal feminists have mainly been concerned with the needs and aspirations of their own middle-class members and supporters.

The fight for the Equal Rights Amendment

As 1982 began just three states were needed to make up the 38 required for the ratification of the ERA by the 30 June deadline. The ERAmerican coalition launched an all-out effort which obscured every other issue on the agenda. Thousands of women abandoned careers, scholarships and families to join the campaign, which was carried into the mass media, including television, almost regardless of the cost. In the final months NOW was receiving *$1.3 million each month* in donations towards the ERA campaign.

The opposition was equally determined. Attempts by federal judges to define the revised time-table as unconstitutional were blocked, but the Moral Majority and its agencies spread the word that the ERA would break up families, deprive women of alimony (which very few could collect anyway) and draft girls into the army. At the 1980 Republican Convention that party repudiated its fifty-year endorsement of the ERA, and the Democrats refused to take it up. Nervous politicians found themselves under pressure not only from the religious new right but from big business leaders. Already feeling the pinch of the recession and forced by civil rights quotas to hire employees from minority groups, corporate leaders believed that constitutional equality for women would make an already crowded labour market intolerably rigid. The resources which the corporations threw into the fight against the ERA virtually assured its defeat.

It could be argued that the long campaign for the ERA drained the energies of the American movement for ten years into an issue which they could not win. The anti-ERA forces had money and connections which enabled them to block the ERA in a few key states almost effortlessly. Feminist organisations, even if they abandoned all other projects and burned up every human and financial resource, could not bring comparable influence to bear on the state politicians whose votes destroyed the ERA.

Although NOW is committed to reviving the ERA fight, a number of legal scholars agree that existing laws and constitutional guarantees could be used to abolish sex discrimination piecemeal through the courts, and even to establish ERAs state by state (in 1982, sixteen states already had an ERA equivalents in their constitutions). Liberal feminists are ready for this long struggle, but are also turning their attention to the possibilities of political power.

Political power

The desperate struggle which the women's movement had to mount to save the ERA reflects its continuing weakness in the centres of political power. With none of the British movement's inhibitions about electoral politics, and indeed with highly professional organisations devoting their time to nothing else, only 19 women sit in the House of Representatives, 4 per cent of the total. The record in local politics is hardly better; the most prominent city leaders like Jane Byrne of Chicago, Dianne Feinstein of San Francisco and Kathy Whitmire of Houston seldom move on to governorships or to Congress.

Recently, Congress has been losing even its few pro-woman members – representatives like Shirley Chisholm and Bella Abzug who could be relied upon to press women's issues – and these are losses which the movement can ill afford.

But the politicisation of women which resulted from the ERA campaign may reverse the trend. After their defeat on the ERA, organisations like NOW and the NWPC moved immediately on to the offensive to reduce the strength of the Republican

Party in Congress. NOW launched a three million dollar drive to support pro-woman Democratic candidates (some of them men) all over the USA. One positive sign for the campaigners was the opening up of a gender gap in voting patterns, with women emerging for the first time as a distinct group opposed to the anti-woman policies of the new right.[22]

Abortion and family policies

At the time of writing, the American movement seems to be losing ground on this issue. While British feminists are fighting an ideological and economic backlash, their American sisters have to contend with one which is also moral and religious, and therefore beyond the scope of rational debate. The neo-conservatives, fundamentalists and Moral Majoritarians have halfway succeeded in reversing the whole libertarian and egalitarian tendency. As of 1982, about one-third of Americans (women and men) believe that abortion should be entirely illegal. Local courts have been increasingly restrictive and punitive in abortion cases and, early in 1982, an anti-abortion constitutional amendment was introduced into Congress closely followed by several other anti-choice amendments and bills.

Feminists had already begun to organise against these threats in 1977, when the proposal to cut financial aid for abortion had surfaced. A liberal/left coalition called the Reproductive Rights National Network (R2N2) was put together to co-ordinate action. Powerful and well-financed groups like Planned Parenthood, the American Civil Liberties Union (ACLU) and the National Abortion Rights Action League (NARAL) have joined in a national effort to protect abortion rights.[23] Radical feminists have generally seen these big organisations as too liberal, and have stayed with their own local campaigns. More recently, liberal feminists have been working to mobilise the two-thirds of voters who would like to preserve the limited abortion rights granted by the 1973 Supreme Court decision. A survey in 1982 suggested that the pro-choice majority felt strongly enough over the abortion issue to allow it to influence their choice of candidates.[24]

The federal budget cuts mounted by the Reagan administration have been directed almost entirely at moderate income and poor families. Aid to pregnant women, food stamps, rent subsidies, child care, community legal services, health care and aid to families with dependent children are just a few of the targets. The 'WORKFARE' programme, which may require welfare recipients to work up to twenty hours a week, is particularly oppressive to single mothers. In Congress the euphemistically titled 'Family Protection Act' has now been introduced twice, and may eventually go through in some form (see Chapter 6).

All such anti-woman initiatives are being vigorously fought but they come so thick and fast, backed by such resources of money and power, that the women's movement is in danger of being choked by them.

Sexual politics and male violence

In this atmosphere, American radical feminists have turned their attention almost entirely to alternative life-styles and to sexual politics. Although the threats to women's rights have, for the first time in many years, brought radicals and liberals together in campaigns and demonstrations, the radicals have not been seduced by mainstream politics but have held to their distinctive concerns.

Among the most visible and active groups have been Women Against Pornography, which mobilised 7,000 women for a march in New York in 1980, Women Against Violence Against Women and a revived troupe of the Women's Liberation Zap Action Brigade. A National Coalition Against Sexual Assault was put together in 1979 to co-ordinate action in this area. The central campaigning issues for radicals have continued to be male violence, rape, pornography and lesbian rights. Most recently a great deal of attention has been paid to sexual harassment at work (a theme quickly taken up by liberal feminists), marital rape and incest, and some legal victories have been scored in feminist-supported cases. But with concerns such as these, radical feminists find themselves even more isolated than liberals in neo-conservative America.

The impulse to collective action is very much a creature of circumstance. In 1968 what was then called simply 'The movement' seemed to be sweeping all of young America along on a tidal wave of protest against the Vietnam war, against racism, against capitalism, against pollution, against the competitive and individualistic culture, and against sexism. But the left/libertarian revolution, and the great hopes which went with it, died somewhere in the 1970s. On 26 August 1980, on the tenth anniversary of the great march of 50,000 women down Fifth Avenue, New York, only 500 turned out to march. Mass action was *passé*, the people were somewhere else now. Out in the backwoods of radical culture, forms of anarchism (including anarcha-feminism) began to reappear, a sure sign of the failure of socialist and liberal solutions.

In the early 1980s the large liberal organisations of American feminism and the few socialist groups are bracing for a political struggle with the forces of the new religious right. In Britain socialist feminist groups with far fewer resources face a more directly economic battle against poverty, unemployment and regressive legislation. Radical feminists in both countries continue to focus on the exposure of male power and violence as the main issues, hoping to raise the consciousness of women in general. The unifying factor in the immediate future may be the threat of war. Since 1980 there has been a great resurgence of non-violent protest and civil disobedience against war and nuclear armaments by women in many countries.

8. Unfinished Business: the Future of Feminism

If the women's liberation movement were dead, this would be the place to bury it with a few appreciative words about its achievements and a respectable historical niche alongside the suffrage movement. Since it is very much alive, the observer's task is more challenging. A living movement is not history but the embodiment of many people's passionate hopes for their futures.

In assessing what the future might hold for feminists, it is necessary to face a contradiction which has been growing through the past three chapters. On the one hand, a picture has emerged of the women's movement as divided, sectarian, weak and isolated from political power; on the other, we have seen that the movement is diverse, creative, full of energy and profoundly committed to the vision of a better life for all women. As a cause, women's liberation is as deep, as wide and as fundamental to human progress as the labour movement ever was. As a movement, it is virtually a textbook case of every problem which has plagued every social movement in history. When we look at the women's movement today, it is hard to know whether we are looking at a great, ongoing force for change or the terminal stage of a form of politics which has been outdated by events.

Liberal feminism in the USA is a success story in so far as it has gained a foothold in mainstream politics and in public consciousness. Yet even this most vigorous branch of the worldwide movement may face critical setbacks in the 1980s as it contends with a national revival of religious conservatism which has as one of its main aims the reassertion of male control over women. In Britain the movement has achieved some integration but is generally more marginal to political debate. The problems which British feminists will face in the immedi-

208

ate future will have more to do with economic decline and public stringency than with a direct ideological attack on women's rights. Nevertheless, the decade will be a bleak one for women unless public and political consciences can be touched by an integrated movement speaking with one firm voice for sexual equality as a fundamental human right. Accordingly, this chapter will focus on the two issues which seem crucial to the strength of the movement, the problem of unity and the problem of organising for political power.

The Search for Unity

In a country the size of the USA the various sectors of feminism are large enough to stand by themselves and to pursue their own separate visions of change; Betty Friedan has argued that the differences are so deep that it is better so. The case is otherwise in Britain, where the smallness and fragility of the movement suggests that unity is the only possible source of strength.

In 1979 a pamphlet appeared with the title *Beyond the Fragments: Feminism and the Making of Socialism*, which generated so much interest that it was soon revised and re-issued as a book.[1] Three long essays by Sheila Rowbotham, Lynne Segal and Hilary Wainwright, each coming from a different socialist perspective, explored the reasons behind the stalemate of British feminism and tried to suggest ways forward. This tripartite structure makes the book hard to summarise, but the central question which it poses is straightforward enough: what kind of organisation can create a socialist feminist movement which is internally unified and positively linked to the other organisations of the political left?

The authors are clear that it will have to be a special kind of organisation, not just an adaptation of the typical Leninist and bureaucratic structures of socialist parties. Such parties, they argue, are designed to sieze power, not to raise consciousness, while the existing patterns of feminist action do the reverse, creating consciousness without being able to turn it into effective political power. *Fragments* does not try to suggest that feminism should be absorbed by the Labour Party, the

Communists or the Trotskyists, recognising that their interests are often in direct conflict. Rather, it looks for a new form of organisation which would reconcile the interests of labour and the interests of women in a new socialist synthesis.

The need for some kind of unified organisation is unarguable. As it is, the women's liberation movement has no collective identity or history and, vitally important for political success, no collective memory. As the authors of *Fragments* point out, the same battles over issues, theory and tactics are fought over and over again within the movement, because each group comes upon them as though they were brand new: 'It is as if the different parts of a piece of cloth – a political organisation – were being woven creatively and with *ad hoc* contact between the weavers, but without anyone having a master plan.'[2]

A *Beyond the Fragments* conference was held in November 1980, and a series of ongoing discussion papers was planned. One of the most persistent criticisms from the male left (aside from hurt protests that male socialists weren't really all *that* bad) was that the book did not live up to its promise. Nowhere was the new form of feminist organisation described in detail; it existed only in vague generalities like 'grass-roots strength' and 'flexibility' which were easier to write down than to put into practice.

But the main debate took shape around the more theoretical question of whether socialism could or should become the underlying principle of all feminism. Groups like the Socialist Workers' Party were understandably enthusiastic, arguing that as women now form nearly half the working class, they will necessarily begin to think of themselves as workers as well as women, wives and mothers. The SWP line was that only through direct pressure from the mass of the working class, including women, could socialism be achieved. As a logical next step, the SWP reabsorbed its separate women's groups into the main party in 1981.

There is no doubt that the broader socialist movement has added women's issues to its agenda. The Labour Party, trade unions and smaller revolutionary and theoretical groups have all begun to give serious attention to the economic inequalities of sex. The question raised by the critics of *Fragments* was whether the left can cope, theoretically or politically, with the non-economic issues that women's liberation entails. Theoretically, a certain pessimism has emerged. For more than a decade socialist feminists have been writing about the synthesis which they hope to achieve between the personal/sexual politics of radical feminism and the economic and political theories of Marxism. No such synthesis has emerged and there is a growing recognition that Marxism may have certain theoretical limitations which just have to be accepted.[3] Intellectual feminists have cleverly adapted Marxism, but have been unable to transform it.

It is by no means clear that unity lies along the path suggested by the *Fragments* debate. One very obvious point is that not all women are or wish to become socialists, and many committed socialists are themselves unhappy about the idea of excluding women who do not share their political perspective.

The divisions within socialism are not the true key to the divisions within feminism. In this book a conventional (and increasingly difficult) distinction has been made between 'socialist feminism' and 'radical feminism', yet even this may not represent the most significant divide. It is frequently claimed that radical feminism is only a special form of socialism, and indeed that it *is* the adaptation of socialism to the problem of gender inequality.[4] Theoretically, these two forms of feminism are not necessarily incompatible. Nor is the major conflict between lesbian and heterosexual feminists, who occupy the whole range of theoretical positions.

What appears to divide the British women's liberation movement most deeply is a question of tactics which cuts across all these boundaries: namely, whether in the pursuit of women's interests, any co-operation with men should be accepted. On the one side are the separatists and revolutionary feminists (predominantly radicals) who reject all co-operation; on the other are the non-separatists (predominantly socialists) who support an autonomous women's movement but declare that limited co-operation with men is possible and necessary.

The reason why this particular division has become so important is that, unlike more abstract theoretical disagreements, it fundamentally affects the whole nature of feminism – its tactics, its campaigns and its identity as an all-women revolutionary movement against the power of men. The danger which the socialist campaign for unity poses for separatists and revolutionary feminists is their belief that such a unity would submerge feminism in the male-dominated politics of the left. The fact that socialist writers have been more successful in getting their views on unity into print has fuelled the fear that, as happened in America in the early 1970s, the most radical forms of women's liberation are about to be written out of history.[5] The sense of threat felt by lesbian separatists is reflected in the setting up of the London Lesbian Offensive Group to 'combat anti-lesbianism in the women's movement'.

Radical separatism can be a problem for other tendencies in the women's movement, both because it is seized on by the press as a stereotype and because the intervention of radicals in campaigns can cause public embarrassment. A vivid example occurred at a National Abortion Campaign rally sponsored by the TUC in 1979. Apart from Women's Aid, the NAC is the only national organisation of women's liberation, and reflects the variety of the movement. But mixed groups like the Socialist Workers' Party and the International Marxist Group have a powerful voice in it, a fact resented by separatists. At the 1979 rally insensitive stewarding by the TUC and the fact that the leaders of the march included men incensed a group of women who rushed to the head of the march. Later, in Trafalgar Square, official TUC speakers were heckled by women carrying women's liberation banners. Such incidents were a gift to the press, who were able to ignore the purpose of the march almost entirely by focusing on them.

This kind of conflict between idealistic and practical politics is hardly new. It surfaces whenever strong beliefs come up against the need for compromise. Yet at one time the promise of feminism was to be the *least* dogmatic of social movements. Its loose, no-leadership structures, its commitment to the political meaning of personal experience and its deep anti-authoritarianism all suggested that feminism would be a movement uniquely tolerant of differences and ambiguities.

And indeed feminism, like socialism, is a broad church with many faiths. As in the USA, a kind of 'unity in diversity' might be possible, if it were not for certain narrowing tendencies which have emerged in the British movement. The individually small and isolated groups, lacking any central direction or authority, quite early began to adopt and defend strong political positions particular to themselves, and therefore not always acceptable to other feminist groups. Thus within the movement, especially after 1975, a struggle appeared over the proper definition of feminism, and who could or could not count herself as a feminist. Was it necessary to be a socialist? Was it necessary to be a lesbian? Was it necessary to be a separatist? The need for each group and tendency to defend its analysis as if it were in a political vacuum (without support from external groups or evidence from history) led inexorably to a hardening of extreme positions and the appearance of strongly held feminist orthodoxies.

Extremism in a good cause, as Senator Goldwater once remarked, is no vice. Some situations demand an extreme response, and it would be cowardly to pretend otherwise. Extremism carried beyond a certain point can taint the whole purpose of a social movement, but there is a compelling logic in the feminist cause which leads the honest enquirer to see the situation of women in radical terms. This comment is not about extremism *per se* but about orthodoxy. If a small movement is fragmented into several strong orthodoxies and no potential convert is accepted unless she at once adopts a full package of predetermined doctrines, the whole possibility of unity is cast into doubt.

The literature and marginalia of the movement are full of protests from women who would like to accept some but not all of its doctrines, and have found themselves rejected by the 'all or nothing' mentality. Janet Radcliffe Richards, writing rather sweepingly about the British movement, speaks of its absolutism and the unwillingness of many feminists to accept mixed feelings about painful questions like abortion.[6] Ann Oakley notes the almost religious 'creed-like qualities' which many theories have acquired in the past few years: 'There is the self-righteous smugness of the believer and the ostracism of the agnostic; the missionary zeal to epistolic conversion and the disenfranchisement and isolation of the sceptic.'[7] There is no virtue in this dogmatism. There is all the difference in the world between movements which raise important issues for debate and those which take a rigid stance and define all alternative views as illegitimate.

In part, this closing-out of discourse has to do with the special language which all social movements create. Strongly held values and beliefs, in politics as in religion, need to be protected against a cynical and hostile world. In social movements this is commonly accomplished by creating a secret world of language and theory which outsiders cannot comprehend, and visiting punishment on those within the movement who do not conform to the rules. The movement is trying to maintain a reality or world-picture very different from the one most people perceive. To do so it must first radically change the world-view of its followers and then help them to maintain their new vision through a special and highly restricted kind of discourse which belongs to them alone. To know the language is to be a part of the group, and to feel secure. Those on the inside claim that only they understand the true situation, and that everyone else is deluded or malicious. This natural partiality for one's own group rather easily develops into a conspiracy theory of the world. Embattled social movements often develop this kind of mentality, seeing everything as evidence of the great conspiracy against them, and thereby confirming their own significance.[8]

Some small but not insignificant tendencies in British feminism have taken steps along this road, and present to the outside world almost the aspect of secret societies. Along with the belief in one's own rightness and the hostility of the world comes a need for internal conformity and discipline. The group is seen to be in such danger that contrary views cannot be allowed within it. Those admitted to the group are progressively selected by various tests of orthodoxy in ideas, behaviour and life-style until the group is composed as nearly as possible of people exactly like one another in every way. This is the classic process of sectarianism, familiar to sociologists and deeply destructive of the political potential of a social movement. Movements which cannot adapt to conflict and change also cannot grow. They can only divide and sub-divide until a tiny group achieves the elusive goal of ideological purity.

For the insider, however, orthodoxy has important compensating virtues. Becoming a feminist opens up a bottomless pit of difficult choices which women in more traditional roles do not have to face: choices about work, family, children, sexuality, which are normally defined by her social situation are suddenly thrown wide open. Conforming to an alternative set of norms narrows the range of choices to manageable proportions once more. Instead of facing a chaos of infinite possibilities, the believer is protected by a clearly defined world-view which tells what is and what is not appropriate. Such is the universal attraction of dogma.

Its less attractive aspects are also well known. Because the believer is righteous and the unbeliever unrighteous, a movement based on an orthodoxy is invariably intolerant. It is often anti-rational and contemptuous of the rules of evidence and logic. It is also often unjust, since such strongly held beliefs may override the more fragile sentiments of balance, sensitivity and fairness.

What has been said most certainly does not apply to all feminists, and indeed is a matter of great concern and debate within the movement. In difficult times, when political initiatives seem to be stalled, the voices of rigid orthodoxy always gain ground; it takes courage to resist them as, for example, feminists like Ann Oakley and Janet Radcliffe Richards have begun to do. Surely, says Richards, liberation should mean *more* options for women, not less, *more* freedom to understand, debate and make choices, not less. Many feminists would agree wholeheartedly.

Public conflicts of this kind have a devastating impact on the image which the movement presents to outsiders, and therefore on the recruitment of new supporters. If the movement is to be more than a forum for consciousness-raising and protest or a safe haven for women in a man's world, it needs to mobilise many more women as participants, demonstrators, fundraisers and voters. It would be unrealistic to expect a mass movement of women at this stage, but neither revolution nor large-scale reform can be launched from the tiny fragmented support base of the present women's liberation movement in Britain.

Betty Friedan has argued in her controversial book *The Second Stage* (1981) that feminism desperately needs to find an image which will not alienate the majority of women. So many women of all ages, races and classes are unhappy with some aspect of their situation as women, but absolutely reject the feminist movement. This is so common that it even has a popular label: the 'I'm not a feminist but . . .' syndrome. This rejection is a response to the stereotypical image of feminism as a secretive, dogmatic, man-hating, elitist, arrogant and humourless movement which could hardly appeal to any sane person. The image shows how thoroughly the media caricature of extreme radical feminism as *all* feminism has been absorbed into the culture, and how the awareness of other forms of feminism has been blocked out.

Even women who get beyond the caricature must be convinced that feminism speaks to their everyday concerns, and one of the strongest cards the movement has is that these everyday lives *do* reveal systematic discrimination, the personal *is* political and the commitment of women to feminism need not be based on some abstract principle. All social movements find it difficult to secure the active support of individuals sometimes because they feel they will reap the benefits (if any) without the need to participate, more often because participation is a big step, takes time and energy and may disrupt one's whole life. To overcome this resistance a movement must be able to offer incentives; few people are moved to action by a sense of injustice alone.

In the early days to be a feminist was to feel that exhilaration of being part of a great new force for social change, and this alone was enough to bring many women to the movement. In more difficult times, when little positive change can be expected, the movement is bound to be smaller and more inward. But, on a more personal level, women can still change their own lives (and men's), and it is still true that conscious-ness can be a subversive and radical force.

A broad-based movement of women could not be as 'political' or as 'radical' as many feminists would like it to be. It would be a thing of compromises and ambiguities covering much of the range of the political spectrum. As NOW in America has discovered, real democracy and real diversity are difficult partners in a social movement. But only by getting women into the movement in the first place can they be enabled to discover just what needs to be done. A tiny vanguard, jealous of its purity, leaves the great majority of women out in the cold. Marxist revolutionary parties have occasionally felt that they could do without the workers until after the revolution, because the workers were full of false consciousness and politically backward. It would be the ultimate irony if the women's movement, starting off from opposite assumptions about the connection between personal life and political theory, should arrive at the same dreary impasse.

The socialist strategy for unity, as outlined in *Beyond the Fragments*, seems unlikely to bring together the many and varied tendencies in the movement, or to provide a basis for the recruitment of many uncommitted women. The self-definitions of feminists are highly complex, based on race, class, sexuality, culture, locality, ethnicity and experience, and many are unwilling to accept any general political label whatsoever. There is a clear need for some such broad basis of agreement as the original 'four demands' intended and which the present 'seven demands' no longer provide, and moves have been made to revive the national conference, suspended since 1978, to discuss a revised programme.

Such a discussion will require compromises from everyone, and will depend on the softening of the most dogmatic and sectarian tendencies in the movement. Their influence in the late 1970s came from the certainty of their message in uncertain times, their power to carry the day at meetings and conferences by being morally and politically positive. The movement in the 1980s seems ready once more to admit the voice of ambiguity in search of a new and more flexible synthesis, so long-sought and so elusive, which will give due respect to the consciousness and experience of all women.

Organising for Change

While the limited appeal and fragmentation of the British movement are indisputably signs of weakness, *full* unity and integration are almost certainly not necessary to its future strength: for any movement which aims to transform the lives of half the population must fight on many fronts. Legal and political reforms are indispensable, but never enough. A full strategy for women's equality would have to include massive changes in occupational and economic *structures*, in the dominating ideas which form society's *ideology*, in the *cultural forms* and practices which are so much a part of ourselves that we are scarcely aware of them, and in the *consciousness* of individual women and men. Changes achieved in any one of these sectors can be neutralised by the relentless persistence of discriminatory attitudes and practices in the others. Equal opportunities in education or employment fail in their purpose if young girls are still taught to see their futures in terms of wifehood and motherhood; similarly, to transform consciousness without transforming the structure of opportunity can create only anger and frustration.

The women's movement has been unique in the breadth of its concerns and strategies for change. Liberals have worked mainly on the legal and political reform issues, socialists on economic and ideological structures, and radicals on culture and consciousness. Even fragmented as they are, these separate forms of action have had a cumulative impact which one alone could not hope for. Yet the forms of organisation which emerged from the 1960s now seem unequal to the challenge of the 1980s, and one of the major debates in the movement today centres on the kinds of organisational structures most likely to sustain and strengthen the drive for women's liberation.

One of the most singular achievements of the feminist movement is virtually unknown and uncelebrated. For more than a decade it has sustained a co-operative, entirely decentralised and leaderless structure which approximates closely to the highest ideals of social anarchism: namely, that people can work together for common goals without the need for a coercive, bureaucratic hierarchy to drive them on. It is an ideal which has been and still is held by many social movements (anti-nuclear and ecology are two examples), but which has never been made to work so long and so effectively. Historians looking back at women's liberation may judge one of its most significant outcomes to have been this demonstration that ultra-democratic structures can be made to work in the cause of social change.

We have seen that the movement's adherence to this ideal has created its own problems. Whether or not these problems are to be regarded as serious depends upon how the process of social change is conceived: as the personal development of individuals, as the demonstration by example that an alternative way of life is possible ('prefigurative politics'), or as creating reformist or revolutionary changes in the whole external society.

The small, autonomous, all-woman group which is at the heart of feminist practice does magnificently what it was intended to do – change consciousness. So long as a group keeps changing and recruiting new members it is a perfect setting both for political education and personal growth. Once groups close themselves to newcomers, a practice which is commonly followed when a stable core has been achieved, their role is less dynamic. The closed group provides friendship, mutual support and an occasional base for political action, but the same few people cannot continue indefinitely to carry on consciousness-raising among themselves. As a way of bringing women into the movement and giving them a new orientation, however, the small group is ideal.

At first, the expectations were greater. By reaching more and more women and raising their consciousness, it was hoped to create a true mass movement to confront the power of men. This was an idealist political strategy, depending as it did on the force of ideas alone to transform society. Idealist movements fitted well with the mood of the late 1960s and, given the right conditions, could be quite dramatic in their effects.[9]

It is now widely accepted that small-group consciousness-raising offers no way of moving from the shared experiences of individuals to political action; it is educational, an end in itself. It was also a dramatically original way of creating authentic and appealing feminist theory directly from women's life-experiences, demonstrating that the personal could indeed be translated into the political.

In some sections of the movement this insight was lost. 'The personal is political' originated in a reaction against male definitions of politics as an abstract activity concerned only with institutional power, which effectively excluded from politics almost everything which concerned women. The new doctrine revealed that personal lives, seen in the aggregate, contained political lessons and could be used to build a responsive political theory. But as it became clear that consciousness-raising could not in itself change things, some radical feminists began to argue that anything personal was *ipso facto* and without translation a political issue, so that consciousness raising on any subject was *ipso facto* a political act. This drains all the meaning out of the word 'political', and condemns those who believe it to political isolation. Socialist feminists in particular have vigorously resisted this line of development.

Related disagreements have surfaced concerning the wisdom of the whole anti-leadership, small-group structure. There is a strong argument that these values are so basic to the movement that they must be maintained whatever the cost. The women's movement must be publicly seen to embody those highly egalitarian and democratic qualities which it publicly promotes, or it would lose all credibility. Two questions may be raised: Does it/can it *in fact* embody those qualities? And is the cost too high?

On the first point, little can be said except that there is no reason to suppose that, just because a group has no men in it, the less attractive forms of human behaviour will vanish. Anarchists and anarcha-feminists (of whom there are a substantial number) are well aware how difficult it is to produce co-operative behaviour in people socialised into a competitive world.

The question of the practical disadvantages of leaderless structures is more open to observation. In the early 1970s, American feminists began to question the no-leadership policy.[10] They charged that, in practice, the policy allowed the development of informal leadership structures and hidden elites who were able to exert considerable control over the movement by virtue of special skills, dedication, determination or powerful personalities. There is enough evidence even in the published debates to suggest that the problem of hidden elites continues to be a thorn in the side of the movement today. The problem is so sensitive that even to accuse someone of elitism is a serious matter. Yet, if we study, for example, the ways in which British national conferences have reached decisions there is no doubt that the influence of a relatively few women in a relatively few groups was disproportionately strong.

The public/political effectiveness of the small, closed group has also been cast in doubt. The intense, personal nature of the group experience may come to absorb nearly all the energies of the people in it, leaving little time for wider political activities: 'A preoccupation with internal processes . . . took precedence over programme or effectiveness. As a result, women's liberation groups tended to oscillate between total formlessness at one extreme and a kind of collective authoritarianism on the other.'[11]

It is a double-edged dilemma, for women who do attain a measure of public recognition as leaders or spokeswomen for the movement risk being labelled as male-identified power-trippers, so there is a strong pressure on de facto leaders to maintain the no-leadership façade even if they can no longer believe in it. The American feminist Kate Millett, who became something of a media celebrity after the publication of her autobiographical book Flying in 1974, had to abdicate the leadership role which the press thrust upon her in order to maintain her identity as a radical feminist.

This question of leadership is the classic anarchist's conundrum, to which there is no answer. Very small, fully autonomous groups may be able to practise absolute democracy by consensus, even though studies show that this is very difficult and time-consuming. But the larger the groups, the more they are connected in networks, the more resources they accumulate and (very important) the more they publish, the more difficult it becomes to keep even a semblance of the ideal. And we also know that the more centralised and bureaucratised a movement, the more it is able to offer strong leadership and selective incentives, the more effective it is likely to be in gaining political concessions.[12]

Without central co-ordination, political campaigns on a regional or national scale are hard to organise and, as anarchists have always found, structureless and leaderless campaigns are easy to divide and next to impossible to unite. In general, in Britain, the more left-dominated the campaign, the more centralised and hierarchical it has been, the National Abortion Campaign being the primary example. Radical campaigns must depend more on self-organisation once the word has been spread by newsletters like WIRES, but this can be effective; simultaneous 'reclaim the night' demonstrations have been mounted in several cities using this structure, for example, without any need for a central leadership.

A proposal at the 1975 national conference to establish a voluntary working party to suggest ways of organising the movement was narrowly defeated by women wary of the dangers of leadership and bureaucracy. Since 1978 there has not been a national conference at which such questions could even be discussed. But it would be a great mistake to believe that better organisation *in itself* would solve the current problems of British feminism. Organisation, however perfect, is no panacea for weakness and lack of numbers. The powerlessness of the highly organised ultra-left confirms this.[13] Radicals claim that their prefigurative style of structureless, no-leadership politics is intrinsic to the nature of feminism, and cannot be integrated into the power politics of socialist movements. Socialists want to break down the isolation of the small-group structure, which they see as a source of individualism, narcissism and self-absorption. Yet radicals claim that the core of their political programme – to involve people and build their consciousness on the basis of experience – is the only way to reveal the true extent of patriarchy and build a mass movement of women against it. The very fact that the women's liberation movement has survived and has enjoyed substantial successes for so long without the public apparatus of structure and leadership suggests that exceptions are possible and that perhaps a viable new political form has been created.

The highly professionalised organisations of American liberal feminism illustrate the alternate strategy. Most have adopted traditional bureaucratic structures with decisions made by formal committees and carried out by salaried staffs. These salaries are low in market terms but entirely adequate, and they come in large part from government, corporate and foundation grants, the balance being made up from voluntary contributions and individual membership fees.[14] This structure, though highly effective in pursuing legal and political reforms, is vulnerable in two ways. First, volunteers and supporters are subject to control and finally to domination by a small group of professional experts. Second, it is entirely at the mercy of grant cutbacks, and the decreases in outside funding which began in 1979 are seriously damaging the liberal feminist organisations at the very moment when their strength is most needed.

Such dangers always exist when a social movement enters the mainstream, becomes professionalised and offers a career structure. In Britain the number of paid jobs for feminists is minimal – a few in publishing, in the Equal Opportunities Commission, the NCCL, Women's Aid, trade unions and the like. In pursuit of legal and political reform and in monitoring existing laws, a greater degree of organisation and professionalisation would probably be beneficial. But there is no evidence that such structures have the potential for achieving any of the more fundamental aims of the women's liberation movement.

Looking at the sheer breadth of the questions raised by this brief discussion of organising for change, it seems unrealistic to suppose that any one form of feminist organisation will predominate in the next decade. These diverse styles of structure and leadership grew up to serve different purposes, and show few signs of converging. While a stronger, more centralised political campaign for women, able to attract substantial resources, would fill an obvious need in Britain, the need for more innovative and radical forms of action would not disappear. Greater organisational diversity, not less, would probably best serve the purposes of the whole movement.

Feminist Futures

Although the potential exists for a mass liberal feminist movement along American lines, the women's liberation movement in Britain is likely to remain for the foreseeable future a loose alliance of tendencies, campaigns and individual groups with no centralised direction. Whatever its exact form, it will be a changed movement, adapted to the fact that harsher economic times have shaped a generation which, according to a *New Society* survey, is more conservative, less sceptical and less likely to rebel than the women of the 1960s who formed the first wave of the new feminism.[15] Feminists cannot control the economic and social context of their struggle, but they can choose how to respond to a changing world. What strategies and what ultimate goals will best serve the needs of the 1980s?

It is no man's business to prescribe futures for the women's movement. What follows is a sketch of the *possibilities* as a political sociologist sees them. The reader will hardly need reminding that the lessons of the past are not an infallible guide to the future. The possibilities outlined fall into two categories: those which concern general strategies for political action, and those which concern the ultimate goals towards which a feminist movement might move.

The political setbacks of recent years have reinforced a deep ambivalence in the movement over whether its present aim should be to reform certain social institutions and cultural habits, to revolutionise the whole society, or simply to provide a satisfying environment for individuals.

A movement which offers a safe space and an alternative culture to individuals is in a strong position to survive and grow. It offers no present threat to the politically powerful and so should attract no repression. As long as it can provide support, solidarity and a meaningful alternative, the life-style and separatist currents in feminism will continue to be a valuable resource for some women. Unless it attracts so many followers as to become a mass movement, however, its potential for creating social change will be slight. Like the hippies and counter-culture people of the 1960s some feminists have chosen to live in a revolutionary way rather than to make revolution.

This leaves us with the two more traditional political options: reform or revolution. In the British movement the two choices often seem to coexist, as limited, reformist demands like equal pay and child care are pressed in the context of a theory which calls for the overthrow of patriarchy or the capitalist state. This poses a dilemma familiar to all political activists: concealing one's true and ultimate aims may cause those aims to become submerged and lost, while revealing them may drive away many potential supporters. Most people are scared by the word 'revolution', and rightly so. The overthrow of a whole social, political and economic system cannot be accomplished without great personal suffering. It is likely also to entail a period of government instability, social chaos and counter-revolutionary struggles extending for a generation or more. Nobody can calmly contemplate the possibility of such events in their lifetime unless they are committed very deeply to the revolutionary cause.

Revolution as an inspiration and a poetic vision has a central place in the rhetoric of radical politics. But as a concrete strategy the idea that the mass of people, or some section of the people, can take control of the modern state by one great act of insurgency is denied by every mass action of modern history, most recently by the fate of the Solidarity movement in Poland. Populations, however angry, are no match for the controlling machineries of the strong state.

This would seem to suggest that only some version of liberal feminism, with egalitarian and reformist goals, could possibly succeed in making a major political impact today. Liberal goals and tactics are widely accepted as legitimate. Indeed, it is just this factor of legitimacy which has led to the near-hegemony of liberal feminism in the USA, and to the radicals' protest that their voice is being smothered. Liberal feminism appears safe, it does not frighten people, and most of its demands are manifestly fair and at least potentially winnable.

The political arguments are also convincing. In the modern world, pluralistic and flexible movements have been the most successful in gaining advantages for their constituencies, because they have not isolated themselves from the sources of power and have not been afraid to compromise when compromise was the only way forward. Indeed, it is difficult to conceive any confrontation with all-pervasive realities like patriarchy or capitalism which would not involve some degree of negotiation and compromise.

So many feminists tend to theorise revolution and act reform, hoping that women will become engaged with the movement on the level of the very concrete issues which affect their lives, and then may be drawn towards a more fully Marxist or radical analysis of the need to change the whole system. It has been argued that only *after* the state has been pushed as far as possible along the road to reform will the limits of reformism be revealed, and the knowledge that formal equality is not enough will generate a new revolutionary consciousness.[16] But this is a speculation supported by no historical examples. All the evidence suggests that elites can manipulate reforms to damp down discontent almost indefinitely, unless they run out of the resources (political or economic) needed to make concessions.

The problem is this: the situation of *most* women will simply not be improved very much by liberal reforms. Middle-class and professional women may make major gains but, as socialists and radicals tirelessly point out, the changes needed to benefit working-class and minority women are so drastic that something like a political revolution is necessary. Feminism has its own logic and, once one has accepted the justice of equal rights, it is hard not to be drawn along a path which leads to a critique of the total social structure. Whether one believes that women are oppressed mainly *as workers* (socialist idea) or mainly *as females* (radical idea), the implications are revolutionary.

It seems unlikely that, in the present political atmosphere, a purely liberal movement can succeed in doing much more than holding the line against the forces of conservatism. On the other hand, we know that, in the British or American setting, revolutionary movements routinely fail, while movements with radical but *non-revolutionary* strategies do much better.[17] Many feminist writers have suggested that what feminism needs now is a renewal of theory which dispenses with dogma, making use of the best of each theoretical tradition but, above all, offering a new theory of social change. For what the revolutionary tendencies in feminism most conspicuously lack is any detailed and realistic plan suggesting how the movement might get from here to there.

While direct revolution against the state entails the exclusiveness and even secrecy of the vanguard group, a strategy for radical reform implies a broad-based movement fighting on many fronts. This in turn suggests that a powerful feminist movement will need more and more active allies than it has hitherto sought or attracted. At the theoretical level the interconnectedness of oppressions is well understood – women's liberation, black liberation, poverty, ecological destruction, the powerlessness of workers and the imperial fantasies of governments are symptoms of a single disease. It has so far proved more difficult to make the day-to-day tactical connections which would join the cause of women to the many other causes of which it is a natural and indispensable part.

Once again, separatism emerges as the crucial point of disagreement. All alliances formed beyond the feminist movement itself will involve men, and many feminists have accepted this. The tenth anniversary edition of *Ms* magazine in August 1982 published a list of forty 'male heroes' of feminism. The argument is an entirely pragmatic one. *If* sexist culture views women as inferior, then a movement composed entirely of women with no male support will *ipso facto* be seen as a derisory movement. Oppressed people cannot pull themselves up entirely by their bootstraps.

But can men ever be true allies of a non-reformist feminist movement? The evidence is slender. In America groups calling themselves Feminist Men have formed to help men shed their oppressive male roles. In Britain between 1973 and 1975 Men Against Sexism tried to find non-patriarchal ways of supporting women's struggles, for example by organising crèches at feminist conferences and, in the early 1980s, the anti-sexist men's movement revived on a small scale. Yet any male intervention divides the movement, any male initiative still tends to steal the limelight and revive old fears that the movement will be taken over. Movement leaders who seek alliances tread a narrow line, gathering support where they can find it but guarding the autonomy which made a women's movement possible.

Whatever strategies and alliances are chosen, there must also be a blue-print of the future. Activism and participation are exciting and satisfying in themselves, but most people will not commit their time or energies to a cause unless they can see it leading towards a better life for themselves or their children. This means, in the fullest and most positive sense, a utopia, and here we enter the greatest area of ambiguity in feminist thought. If women's liberation implies a destination, some final ideal state, it remains unspecified. If it implies choices *beyond* those which now exist – choices which are not now available to anyone – these too remain obscure. Marx's vision of the classless society was sketchily drawn, but its essential outlines were clear enough to inspire generations of working people. The dreamers of the nineteenth century like Fourier, Cabet,

Owen and Thoreau gave utopia a bad name with their obsessive fantasies of controlled and orderly human societies. And yet, as Oscar Wilde said, no map of the world is worth a glance which hasn't utopia on it, and a movement which aims at the radical transformation of the world must show that the dream has shape and substance, that it is possible, and that people would want to live there.

In modern feminist thought three kinds of futures can be discerned: an integrated or egalitarian society where sex differences no longer count; an androgynous society where sex differences no longer exist; and a separatist society where men and women no longer share the same social world. By their nature these futures pose the fundamental but unanswerable question of whether women are the same as men in all but the most superficial biological details, or whether they are in some ways profoundly different. Feminists have historically always divided along these lines, with equal rights campaigners claiming the essential similarity of the sexes and more radical crusaders claiming that women have a separate and distinctive nature, and thus a special role in the world.

Equality, of course, is an absolute. Since it is impossible to imagine every individual being equal in every way, this goal is usually specified and restricted to mean equality of opportunity, equality of income, equality of class, of status, or whatever. The liberal feminist goal, now widely accepted, is equality of opportunity. It rests on the liberal individualist position so eloquently argued by John Stuart Mill (p. 64) that, since we cannot know whether women's inequality is a product of nature or culture, no harm can come from removing all social barriers which limit women and acting *as if* women and men are the same. It is the same principle used by campaigners for black civil rights in the USA and subsequently adopted by liberal feminists: biological differences have nothing to do with political justice. Equality of opportunity, in this form, would allow women to make the same choices which men make, no more and no less.

Yet women's *liberation* seems to imply something more, and for socialist and radical feminists equality has a stronger meaning. The debate within socialism about the true relationship between class equality and sexual equality has often been referred to and is unresolved, but it can be said that the socialist vision of the future would at minimum include an end to the economic exploitation of women *and* men and, on the basis of that economic equality, would anticipate an end to the patriarchal power of men also.

We are left with a demand often heard in the women's liberation movement for sexual equality. This is sometimes used to mean equal treatment for both sexes, sometimes the more androgynous ideal of the elimination of all important differences. Both usages are understandable, even if the terminology could be clearer.

The problem arises when sexual equality is stated as the major goal of feminism without further explanation. The difficulty is both logical and interpretive. Does this mean that all women should be equal to all men? Or all women equal to some men (the most advantaged)? Or that men and women in different class positions should be equal to one another? Like racial equality, sexual equality can imply infinitely varied meanings and, in times of scarcity and economic competition, the state symbolised by the term 'sexual equality' becomes particularly problematic to outsiders unless both its meaning and its exact implications are specified.

Beyond equality we find ourselves in still more difficult territory. While the debate on equality has a long history in philosophy and politics, both androgyny and separatism are utopias without a political history. What they might mean can be glimpsed mainly through works of literature and imagination.

Androgyny, meaning to have the characteristics of both male and female, has been a popular science fiction theme since Aldous Huxley wrote *Brave New World* in 1946. The sexless denizens of his dystopia were literally as well as metaphorically beyond biological distinctions. In the 1970s we see this theme taken up by feminist science fiction writers like Joanna Russ, Ursula LeGuin and Marge Piercy.[18] A less drastic version may be found in one of the few non-fiction books on the subject, *Towards a Recognition of Androgyny* by Carolyn G. Heilbrun, in which she argues simply for a world in which personal behaviour is not defined by biological sex, so that both men and women may have the full range of human feelings and experiences. In this moderated form, androgyny is simply an extended version of the egalitarian/integrationist utopia.

Many feminists, both liberals and socialist, would probably agree that this was a desirable goal. Others might argue that so to erode the differences between women and men would take away one of life's more exquisite pleasures, leaving the world dull and flat. And this locates the main political problem for the androgynous perspective, namely that most people find it very unattractive as well as unrealistic. Unlike the other feminist visions of an ideal society, androgyny depends on the premiss that women and men are really just the same. This may not contradict biology (we don't know) but it does fly in the face of the entire known cultural history of the human race. As a goal, therefore, the fully androgynous society is so infinitely remote and strange as to offer no possibilities for present action.

Within the feminist movement voices are raised against the androgynous idea not just from sceptics and wary heterosexuals but from the radical separatist side also. Those who are interested in building a specifically *women's* movement, a *women's* culture and ultimately a *women's* world are clearly at odds with the idea that women and men are the same. Once again, if we look first to science fiction for clues to the utopia, we find portraits of matriarchal or Amazonian cultures without men, or female supremacist cultures in which men have been reduced to servitude. The assumptions here are very different: men are defined not only as unlike women but also as inferior. Given the strength of this separatist current within modern feminism, it is worth spending some time to explore its implications for women's liberation as a political movement with political aims.

When the British movement began in 1969 separatism was not the major issue which it had been in America from the outset. The rhetoric of class logically entailed that the purpose of the movement should be to dissolve the connection between gender and economic power. It was acknowledged that most men, like most women, are workers and that the key to women's economic oppression lay in the unification of the *whole* working class. When separatism became a powerful force in the mid-1970s, socialists argued that the separation of women from men would simply play into the hands of the state by dividing the working class.

Separatism in Britain was profoundly influenced by the published works and political practices of American radical feminists who, as we have noted before, adopted the rhetoric of race for their primary analysis. Like the cultural separatists of the black power movement, they argued that the two groups (black and white, men and women) were unalterably opposed, both by their innate differences and by the long history of their conflict.

The separatist line was adopted in different forms and under different labels by many radical feminists in America and Britain. Its attraction lay in it being a logical extension of the radical position (men are the enemy) and also in it being a strong position for women to adopt. It had shock value, as well as consciousness-raising value.

Paradoxically, another consequence was to encourage the development of a female sub-culture in which traits held to be feminine – like emotional expressiveness, qualities of nurturance and personal involvement – were glorified, while traits held to be masculine were denigrated. Unfortunately, many of these supposedly masculine characteristics were precisely those which allowed men to dominate and control: impersonal efficiency, objectivity and distancing, instrumentalism. In recent years the argument has come full circle as a few separatists have asserted their right to use some of the more unpleasant qualities of masculinity (aggression, even violence) in order to combat patriarchal power. This 'female supremacism' elevates an abstract feminine principle as the source of goodness, morality and power and seeks not to abolish inequality but to reverse it. Injustices done to women in the past are held to cancel out any injustices which women might do to others in the present, and the situation is defined as one of total war between women and men. Supremacism is quite distinct from other forms of separatism, since it denies that feminine qualities (as at present defined) are morally superior to masculine qualities. It remains very much a minority tendency.

In general, it is probably appropriate to understand separatist feminism as a tendency with fundamentally different logic and different goals. No longer a social movement for change, it has become a means for creating and defending a life-style choice and a particular identity for individuals. American social scientist Albert Hirschman has demonstrated that social movements typically go through a cyclical development in which phases of public and political action alternate with phases in which private and personal goals predominate.[19] Separatism may well be a symptom of this latter phase in feminism, though the separatist theory in itself tends to block out the possibility of political dialogue.

Each feminist future – equality, androgyny or separatism – can therefore be seen to pose rather precise political questions and to entail definite political consequences. Each individual will read their promise in her own way. Yet we know from political history that the dreams which move people have a sharpness of definition and even a certain down-to-earth, practical quality which the utopias of feminism have not yet fully achieved.

Concluding Note

Because women are still underpaid at work and under-valued at home, because so few have attained positions of power and influence and because so many are still subject to discrimination and violence from men, it is easy to imagine that the women's liberation movement was never more than a kind of millennial religion, a dream of impossible futures. But in terms of the real life-experiences and expectations of women, the changes wrought by the two waves of feminism have indeed been revolutionary.

From the suffragettes to the revolutionary feminists, each wave of feminism has left a mark on the culture and has provided a foundation, or more properly a launching-pad, for the next. Like socialism, it has been a movement of cumulative force, chipping away at an edifice which seems impregnable at any given moment but which in retrospect has always been vulnerable.

'What do women want?', men ask, bemused by the negative stereotypes of feminism they find in the media. What women want, first of all, are a number of explicit and positive changes in social policy. The politically negotiable issues are what they always were: equal pay, opportunities and education, financial and legal independence, reproductive rights and better child care. These are part of a continuing struggle for equal rights which goes back to the earliest history of feminism.

What women also want is human equality, which means a broader revolution in culture and in the attitudes of men. This radical or liberationist impulse in feminism also goes back to the nineteenth century but has come out much more strongly in the feminisms of the twentieth. What it demands, governments cannot legislate but people can create.

We therefore see one movement on two levels, reformist and radical, with these two aspects intimately bound together. Each reform changes the context of the struggle and the consciousness of the participants; each new vision of the future contributes to a better understanding of the present.

Feminism has always been a fluid movement with a rare degree of creativity and adaptiveness. In Britain and America in the 1980s the feminist movement may be going through another change and offering a new kind of challenge to women and men whose consciousness has been raised by the first decade. What a great many people now recognise is that feminism at its best represents a long-overdue step towards equality and sanity in human relationships. That is something worth fighting for.

Further Reading

Women's History

One of the best histories of the women's suffrage movement in Britain is still Ray Strachey's *The Cause*, originally published in 1928 (London: Virago, 1978). For a more modern and committed feminist view of the suffragettes, readers should turn to Jill Liddington and Jill Norris, *One Hand Tied Behind Us* (London: Virago, 1978), and a systematic sociological analysis of the early movements can be found in Olive Banks, *Faces of Feminism* (London: Martin Robertson, 1981), which also has some commentary on the modern period.

The American movement is best approached via Eleanor Flexner's *Century of Struggle* (Cambridge, Mass.: Belknap Press, 1975), which offers a thorough historical account. For a more idiosyncratic and critical view, see William L. O'Neill, *Everyone Was Brave* (New York: Quadrangle, 1969).

O'Neill also authored one of the few studies which compares early feminism in Britain and the USA, *The Woman Movement* (London: Allen & Unwin, 1969). For a wider comparative view and interpretation of feminist movements in many parts of the world, Richard J. Evans's *The Feminists* (London: Croom Helm, 1977) is a useful resource that identifies the various philosophical and political doctrines used by women's movements in the past.

The post-1920s period has, until very recently, been somewhat neglected by students of women's issues. Two books, however, are especially noteworthy: Elizabeth Wilson's *Halfway to Paradise* (London: Tavistock, 1980) is a scholarly examination of women's lives in post-war Britain, and Ruth Adam's *A Woman's Place* (New York: Norton, 1977) offers a panoramic narrative of changes in the conditions of women between 1910 and 1975. Both books are important background for a proper understanding of the origins of modern feminism, and an American counterpart to Ruth Adam's study is William H. Chafe's *The American Woman* (New York: Oxford University Press, 1972) which covers the years between 1920 and 1970.

234

Feminist Theory

A seminal book in the changing consciousness of the post-war period was Simone de Beauvoir's *The Second Sex* (Harmondsworth: Penguin, 1972), originally published in English in 1952, and still an essential starting-point for an exploration of feminist theory. Readers who would like a general introduction to the whole topic of sex role divisions might begin with Ann Oakley's influential textbook, *Sex, Gender and Society* (London: Temple Smith, 1972). The scientific issues are further explored in Brian Easlea's *Science and Sexual Oppression* (London: Weidenfeld & Nicolson, 1981) and Janet Sayers's *Biological Politics* (London: Tavistock, 1982).

Liberals tend to be more interested in practical politics than in elaborating theory so there are few works which deal specifically with theories of liberal feminism. Insights can be gained from the works of Betty Friedan, Jo Freeman, Judith Hole and Ellen Levine which are listed under 'The Feminist Movement in the USA'. John Charvet provides a useful comparative introduction to the origins of liberal feminism in *Feminism* (London: Dent, 1982) and a more detailed critical survey can be found in Zillah Eisenstein's *The Radical Future of Liberal Feminism* (London: Longman, 1981). A philosophical defence of essentially liberal values is the basis of Janet Radcliffe Richards's controversial study, *The Sceptical Feminist* (London: Routledge & Kegan Paul, 1980).

Socialist feminism, by contrast, has generated a vast theoretical literature. An exploration might begin with Juliet Mitchell's early analysis in *Woman's Estate* (Harmondsworth: Penguin, 1970) and Sheila Rowbotham's *Woman's Consciousness, Man's World* (Harmondsworth: Penguin, 1973). Mitchell has also written one of the most interesting attempts to link Marxism with psychological perspectives in *Psychoanalysis and Feminism* (Harmondsworth: Penguin, 1975), and this argument is pursued in Ann Foreman's *Femininity as Alienation* (London: Pluto Press, 1977). The Marxist feminist perspective on ideology can be approached via an excellent collection of articles edited by the Women's Studies Group of the Centre for Contemporary Cultural Studies in Birmingham, *Women Take Issue* (London: Hutchinson, 1978). Recent theoretical work in the Marxist tradition, not always easy reading, are Michèle Barrett's *Women's Oppression Today* (London: Verso, 1980) and a collection edited by Annette Kuhn and Anne Marie Wolpe, *Feminism and Materialism* (London: Routledge & Kegan Paul, 1978).

The relationship between patriarchy and capitalism is analysed in a widely discussed book by Heidi Hartmann, *The Unhappy Marriage of Marxism and Feminism* (London: Pluto Press, 1981). A Marxist perspective on the family is developed in *The Anti-Social Family* by Michèle Barrett and Mary McIntosh (London: Verso, 1982). And, once again, John Charvet's *Feminism* gives a straightforward introduction to the history of socialist feminist thought.

The major commercially published works of radical feminist theory come from the USA. Much of it has appeared in the form of pamphlets, journals and occasional writings, and is not easily accessible. A strong collection from the early days is *Radical Feminism*, edited by Anne Koedt *et al.* (New York: Quadrangle, 1973), though the reader should note that some radicals claim that the selection of material is biased towards a more 'liberal' line. Shulamith Firestone's *The Dialectic of Sex* (New York: Bantam Books, 1971), is absolutely indispensable reading, and remains one of the most systematic statements of a radical theory, though its biological determinism is rejected by some. On patriarchy, a good starting-point is Eva Figes's *Patriarchal Attitudes* (Greenwich, Conn: Fawcett, 1971) and a stronger, polemical treatment will be found in Mary Daly's *Gyn/Ecology* (London: Women's Press, 1979). The argument for lesbianism and a woman-centred society is expressed in the poetry and prose of Adrienne Rich, especially *On Lies, Secrets, Silence* (London: Virago, 1980) and *Compulsory Heterosexuality and Lesbian Existence* (London: Onlywoman Press, 1981). A sociological treatment of this subject is E. M. Ettorre's *Lesbians, Women and Society* (London: Routledge & Kegan Paul, 1980).

Germaine Greer's *The Female Eunuch* (London: MacGibbon & Kee, 1970) is difficult to classify, in so far as it projects an aggressive, heterosexual feminism unlike anything which subsequently developed; but it is still well worth reading for its treatment of female passivity.

The Feminist Movement in the USA

Betty Friedan's path-breaking book *The Feminine Mystique* (Harmondsworth: Penguin, 1975) still gives a vivid sense of the social conditions which made a feminist movement necessary. Her autobiographical collection *It Changed My Life* (New York: Random House, 1976) tells the insider's story of the formation and early years of the National Organisation for Women, and offers a rather jaundiced view of the role of more radical feminists during that period.

The most scholarly, readable and thorough study of the American feminist movement up to 1971 is *The Rebirth of Feminism* by Judith Hole and Ellen Levine (New York: Quadrangle, 1971). Aside from this indispensable guide, some collections of readings from the early years give an insight into the richness and variety of feminist thought and writing. Among the best are: Robin Morgan (ed.), *Sisterhood is Powerful* (New York: Vintage, 1970); Leslie B. Tanner (ed.), *Voices from Women's Liberation* (New York: Mentor, 1971).

Sara Evans provides a critical view of the origins of the American movement and its subsequent career in *Personal Politics* (New York: Vintage, 1980), and a careful analysis of the political context of the emerging movement is Jo Freeman's *The Politics of Women's Liberation* (New York: McKay, 1975). More recently, Joyce Gelb and Marian Lief Palley have charted the movement's progress in *Women and Public Policies* (Princeton University Press, 1982). And Betty Friedan has issued a new challenge to the women's movement and a new programme for its future in *The Second Stage* (New York: Summit, 1981).

The Women's Movement in Britain

The first years of feminism in Britain have so far been less well documented, at least in book form. The ideas and struggles of the early days are recaptured in Juliet Mitchell's *Woman's Estate* (Harmondsworth: Penguin, 1971) and there is a useful collection of writings compiled by Micheline Wandor under the title *The Body Politic: Writings from the Women's Liberation Movement in Britain, 1969–1970* (London: Stage 1, 1972). The latter contains Sheila Rowbotham's essay, 'The Beginnings of Women's Liberation in Britain'. Subsequent collections give an overview of the developing movement: *Conditions of Illusion* by the Feminist Books Collective (Leeds: Feminist Books, 1974); *No Turning Back* edited by the Feminist Books Collective which covers the years 1975–80 (London: Women's Press, 1981) and the *Spare Rib Reader* edited by Marsha Rowe (Harmondsworth: Penguin, 1982). The prevalence of collections of writings reflects the preference in the British movement for collective rather than individual presentations of feminist thought. An exception is *Sweet Freedom* by Anna Coote and Beatrix Campbell, which documents the history of the movement from a Marxist perspective (London: Picador, 1982). The relationship between socialism and feminism in Britain is explored in a collection of long articles by Sheila Rowbotham, Lynne Segal and Hilary Wainwright, *Beyond the Fragments* (London: Merlin Press, 1979). The influence of feminism on women's political participation is debated in *Women and Politics* by Vicky Randall (London: Macmillan, 1982) and in international perspective in *The Politics of the Second Electorate* edited by

Joni Lovenduski and Jill Hills (London: Routledge & Kegan Paul, 1981).

Readers wishing to explore the current ideas and actions of the British movement cannot do better than to read its journals and periodicals: *Spare Rib*, *Women's Voice*, *Feminist Review*, *M/F*, the *WIRES Newsletter* (for women only) and other publications which can be found in feminist and alternative bookshops.

References

1. False Promises: the Liberation and Domestication of Women

1. Ray Strachey, *The Cause: A Short History of the Women's Movement in Great Britain* (London: Virago, 1978) p. 384.
2. *Spare Rib*, no. 73, August 1978, p. 4.
3. Alexis de Tocqueville, *Democracy in America* (New York: Vintage Books, 1945) vol. II, p. 224.
4. E. Sylvia Pankhurst, *The Suffragette Movement* (London: Virago, 1977).
5. Quoted from *Rosie the Riveter*, a film on women's work in the USA during the Second World War.
6. Elizabeth Wilson, *Only Halfway to Paradise* (London: Tavistock, 1980) pp. 41–59.
7. Friedrich Engels, *On the Origin of the Family, Private Property and the State* (London: Lawrence & Wishart, 1972).
8. Dr Benjamin Spock, *Baby and Child Care* (New York: Pocket Books, 1946) p. 460.
9. Wilson, *Only Halfway to Paradise*, pp. 146–61.
10. Roxanne Dunbar, 'The Second Sex', *No More Fun and Games*, issue 2, Boston, 1969.

2. New Beginnings: the Rebirth of Feminism, 1963–9

1. Betty Friedan, *The Feminine Mystique* (Harmondsworth: Penguin, 1975) p. 32.
2. Betty Friedan, *It Changed My Life* (New York: Random House, 1976) p. 18.
3. Daniel Bell, *The End of Ideology* (New York: Free Press, 1960).
4. *Shrew*, July 1969.
5. Ibid.
6. *Spare Rib*, no. 69, April 1978, p. 41.

3. Mixed Messages: Theories of Modern Feminism

1. Juliet Mitchell, *Woman's Estate* (Harmondsworth: Penguin, 1971) p. 64.
2. John Stuart Mill (with Harriet Taylor), *On the Subjection of Women* (Greenwich, Conn: Fawcett, 1971) p. 145.
3. John Charvet, *Feminism* (London: Dent, 1982) pp. 48–96.
4. Friedrich Engels, *On the Origin of the Family, Private Property and the State* (London: Lawrence & Wishart, 1972) p. 235.
5. Mitchell, *Woman's Estate*, p. 17.
6. Sheila Rowbotham, *Woman's Consciousness, Man's World* (Harmondsworth, Penguin, 1973) p. 124.
7. V. I. Lenin, 'A Great Beginning', in *Selected Works* (Moscow: Progress Publishers, 1967) p. 492.
8. Mitchell, *Woman's Estate*, p. 162.
9. Michèle Barrett and Mary McIntosh, *The Anti-Social Family* (London: Verso, 1982).
10. Juliet Mitchell, *Women: The Longest Revolution* (Boston: New England Free Press, 1966).
11. Juliet Mitchell, *Psychoanalysis and Feminism* (Harmondsworth: Penguin, 1975).
12. Sheila Rowbotham, *Women's Liberation and the New Politics* (Nottingham: Bertrand Russell Peace Foundation, 1971) p. 25.
13. *Manifesto of the New York Radical Feminists*, quoted in Anne Koedt, Ellen Levine and Anita Rapone (eds), *Radical Feminism* (New York: Quadrangle, 1973) p. 379.
14. *Redstockings Manifesto* (New York: Redstockings, 1979).
15. See Kate Millett, *Sexual Politics* (London: Hart Davis, 1971).
16. Shulamith Firestone, *The Dialectic of Sex* (New York: Morrow, 1980).
17. *Feminist's Manifesto* (New York: New York Radical Feminists, 1969), reprinted in *Notes from the Second Year* (1970).
18. Sheila Cronan, 'Marriage', in Koedt *et al.*, *Radical Feminism*.
19. Anne Koedt, 'The Myth of the Vaginal Orgasm', in *Notes from the Second Year* (1970) and widely reprinted.
20. W. H. Masters and V. E. Johnson, *Human Sexual Response* (Boston: Little, Brown, 1966).
21. Charlene Spretnak (ed.), *The Politics of Women's Spirituality* (New York: Anchor/Doubleday, 1982); and Elizabeth Gould Davis, *The First Sex* (Harmondsworth: Penguin, 1971).
22. Evelyn Reed, *Problems of Women's Liberation* (New York: Pathfinder Press, 1969) p. 75.
23. Quoted in Carol Ehrlich, *Socialism, Anarchism and Feminism* (London: Black Bear, 1978) p. 8.

24. *Redstockings Manifesto.*
25. See Heidi Hartmann, *The Unhappy Marriage of Marxism and Feminism* (London: Pluto Press, 1981).

4. High Hopes: the Growth of Feminism, 1970–5

1. Jo Freeman, *The Politics of Women's Liberation* (New York: David McKay, 1975) p. 148.
2. *Shrew*, April 1970, p. 4.
3. A full account of the Night Cleaners' Campaign can be found in *Shrew*, December 1971, and is reprinted in Micheline Wandor (ed.), *The Body Politic* (London: Stage 1, 1972) pp. 225–34, and in Sandra Allen, Lee Sanders and Jan Wallis (eds), *Conditions of Illusion* (Leeds: Feminist Books, 1974) pp. 309–25.
4. Allen *et al.*, *Conditions of Illusion*, pp. 332–46.
5. *Spare Rib*, no. 24, 1974, p. 19.
6. George H. Gallup (ed.), *International Public Opinion Polls 1937–1975* (New York: Random House, 1976).
7. See D. Marsh and J. Chambers, *Abortion Politics* (London: Junction Books, 1981).
8. Gallup, *International Public Opinion Polls.*
9. Germaine Greer, *The Female Eunuch* (London: Paladin, 1971).
10. Erica Jong, *Fear of Flying* (New York: Holt, Rinehart & Winston, 1973).
11. Betty Friedan, *It Changed My Life* (New York: Random House, 1976) p. 158.
12. See Anna Coote and Beatrix Campbell, *Sweet Freedom* (London: Picador, 1982) pp. 103–41.
13. George H. Gallup, *International Public Opinion Polls 1976* (West Point, Conn.: Greenwood Press, 1977).
14. *Ms*, December 1979.
15. Freeman, *The Politics of Women's Liberation*, pp. 91–2.
16. Friedan, *It Changed My Life*, p. 374.

5. New Directions: Policy Conflicts and Fresh Campaigns, 1976–8

1. *Spare Rib*, no. 70, May 1978, p. 17.
2. The *WIRES Newsletter* is not available to men. The debate was subsequently published in a pamphlet, *Love Your Enemy?* (London: Onlywoman Press, 1981).

3. Beatrix Campbell, 'A Feminist Sexual Politics: Now You See It, Now You Don't', *Feminist Review*, no. 5, 1980, p. 1.

4. See Carol Lipman, 'Red Baiting in the Women's Movement', in Robert R. Evans (ed.), *Social Movements* (Chicago: Rand McNally, 1973); Robin Morgan, 'Goodbye to All That', in Robin Morgan (ed.), *Sisterhood is Powerful* (New York: Vintage, 1970).

5. David Bouchier, 'The Deradicalisation of Feminism: Ideology and Utopia in Action', *Sociology*, vol. 13, no. 3, September 1979.

6. Anne Koedt, Ellen Levine and Anita Rapone (eds), *Radical Feminism* (New York: Quadrangle, 1973).

7. Betty Friedan, *It Changed My Life* (New York: Random House, 1976) pp. 383–4.

8. Erin Pizzey, letter to *The Guardian*, 4 February 1982. See also Erin Pizzey and Jeff Shapiro, *Prone to Violence* (London: Hamlyn, 1982).

9. Rosalind Coward, 'Sexual Violence and Sexuality', *Feminist Review*, no. 11, Summer 1982, pp. 9–22.

10. David Bouchier, *Idealism and Revolution* (London: Edward Arnold, 1978).

11. *Spare Rib*, no. 73, August 1978, p. 4.

6. Hostile Responses: the Enemies of Women's Liberation

1. Warren Farrell, *The Liberated Man* (New York: Random House, 1974) pp. 162–77.

2. See, for example, Ann Oakley, *Subject Women* (London: Fontana, 1982); and Sara Delamont, *The Sociology of Women* (London: Allen & Unwin, 1980).

3. These generalisations on male consciousness-raising come from the author's own experience.

4. Fatima Mernissi, *Beyond the Veil* (New York: Wiley, 1975) pp. 3–6.

5. See Wolfgang Lederer, *The Fear of Women* (New York: Harcourt Brace Jovanovich, 1968).

6. Gene Marine, *A Male Guide to Women's Liberation* (New York: Holt, Rinehart & Winston, 1972) pp. 147–8; John Gordon, *The Myth of the Monstrous Male and Other Feminist Fables* (New York: Playboy Press, 1982).

7. Kirkpatrick Sale, *SDS* (New York: Vintage, 1974) pp. 418–21; David Bouchier, *Idealism and Revolution* (London: Edward Arnold, 1978) p. 73.

8. Anne Koedt *et al.*, *Radical Feminism* (New York: Quadrangle, 1973).

9. *Spare Rib*, no. 94, May 1980, p. 23 (based on research by Diana Leonard).
10. *The Gallup Poll 1981* (Wilmington, Delaware: Scholarly Resources, 1982).
11. Colette Dowling, *The Cinderella Complex: Women's Hidden Fear of Independence* (New York: Summit, 1981).
12. See, for example, *Spare Rib*, no. 89, p. 5; no. 106, p. 5; no. 107, p. 4.
13. Andrew H. Morton, *Enemies of Choice: The Right to Life Movement and the Threat to Abortion* (Boston: Beacon, 1981).
14. *The Gallup Poll 1981*.
15. Michèle Barrett and Mary McIntosh, *The Anti-Social Family* (London: Verso, 1982) pp. 11–13.
16. *Ms*, July–August 1982, p. 221.
17. Walda Katz Fishman, *The New Right: Unravelling the Opposition to Women's Equality* (New York: Praeger, 1982).
18. Judith Hole and Ellen Levine, *The Rebirth of Feminism* (New York: Quadrangle, 1971) p. 226.
19. See Todd Gitlin, *The Whole World is Watching* (Berkeley: University of California Press, 1980).
20. Anna Coote and Beatrix Campbell, *Sweet Freedom* (London: Picador, 1982) pp. 192–3.
21. Trevor Millum, *Images of Women* (London: Chatto, 1975); Erving Goffman, *Gender Advertisements* (New York: Harper & Row, 1975).
22. Steven Goldberg, *The Inevitability of Patriarchy* (New York: William Morrow, 1973) p. 98.
23. E. O. Wilson, *Sociobiology* (Cambridge, Mass.: Harvard University Press, 1975).
24. Janet Sayers, *Biological Politics* (London: Tavistock, 1982).
25. George F. Gilder, *Sexual Suicide* (New York: Quadrangle, 1973).
26. George F. Gilder, *Wealth and Poverty* (New York: Basic, 1981).
27. Midge Decter, *The New Chastity and Other Arguments Against Women's Liberation* (London: Wildwood House, 1973) p. 179.
28. Joan Didion, *The White Album* (New York: Simon & Schuster, 1979) pp. 109–18.

7. Testing Times: the Women's Movement Today

1. *The Gallup Poll 1981* (Wilmington, Delaware: Scholarly Resources, 1982).
2. *New Earnings Survey 1982* (London: HMSO, 1983).
3. Anna Coote and Beatrix Campbell, *Sweet Freedom* (London: Picador, 1982) pp. 48–101; also Hilary Wainwright, 'Women and the Division of Labour', in Philip Adams (ed.), *Work, Urbanism and Inequality* (London: Weidenfeld & Nicolson, 1978).

4. *Employment Gazette* (London: Department of Employment, November 1980).
5. Micheline Wandor, 'Where to Next?', *Spare Rib*, April 1981, pp. 40–1.
6. D. Spender and Elizabeth Sarah (eds), *Learning to Lose* (London: Women's Press, 1980); M. Stanworth, *Gender and Schooling* (London: Women's Research and Resources Centre, 1980); Coote and Campbell, *Sweet Freedom*, pp. 171–88.
7. Ann Oakley, *Subject Women* (London: Fontana, 1982) p. 134.
8. Bobbie Jackson, *The Ladykillers* (London: Pluto Press, 1981).
9. Susan Orbach, *Fat is a Feminist Issue* (New York: Paddington Press, 1978).
10. *Spare Rib*, no. 101, December 1980, pp. 24–7; see also nos 102 and 103.
11. Joni Lovenduski and Jill Hills (eds), *The Politics of the Second Electorate* (London: Routledge & Kegan Paul, 1981) p. 16; and Vicky Randall, *Women and Politics* (London: Macmillan, 1982) pp. 44–53.
12. *Guardian* Marplan Poll, 7 February 1983, p. 4.
13. Lovenduski and Hills, *The Politics of the Second Electorate*, pp. 20–5.
14. Vicky Randall, *Women and Politics* (London: Macmillan, 1982) p. 78.
15. Coote and Campbell, *Sweet Freedom*, p. 240.
16. *The Gallup Poll 1980* (Wilmington, Delaware: Scholarly Resources, 1981).
17. Michèle Barrett and Mary McIntosh, *The Anti-Social Family* (London: Verso, 1982).
18. Ibid, p. 80.
19. Stephanie Dowrick and Sibyl Grundberg, *Why Children?* (London: Women's Press, 1981).
20. *Social Trends*, 13th edn (London: HMSO, 1982); R. N. Rapaport and M. T. Fogarty, *Families in Britain* (London: Routledge & Kegan Paul, 1982).
21. *The Sunday Times* Family Poll, 2 May 1982.
22. *The Guardian*, 3 November 1982, p. 9.
23. Joyce Gelb and Marian Lief Palley, *Women and Public Policies* (Princeton University Press, 1982).
24. *Ms*, July–August 1982, p. 70.

8. Unfinished Business: the Future of Feminism

1. Sheila Rowbotham, Lynne Segal and Hilary Wainwright, *Beyond the Fragments* (London: Merlin Press, 1979).
2. Ibid, p. 225.

3. Heidi Hartmann, *The Unhappy Marriage of Marxism and Feminism* (London: Pluto Press, 1981).
4. John Charvet, *Feminism* (London: Dent, 1982) p. 130.
5. *Spare Rib*, no. 123, October 1982, pp. 26–7.
6. Janet Radcliffe Richards, *The Sceptical Feminist* (London: Routledge & Kegan Paul, 1980) p. 287.
7. Ann Oakley, *Subject Women* (London: Fontana, 1982) p. 340.
8. Robert R. Evans (ed.), *Social Movements* (Chicago, Rand McNally, 1973) pp. 43, 45, 452.
9. David Bouchier, *Idealism and Revolution* (London: Edward Arnold, 1978) pp. 175–8.
10. See Anselma Dell'Olio, 'Divisiveness and Self-Destruction in the Women's Movement', *Chicago Women's Liberation Newsletter*, August 1970; and Joreen, 'The Tyranny of Structurelessness', reprinted in Anne Koedt *et al.*, *Radical Feminism* (New York: Quadrangle, 1973) pp. 285–99.
11. Sara Evans, *Personal Politics* (New York: Vintage, 1980) pp. 222–3.
12. See William A. Gamson, *The Strategy of Social Protest* (Homewood, Ill.: Dorsey, 1975); and Theodore Abel, 'The Pattern of a Successful Political Movement' and Mayer N. Zald and Roberta Ash, 'Social Movement Organizations: Growth, Decay and Change', both in Evans (ed.), *Social Movements*.
13. See F. F. Piven and R. A. Cloward, *Poor People's Movements: How They Succeed and Why They Fail* (New York: Vintage, 1979).
14. Joyce Gelb and Marian Lief Palley, *Women and Public Policies* (Princeton University Press, 1982) pp. 37–61.
15. *New Society*, 25 November 1982, p. 332.
16. Zillah Eisenstein, *The Radical Future of Liberal Feminism* (London: Longman, 1981) p. 222.
17. Gamson, *The Strategy of Social Protest*, pp. 46–9.
18. Oakley, *Subject Women*, pp. 340–1.
19. Albert Hirschman, *Shifting Involvements: Private Interest and Public Action* (London: Martin Robertson, 1981).

Index

246